Camille

AND OTHER PLAYS

Camille

AND OTHER PLAYS

Edited, with an Introduction to the well-made play

by

STEPHEN S. STANTON

A MERMAID DRAMABOOK

HILL AND WANG · NEW YORK

A DIVISION OF FARRAR, STRAUS AND GIROUX

All rights to three of the plays in this volume, including performance rights, are protected by their individual copyright. On the title page of these three plays, it is indicated from whom permissions to print have been obtained and to whom inquiries about performing rights should be directed. Producers, professional and amateur, are expressly warned that performance rights cover not only production but also readings.

Stephen S. Stanton was born in 1915 at Ann Arbor, Michigan. Graduating from Harvard in 1938, he taught English at St. Paul's School, Concord, N. H., and acquired a Master's Degree from the University of Michigan before he joined the Naval Reserve in 1942. After the War Mr. Stanton was an instructor in English at Williams College, the University of Michigan, and Barnard College. In 1955 he received his doctorate in English and comparative literature from Columbia University. At the present time he is assistant professor of English in the College of Engineering, University of Michigan.

FIRST DRAMABOOK EDITION JANUARY 1957

Standard Book Number: 8090-0706-1

Library of Congress Catalog Card No.: 57-5843

Twenty-sixth printing, 1989

CONTENTS

ACKNOWLEDGMENTS

To Eric Bentley go my thanks for making possible this anthology of French plays and for helpful suggestions too numerous to count. Maurice Valency, however, first inspired me to study a vital but neglected side of the drama and made me appreciate how vital technical proficiency —or what may be called a sense of theatre—is to all great dramatic art.

I am grateful to Stephen Xydis and Patricia Irwin for editorial advice, and to Arthur Wang for the benefit of his experience and understanding.

Staff members of The Library of Congress, The New York Public Library, and the libraries of Columbia University and The University of Michigan cheerfully assisted in running down evasive scripts and in obtaining material whose recent publication made examination difficult before I sent the MS. of this book to the printer.

S.S.S.

INTRODUCTION

The Well-Made Play and the Modern Theatre

JOHN VAN DRUTEN, in his useful and entertaining book *Playwright at Work*, maintains that we have come to frown on the "well-made" play—the play that by strict definition adheres to an ingenious, commercially successful pattern of construction and usually contains at least a dash of moral or thesis, a lesson taught satirically and amusingly though not unduly insisted upon. This variety of dramatic entertainment was once the darling of the theatre. Mr. van Druten quotes the British playwright and poet Clifford Bax: "We ought to admire the well-made play as we admire a well-made man, and if we were to elaborate this analogy we should find that many modern plays are skinny creatures or cripples or over-large in the head." [1] Mr. van Druten comments that all of us have met well-made men with symmetrical but empty heads. Here is the principal argument against the well-made play. The term has become synonymous with trashy playwriting—with the play that amuses but says nothing. When Eugène Scribe (1791–1861), father of the *pièce bien faite* in France, insisted before the French Academy in 1836 that the theatre should be a place of entertainment and not a college classroom,[2] he was saying nothing that Molière had not said in his *Critique de l'Ecole des Femmes* (1663). Yet Scribe was blamed for heterodoxy, and the fact that he gave the theatre a viable dramatic form—indeed, one that is always sure to satisfy the box office—coupled with a sane, though certainly not weighty, moral content is generally ignored.

Mr. van Druten and many other reputable critics and

---

[1] *Playwright at Work* (New York, 1953), pp. 66–67.
[2] "You go to the theatre for relaxation and amusement, not for instruction or correction. Now what most amuses you is not truth but fiction. . . . The theatre is therefore rarely the direct expression of social life . . . it is often the inverse expression." (My translation.) *Oeuvres Complètes de Eugène Scribe*, ed. E. Dentu (Paris, 1874), I, xxiv. (The standard complete edition in 76 vols.)

dramatists admit the importance, even the necessity, of this kind of theatre. "I am inclined to think," says Mr. van Druten, "that an acquaintance with the older rules of the well-made play is still a good basis for learning how to break them." And he mentions his early dependence on the dramatic technique of Ibsen, who built his own first dramas painstakingly on Scribean foundations.

But Eric Bentley, in reviewing an "ill-made" play, takes issue with the official rule book of Broadway's New Drama, for which Mr. van Druten is a leading spokesman: ". . . the new plays have the structure of a short story. And there is nothing to be said against this structure except that it has no room for the major matters of drama and the novel." [3]

The social play (*pièce à thèse*) has been a staple of European and American drama since 1850, but it could not have existed without the formula of the well-made play. Although Mr. Average Playgoer looks for entertainment and not social enlightenment, he will probably accept some—perhaps much—moralizing if it is disguised and made amusing. Molière shrewdly observed that the hearty ridicule of human folly humorously exaggerated is therapeutic. Realizing this truth, both Alexandre Dumas *fils* (1824–95) and Emile Augier (1820–89), who nurtured the thesis play in its infancy, depended heavily on the technique of Scribe's plays. It is not too much to say that the technical proficiency of Scribe and Victorien Sardou (1831–1908) and the psychological acumen of Augier and Dumas were the two most important contributions to French drama during the nineteenth century.[4] "The dramatist who knows *man* as Balzac did," said Dumas in 1868 (and Augier would have agreed), "and the *theatre* as Scribe did, will be the greatest of the world's dramatists." [5] In truth the *pièce bien faite*, as Scribe had established it, was somewhat shallow, though not so shallow as most critics would have us believe. Only with Dumas, Augier, and their followers did the form come to be the accepted one for social drama.

---

[3] *The Dramatic Event* (Boston, 1956), p. 177.
[4] See Marvin Felheim, *The Theater of Augustin Daly: An Account of the Late Nineteenth-Century American Stage* (Cambridge, Mass., 1956), p. 189.
[5] Preface to *Un Père Prodigue*. (My translation; Dumas' italics.)

Indeed, playwrights who preached the new social gospel were able to reach a popular audience only by coating their bitter and often repugnant contents with the sugar of theatrical tricks and surprises. Thus instruction in the theatre was disguised as sheer entertainment. By these means Augier's *Gabrielle* (first performance 1849), Dumas' *Diane de Lys* (1853) and *Francillon* (1887), Oscar Wilde's *Lady Windermere's Fan* (1892), aṅd Arthur Wing Pinero's *Mid-Channel* (1909) attack adultery; Dumas' *Camille* (1852), Augier's *Les Lionnes Pauvres* (1858), and George Bernard Shaw's *Mrs. Warren's Profession* (1893) exposed to shocked and uncomprehending audiences the dangers of prostitution or free love; in Dumas' *Le Demi-Monde* (1855), Augier's *Un Beau Mariage* (1859), Shaw's *Widowers' Houses* (1892), and Pinero's *The Second Mrs. Tanqueray* (1892) the hypocrisy and deceit behind outwardly respectable society was discovered; marriage was critically examined in Augier's *Madam Caverlet* (1876) and Shaw's *Candida* (1895). The possibility of saving the fallen woman was treated in a number of plays. In Dumas' first plays the theme of illicit love was borrowed from the dying romantic drama; passion was transposed from Hugo's dramas and the novels of the elder Dumas; and the cleverly contrived but mildly didactic plot of intrigue and suspense was taken from Scribe. The reason the social dramatists adopted Scribe's technique was that he had evolved a very tricky, though essentially mechanical method of dealing with lightly social and moral themes, so as to make them seem amusing to a jaded and blasé society.

Before international copyright laws were established in 1877, mediocre English dramatists claimed the authorship of hundreds of French plays that they had translated; for only in France did drama have at this time a high rating as successful theatre. Despite Shaw's rhetorical question to his biographer, "Who was Scribe that he should dictate to me or anyone else how a play should be written?" the best playwrights—Wilde, Pinero, Shaw—turned the well-made play to their own uses. From childhood Shaw had been immersed in the Scribean stage devices; they filled the plays of Tom Taylor and other stage favorites of the day. Shaw deliberately built some of his most popular works—*Arms and the Man* (1894), *Candida, The Devil's Disciple* (1897), *Man and Superman* (1903), and *Major Barbara* (1906)—out of materials from the house of Scribe. But he combined them differently, so as to ridicule with an ironic twist both the audience's acceptance of conventional thrills and suspense and the Victorian attitudes that enabled them to accept these conventions.

In America during this period the situation was much the same. The volumes of George Odell's *Annals of the New York Stage* record frequent revivals of plays by Scribe and by dramatists who used his technique.[6]

Despite a gradual shift after the First World War from the play with a well-made plot toward the play of mood, the Scribean play has not been demolished. Entertaining, even edifying English and American dramas are still constructed with the same builder's craftsmanship: witness *The Circle* (1921), by Somerset Maugham; *Dangerous Corner* (1931), by J. B. Priestley; *The Little Foxes* (1939) and *Watch on the Rhine* (1941), by Lillian Hellman; *All My Sons* (1946), by Arthur Miller; *Affairs of State* (1950), by Louis Verneuil; *The Confidential Clerk* (1952), by T. S. Eliot; *Anastasia* (1955), by M. Maurette and Guy Bolton. Jean Cocteau, championing a new *poésie de théâtre* for our time, one that substitutes surrealistic effects and a reworking of ancient myths for verse dialogue, deliberately adopts and rearranges a well-made plot in *La Machine à Ecrire* (1941), produced in New York in 1955 as *The Typewriter*. He expressively manipulates stage movement so as to parody the melodrama of the conventional detective story and satirize the hypocrisy of the small town. Scribean logic and action are oddly distorted to give the "whodunit" another twist for extra suspense and satire.

The well-made play, then, has "paid off" in the theatre. Every successful modern dramatist, beginning with the younger Dumas, has had to reckon with Scribean theatre, whether in principle he favored or denounced it, and to admit its vitality. Hundreds of French plays, from the farces of Eugène Labiche to Emile Zola's iconoclastic *Thérèse*

---

[6] For an informative general account of American productions of French plays at this time, consult Felheim, *Theater of Daly*, chap. 5. Daly produced 65 French plays, including two by Scribe, four by Dumas *fils*, and twelve by Sardou: pp. 204–5.

Raquin (1873), made some use of the well-made pattern. Indeed, the most significant dramas of the late nineteenth and early twentieth centuries in France, England, and America were born out of the union of a specific and amusing technical form perfected by one man—the *pièce bien faite* —with serious social or psychological subject matter. In a dramaturgical sense, they sprang well-made from the mind of Scribe as the armored Athena sprang from the brow of Zeus.

Eugène Scribe and Victorien Sardou: The Technique of the Well-Made Play

Augustin-Eugène Scribe was one of the most indefatigable and prolific playwrights the stage has ever known. He created and for the most part saw produced 216 *comédies-vaudevilles* (most of them in one act), 35 full-length plays, and libretti for 28 grand operas, 86 *opéras-comiques*, and 9 *opéra-ballets* or *ballets-pantomimes*.[7] His works for the theatre totaled 374. In the entire history of the drama this output has probably been equaled only by that of Lope de Vega, Tirso de Molina, and Alexandre Hardy.

Comédies-vaudevilles were simple plays in which comic and serious scenes were bound together by satirical or jovial songs (originally composed about famous people and rhymed to old popular airs) known as *vaudevilles*.[8] Scribe combined the light satirical spirit that had characterized these songs and an intricate technique. The technique he inherited from the French *comédie d'intrigue*, as developed by his predecessors in the theatre from Plautus to Beaumarchais. *Comédie d'intrigue* is directly descended from classical comedy by way of the literary and popular drama of Italy and Spain. In this kind of comedy the action—all the structure of complication and reversal that sustains suspense and delays the resolution—dominates everything else. After the early successes the songs gradually disappeared,

---

[7] For an understanding of these genres Neil C. Arvin's *Eugène Scribe and the French Theatre, 1815–1860* (Cambridge, Mass., 1924) should be consulted.

[8] Not until 1792 did the name "vaudeville" come into current usage to designate light comedies containing *vaudevilles*. Before this date such plays were known as *comédies en vaudevilles* or *pièces en vaudevilles*. But "vaudeville" in our modern American sense has no connection with these French forms

though Scribe continued to ridicule and expose charlatan-
ism and various forms of pretentiousness.

By 1811, when Scribe first began to write for the stage,
the *comédie-vaudeville* was already one of the most popular
forms of light dramatic entertainment in France. During
the next fifty years Scribe, with some help from a dozen or
more collaborators, revolutionized and improved it and
also developed these light sketches of manners into the long
comedies of manners that became the established proto-
types of the *pièce bien faite*.

Nevertheless, with a few exceptions to be mentioned at
the end of this section, the characters and the situations of
his individual works have become indistinguishable. It is
curious that a playwright with so tremendous and varied a
talent should be remembered today rather for his impact
on the modern theatre than for his own plays. For an understanding of Scribe's truly extraordinary influence the
special characteristics of the well-made play must be examined.

True examples of such drama display seven structural
features: [1] a plot based on a secret known to the audience
but withheld from certain characters (who have long been
engaged [9] in a battle of wits) until its revelation (or the
direct consequence thereof) in the climactic scene serves
to unmask a fraudulent character and restore to good fortune the suffering hero, with whom the audience has been
made to sympathize; [2] a pattern of increasingly intense
action and suspense, prepared by exposition (this pattern
assisted by contrived entrances and exits, letters, and other
devices); [3] a series of ups and downs in the hero's fortunes, caused by his conflict with an adversary; [4] the coun-
terpunch of peripeteia[10] and *scène à faire*,[11] marking, re-
spectively, the lowest and the highest point in the hero's

[9] The play deals with the culmination of a long story, the greater part
of which has occurred before the curtain goes up. This late beginning
of the play is called a late *point of attack*. The action is through exposition always delayed until the foregoing events have been related for
the audience's benefit. See William Archer, *Playmaking, A Manual of
Craftsmanship* (New York, 1928), pp. 85–110.
[10] The term peripeteia refers here to the greatest in a series of mishaps
suffered by the hero. See Archer, *ibid.*, pp. 260–74.
[11] *Scène à faire*: a term invented by the nineteenth-century French
critic Francisque Sarcey. See Archer's discussion of the "obligatory"
scene, *ibid.*, pp. 225–59.

adventures, and brought about by the disclosure of secrets to the opposing side; [5] a central misunderstanding or *quiproquo*,[12] made obvious to the spectator but withheld from the participants; [6] a logical and credible dénouement; and [7] the reproduction of the overall action pattern in the individual acts.

In what way do these features differ from those used by Scribe's predecessors? Scribe invented nothing. He used the technical methods of all the great writers of comedy, but he kept *all* their tricks in use *all* the time in his plays. He was the theatrical juggler supreme.

His plots were nevertheless more complicated than those of Beaumarchais, Molière, and Plautus, dramatists who, like Scribe, belonged to the classical tradition. Plautus wrote farces according to the conventions of his day, using the stock characters, the odd coincidences, and the singular situations that his audiences enjoyed. He employed the devices just listed, but he imposed them arbitrarily on the characters. Despite realistic touches here and there, the characters are not realistic, the events are not logical. Farce is a one-dimensional medium, founded on an improbability. Molière, also writing comedies according to classical conventions, used simple plots many of which were taken from the Renaissance farce, but he gave them happy endings: happy endings were expected. He did not write problem plays; these were unknown in his day. He treated social pretentiousness satirically; he exposed hypocrisy; but he maintained a comic point of view. He did not explore consequences, nor did he regard foibles as fatal. Once exposed, they could be dispensed with, everyone the wiser and the healthier for a good laugh. Hence, for Molière logic was not required. The situations and the treatment were intentionally artificial. Beaumarchais, under the impetus of late eighteenth-century rationalism in the drama, refined the conventional plot of intrigue, but he used the simple, artificial situations and characters of traditional farce as a

---

[12] *Quiproquo* [Latin *quid pro quo*]: literally, "something for something"; two or more characters interpret a word or, by extension, a situation in different ways, all the time assuming that their interpretations are the same. This form of humor is one of the most durable in the history of the theatre; it delights Broadway as much as it delighted Rome in Plautus' day. See discussion of *The Glass of Water* and *A Scrap of Paper* for examples in this volume.

political engine. He loaded the dialogue of his plots with gibes at the incompetence of the aristocracy. He too was bent on social ends rather than on logically handled means.

All these dramatists employed the same general methods, but Scribe alone imparted to them a probability and a logic previously unknown in the theatre. Though his plots and characters were contrived, they were plausible; they followed the demands of common sense. His dénouements were not tacked on, but evolved inevitably from the events of the plot. His expository preparations were careful and precise. For these reasons the *pièce bien faite* was more suited than any other to the demands of the nineteenth-century problem play.

No piece, then, can be said to fit the Procrustean bed of the well-made play unless, besides exhibiting these features in the precise pattern just described, it also combines them in a manner that seems convincing and logical, or unless the *scène à faire* takes the form of a *coup de théâtre* —the disclosure of a withheld truth that contains a moral judgment. This judgment need not necessarily be profound, and in Scribe it is often frankly trivial; but at least the moral dimensions are clearly specified.

Now for a closer look at this dramatic method. As the play opens, the likable but helpless hero is overwhelmed by adverse circumstances and dominated by an opposing character. Because the play presents only the crisis of the whole story, the first act is almost entirely expository; it corresponds in a general way to the protasis of classical comedy.[13] Much information is offered about characters and events; and all this information prepares the outcome of the action and helps the audience anticipate the final revelation of the secret. The action itself begins near the end of the first act and progresses in the form of a battle of wits and of skillful strategy between two formidable contestants: (A) the hero or his clever and more worldly representative and (B) his antagonist, the hostile rival force. Often the hero is loved by two women: a naïve girl whom he wishes to marry and an older woman to whom he is in some way obligated and who objects to his marriage. His

[13] The technical features of classical comedy here alluded to are discussed in G. E. Duckworth, *The Nature of Roman Comedy* (Princeton, 1952).

problem is to extricate himself from these entanglements without embarrassment and without compromising himself or the lady. As the action begins he gains a victory and his rival suffers a defeat; then vice versa. The contest is a seesaw, with first one side mastering the situation and then the other. The conflict becomes more and more rapid, exciting, and productive of suspense as dominance shuttles from one side to the other. After several such alternations the hero undergoes an unexpected reversal of fortune—the peripeteia of classical tragedy. Thereupon a secret baneful to the opposing interest is suddenly released, and the hero's enemy suffers a crushing defeat. This scene of the hero's or his representative's greatest triumph is the *scène à faire* or "obligatory" scene. After it, only some comparatively minor matters need clearing up. They are resolved in a climactic extension or "recognition" scene—the anagnorisis of classical tragedy—usually to the hero's gain, occasionally to his unexpected loss. Additional information is divulged— some long-obscured secret of moment to the hero's fortunes. The dénouement follows at once, with appropriate dispensations to the good and the bad characters.

Throughout the fluctuation of the hero's fortunes excitement is produced by precise timing. The playwright creates suspense partly by providing, especially in the first act, clues to impending events, thereby coaching the audience to anticipate these events, and partly by withholding from certain of the characters until the crucial moment vital information known to the audience all along. The machinery of complication is often misdelivery of a letter or other document; some trifling incident or detail of which we may be casually, almost accidentally, informed turns out in the *scène à faire* or the recognition scene to have overwhelming significance.

It is to be noted that the will of the characters in this type of drama is always subordinate to the exigencies of the plot and to the artifices employed by the author. Factitiously conceived though they are, these pasteboard personages occasionally assume the color and conviction of life, and the artificial bravura of many roles appears emotionally convincing when the roles are interpreted by great actors.

A brief analysis of *The Glass of Water*, one of Scribe's

most typical dramas, will serve to illustrate his dramatic method, which remains constant in all his plays.

Act I, Scene i (Act I in Scribe). Bolingbroke and Masham (hero) discuss the obstacles to their success (exposition). Bolingbroke's difficulty: the weak Queen Anne is controlled by the selfish Duke and Duchess of Marlborough. Masham loves Abigail, a poor shopgirl (heroine), but his marriage has been thwarted by an unknown enemy (late point of attack). Bolingbroke tells how a series of trivial incidents led to his becoming an important political figure (small causes produce great events). He agrees to help Masham's fiancée get a court position. A battle of wits begins between Bolingbroke and the Duchess. Unless she will help Abigail obtain a position as lady in waiting to the Queen, he will reveal her relationship to the poor shop assistant. The Duchess, in turn, threatens to reveal Bolingbroke's debts. Masham kills his rival in a duel (action begins).

Act I, Scene ii (Act II in Scribe). The Duchess persuades the Queen not to favor Abigail (seesaw begins: down). Masham wins the Queen's support (up). The Duchess secretly sends a military promotion to Masham, whom she loves (down), but Bolingbroke threatens to reveal her secret (up) unless she helps Abigail. *Act II, Scene i* (Act III in Scribe). The Queen admits to Abigail a secret love (preparation for *scène à faire*). The Duchess and the Queen engage in further hostilities (seesaw). The Queen, not knowing of the love between Masham and Abigail, reveals to the latter her own secret love for him (peripeteia: lowest point in the heroine's fortunes; disclosure of the withheld secret).

Act II, Scene ii (Act IV in Scribe). Worrying momentarily about Masham's constancy, Abigail, who knows he is being pursued by the Queen and the Duchess, devises with Bolingbroke the glass of water trick whereby the two jealous women will become entangled in their own petty rivalry. Bolingbroke tells the Duchess that her rival will ask Masham for a glass of water during a reception for the French ambassador. Abigail suggests that the Queen use the trick to arrange a rendezvous with Masham. When the Duchess learns that the Queen is her rival, she resigns her position, overcome by jealousy (*scène à faire*: exposure of rival force). In revenge she reveals that Masham has killed Bolingbroke's wicked cousin in the duel.

Act III (Act V in Scribe). Masham tells the Queen he loves a lady at court; she supposes he is referring to herself (*quiproquo*). The Duchess surprises Masham in the Queen's apartments. But Bolingbroke explains everything. The Queen resignedly unites the lovers; the Duke and Duchess fall from grace;[14] Bolingbroke becomes the new minister under the Queen (dénouement).

[1] We see that the story of *The Glass of Water* has actually begun long before the curtain rises.[15] Masham and Bolingbroke have failed in their affairs. The exposition of just how this has happened monopolizes most of the first act. The secret withheld from the Duchess until the *scène à faire* is of course the Queen's love for Masham. Revelation of it unmasks the Duchess (and the Queen's weakness) and leads, through the Duchess' attempted revenge, to the disclosure that Masham loves Abigail. All this has an appearance of realism that is lacking in the stylized traditional plots of Beaumarchais, Molière, and Plautus. Everything is of course contrived, yet completely logical.

[2] Suspense develops in Act II, Scene i from the increasing ambiguity of Masham's relationship to both the Duchess and the Queen and from the resulting distress of Abigail. By the conclusion of Act II, Scene ii we learn that the Queen, too, is to be a rival for Masham's love. The suspense results from the Queen's and Masham's ignorance of the true state of affairs: the Queen loves him, but he, without knowing this, loves Abigail. Bolingbroke's intrusion upon the Queen in Act II, Scene i thwarts Masham's attempt to tell her of his love for Abigail. Though Bolingbroke's entrance is obviously a contrived interruption of suspense, it seems a perfectly logical action, for England's military plight demands his consultation with the Queen. But she, because she knows nothing of Masham's or the Duchess' love, will feel free to ask Masham for the glass of water (and a rendezvous) in the *scène à faire*. The au-

---

[14] In the Bodeen version of the play the Duchess and Bolingbroke are reconciled; in Scribe they are not.
[15] The numerals accompanying this analysis correspond for easy reference to the seven structural features listed above.

dience anticipates this scene, desiring to see the exposure of the Duchess. It also relishes the imbroglio between these two great ladies, for it knows the contents of the Duchess' secret letters to Masham.

[3] From the end of Act I, Scene i to the *scène à faire* Bolingbroke and the Duchess are locked in a deadly contest. Even with the Duchess in disgrace for having spilled the glass of water, the conflict is not ended. Only in the last act are the scales tipped decisively against her.

[4] The *scène à faire* in Scribe's play is more believable than in the plays of Beaumarchais or Plautus, though all playwrights who followed the tradition of classical comedy used this scene to ridicule a foolish or an immoral character. Although we desire the defeat of the Duchess by the Queen, we now construe the Queen's amorous interest in Abigail's fiancé as another manifestation of weakness in a royal personage. The *coup de théâtre* of the glass of water focuses attention on her frivolity and poor judgment at a moment when all her powers are challenged by the Anglo-French situation. Both ladies are amusingly censured; honest and sincere underlings are rewarded.

The obligatory scene of a Beaumarchais play is based on farcical improbabilities like those of Latin comedy. In *The Glass of Water* this scene, for all its dependence on a hand prop and its skillful timing, seems more credible and not just another variation of a standard farce plot. The crucial scene is led up to by everything in Scribe's play— Bolingbroke's speech in the first scene explaining that great events are produced by trivial causes, his exposure of the Duchess' secret interest in Masham, the Queen's admission to Abigail that she loves Masham, the hostility of the Duchess and the Queen. The play advances with the precision of a chess game; each character acts according to the author's predetermined plan. The well-made play is, in fact, generally worked out backward from its crucial scene.

[5] The comic suspense at this point depends on the use of *quiproquo*. The romantic Queen, interpreting Masham's equivocal allusions to love as meaning that he loves her, palpitates with excitement; the hero, absorbed in his own amorous thoughts, never suspects that his sovereign is experiencing emotional high blood pressure.

[6] The dénouement in which all misunderstandings are unraveled seems inevitable. After the obligatory scene the Duchess, seeking revenge, discovers Masham in the Queen's apartments; only then does Bolingbroke, to save the lovers, reveal the whole truth. In Molière's *Tartuffe* and *Les Femmes Savantes*, on the other hand, the endings seem arbitrarily imposed, in the first by a warrant for arrest, in the second by letters; and the plot of *Le Misanthrope* likewise seems to modern spectators loosely constructed.

[7] Each act of *The Glass of Water*, or of any play by Scribe, comprises the same pattern of action as the whole. The developments, interspersed with upsets and reversals, accelerate steadily to the crisis. The first act is slow, the action static, while information withheld from the characters is explained to the audience. Toward the end the plot gathers momentum with an important step taken by the hero. The succeeding acts diminish in length and increase in intensity. The final act discloses the withheld secrets in a flurry of excitement.

Scribe composed his plays, then, according to a precise formula. In the better ones he may be said to have fulfilled his purpose of amusing his audience with ingeniously constructed plots and entertaining characters and, through the ridicule of foibles, instructing them with healthy laughter.

So much for Scribe's technique. When we examine the scope and content of his well-made plays, we find them nearly always lightly satirical but focused on no special subject matter that distinguishes them from dramas of another type. Most of the early ones either portray social vices and weaknesses—unethical business methods, speculation, gambling, and the like—or else state marital problems. *Le Mariage de Raison* (1826) and *Malvina, ou le Mariage d'Inclination* (1828), each in two acts, and *Le Famille Riquebourg, ou le Mariage mal Assorti* (1831) treat this subject more seriously than is customary in the genre, besides illustrating Scribe's tighter and more logical plot construction. The first applauds a sensible marriage founded on social equality, propriety, and parental approval instead of on passion and impulse. The same theme is more graphically stated in *Malvina*, in which the headstrong, romantic heroine faces a life of misery to pay for eloping with a worthless rake, whereas her level-headed cousin makes an unexciting but durable match. To Scribe, similarity of education and tastes, the domestic virtues, and the security of a comfortable dowry are prerequisites for marital happiness. These solid values are exhibited in *La Frontière de Savoie* (1834), *A Peculiar Position*,[16] a diverting farce and an anticipation of Scribe's best-known play, *Bataille de Dames* (1851),[17] written with Ernest Legouvé. Scribe took from Plautus (*The Captives*) the central comic situation of both plays: the clever use by two women of a ridiculous admirer as a decoy to save their lovers or husbands from a pursuer.

Through his light but effective satire of middle-class peccadilloes, and his structural refinement of the *comédie-vaudeville*, Scribe was preparing the way for his more ambitious comedies. Turning to these in 1827, he continued for the rest of his life to write simultaneously *vaudevilles*, dramas, and opera libretti. Most of the ambitious plays, beginning with *Le Mariage d'Argent* (1827), were produced at the Théâtre Français. He is frequently charged with being shallow and "materialistic": nevertheless his point in this drama is that a mercenary marriage brings unhappiness to both parties. Political conspiracy and intrigue are cleverly handled in *Bertrand et Raton* (1833), the first of his "historical" plays, of which *Le Verre d'Eau* (1840), *The Glass of Water*, is an outstanding example. In these dramas historical fidelity is sacrificed to the tightly integrated mechanism of the plot—that is, to entertainment. A passage of history is reduced to a chain of events in which a trivial accident leads to some overwhelming consequence: a sudden arrest reverses the tide of a revolution, a glass of water affects the fate of a nation. *Adrienne Lecouvreur* (1849), another play written in collaboration with Legouvé and Scribe's only tragedy, is a strained and melodramatic piece that nevertheless provides a telling part

---

[16] Dates, records of notable performances, and other information about the plays in this volume will be found in the Notes.
[17] Imaginatively adapted by Maurice Valency as *The Queen's Gambit* (New York, Samuel French, Inc., 1956). See Eric Bentley's review of the New York production in *What Is Theatre?* (Boston, Beacon Press, 1956).

for a versatile actress. A number of social evils are attacked by means of the well-made formula, some more seriously than others: in *L'Ambitieux* (1834), political ambition; in *La Camaraderie* (1837), political fraud; in *La Calomnie* (1840), slander; in *Une Chaîne* (1841), adultery; in *Le Puff* (1848), literary imposture.

The career of Sardou, Scribe's chief disciple, embraced the most popular period of the *pièce bien faite* in all countries of the Western world. Several of his successes were adapted half a dozen times apiece in England and the United States. He emerged from obscurity only when the popular actress Virginie Déjazet, a friend of his wife, starred in *Les Premières Armes de Figaro* (1859) and others of his early plays. Here he demonstrated a sense of theatre, without which the greatest literary genius will fail as a dramatist. Though he was no profound thinker, Sardou possessed great talent, and he was indeed, as Henry James said of him, a "supremely skillful contriver and arranger . . . a man who has more of the light, and less of the heat, of cleverness, than anyone else." [18] He treated a variety of subjects with Scribe's dramaturgy, but he was inclined to weigh down his well-made plots with theatrical effects for their own sake. Two of his best-known plays in England and America were among his early successes: *Les Pattes de Mouche*[19] (1860), *A Scrap of Paper*, and *Nos Intimes* (1861). *La Famille Benoîton* (1865), a satire of social life during the Second Empire, demonstrated his occasional ability to approach Augier's mastery of social comedy. But it was in historical spectacle that his ingenuity and skill went unchallenged. *Patrie!* (1869), his outstanding contribution to this genre, shows him a more versatile, though not a better, technician than Scribe. *Dora* (1877), crudely adapted for the London and New York stages as *Diplomacy* (1878) by Clement Scott and B. C. Stephenson, probably served Oscar Wilde as a model for *An Ideal Husband* (1895). Sardou followed *Daniel Rochat* (1880), a tedious and unconvincing defense of religion as a binding force in marriage, with the risqué farce *Divorçons* in the same year.

[18] *The Scenic Art. Notes on Acting and the Drama: 1872–1901*, ed. Allan Wade (New York, 1957), p. 40.
[19] "Pattes de mouche": literally, "fly-tracks"; hence, scrawl, carelessly written message.

But he no more wanted to be a consistent social dramatist than Scribe wanted to be a great stage moralist. Near the end of his career Sardou fabricated several acting vehicles for Sarah Bernhardt, of which *Fédora* (1882), *Théodora* (1884), and *La Tosca* (1887) are the most impressive. Several of them called for incidental music; one, *La Tosca*, yielded an opera that still lives. Sardou's last piece was *L'Affaire des Poisons* (1907).

Bernard Shaw, writing in *The Saturday Review* in the '90's, derided Sardou for the extravagance and implausibility of his plots, and the barb stuck when he flung the word "Sardoodledom." [20] Barrett H. Clark has shown, however, that Sardou's English detractors generally knew his work in wretched adaptations, many of them produced in London before the originals were even published. [21]

It is incontestable that Sardou follows closely the dramatic methods of his master, Scribe. He builds an elaborate plot on some trivial, apparently insignificant fact. In Scribe, a glass of water changes England's political situation; in Sardou a lost love letter turns a household upside down. The plays of both usually depend on some *quiproquo*: in *A Scrap of Paper* Vanhove and Prosper fail to understand each other because Prosper thinks Vanhove is speaking about the latter's wife and is amazed at what he hears; Vanhove assumes with the same result that Prosper is referring to Suzanne.

Another device common to Sardou and Scribe is the plot pattern involving the pursuit of a phantom object and based on withheld information. A loves B; B is opposed by C; A, pursuing reprisal against C, is victim of a misconception, for C is actually a friend (many variations). [22] In *The Glass of Water* the Duchess loves Masham; he is also secretly loved by the Queen; in plotting vengeance against her unknown rival, the Duchess learns belatedly, and with

[20] Bernard Shaw, *Dramatic Opinions and Essays* (London, 1909), Vol. I, p. 115.
[21] Introduction to Sardou's *Patrie!*, translated by B. H. Clark (Garden City, New York, 1915), pp. vii–viii.
[22] For further discussion see Armand Praviel, "Victorien Sardou," *Le Correspondant* 324: 515–28 (August 25, 1931). This formula furnishes the central situation of the ever-popular *An Italian Straw Hat* (1851), by Eugène Labiche and Marc-Michel, included in *The Modern Theatre*, ed. Eric Bentley. Garden City, New York, 1955. (Doubleday Anchor Books, Vol. 3.)

dire consequences, that her enemy is none other than her sovereign. Prosper, in *A Scrap of Paper*, wants Marthe for his wife, but Suzanne opposes his design. In the struggle that ensues Prosper and Susanne discover that they are in love. Sardou once explained that he had trained himself to read the first act of a play by Scribe, put it aside, plot the rest of the play, and compare his result with the original.[23] Logic, then, was what concerned Sardou. Given a basic situation, knowledge of which has been denied to certain persons, what will be the inevitable result? Sardou did not adapt a situation to fully conceived characters, as the greatest dramatists do: rather, he improvised puppet-like figures around the core of the plot. (Suzanne is an exception.) In writing a play, he tells us in the preface to *La Haine*, he always first established the *scène à faire* and from this crisis worked out his entire plot in reverse.[24]

But Sardou emphasized even more than Scribe the chance vicissitudes of a hand prop, such as a shawl or document, as a way of arousing suspense. In welcoming him to the French Academy in 1878 the director commented: "The letter! It plays a major part in most of your plots, and every detail of it is vital, container and contents. The envelope, the seal, the wax, the stamp, the postmark, the shade of the paper, and the perfume that clings to it. . . ."[25] Though Sardou derived his plots from Scribe, he had a wider dramatic range, and he could portray his heroines with a Gallic zest peculiar to himself. Suzanne is a good example. She is charming, witty, and audacious, with a dash of the ingénue but a bit more tang, susceptible to love without knowing it. Sardou could intoxicate an audience with fantastic mixtures of incompatible genres (tragical-comical-historical-melodramatic) tricked out with lavish *mise en scène*. *Théodora* and *Patrie!* eminently display his gift for manipulating vast historical pageants. *Patrie!* best illustrates this knack; it indulges the most

[23] See Arthur Hornblow, "Contemporary French Dramatists," *Cosmopolitan Magazine* 15: 108 (May, 1893).
[24] See C. E. Montague's brilliant analysis of Sardou's *La Sorcière* in *Dramatic Values* (London, 1911), p. 64. Reprinted in van Druten, *Playwright at Work*, p. 32.
[25] Charles Blanc, *Discours en réponse au discours prononcé par M. Victorien Sardou, pour sa réception à l'Académie Française, le 23 Mai, 1878* (Paris, 1878), p. 48. (My translation.)

variegated caprices of the audience by assembling with vast gusts an overpowering mélange of theatrical trappings— gaudy spectacles and melodramatic thrills, a triangle plot of guilty passion, the pathos of filial devotion, the nobility of patriotism; the whole seasoned with comic relief, punctuated with grandiose sound effects including musical motifs, smothered cries, and a thunder of massed crowds giving voice to their emotions in unison, and culminating in a turbulent death scene charged with passions of hate, love, remorse, and vengeance and involving a suicide. Indeed, Sardou in the legitimate theatre anticipated by some fifty years the historical panorama as evolved by Hollywood.

None of these stupefying expedients is to be found in A *Scrap of Paper*, as deft and actable a comedy as exists. Here Sardou employs the restraint and economy that distinguish the best work of his tutor. The plot, after a slow start, gathers incredible speed. The exposition, never slow or heavy as it sometimes is in the earlier playwright, unfolds a dilemma created for the hero by the eccentric demands of his uncle. Act I occurs three years after the separation of two lovers, Prosper and Clarisse, the present Mme. Vanhove. Her love note comes belatedly into Prosper's possession, and she has to help him get married lest he reveal it. Attention is focused early on the Sèvres statuette; the race between Prosper and Clarisse for the letter underneath it evokes suspense, because our sympathies are with Prosper. At the end of Act I Suzanne and Prosper vie for possession of the letter containing the well-made secret. The action, delayed until just before the curtain, begins with Prosper confident of gaining a bride and satisfying the demands of his surly uncle.

The prospect of a duel lessens the hero's chances early in the second act (seesaw begins: his end down). He promises to destroy the letter if he relinquishes Marthe (up). Suzanne finds the letter (down). Vanhove, nearly catching his wife in Prosper's apartment, now suspects her; to prove her innocence, Clarisse is more constrained than ever to help Prosper (up). Things look grim when Suzanne, to extricate herself from having to marry Prosper, will force him to go away (down). More suspense, after which

Prosper excitedly throws the letter out the window, thereby placing himself at Vanhove's mercy (peripeteia).

The seesaw accelerates in Act III with Paul's interception of the letter. Amid the excitement dinner is announced, and the suspense is broken off just before the final burst of activity that culminates in the *scène à faire* (Thirion and Vanhove both reading the letter and Vanhove *almost* comprehending); but not before Vanhove and Prosper have become involved in an exchange about Prosper's affair with an unnamed lady about whose identity the two make quite different assumptions—a *quiproquo* in the style of Plautus or Molière. The dénouement unites Prosper and Suzanne, and the disheveled and perspiring hero, the poorer by a good dinner, recovers his customary eupeptic buoyancy on finding himself the richer by addition of the charming Suzanne to his collection of curios.

"Camille": Strong Wine in a Tempting Bottle

The Broadway critics, reviewing a recent New York production of *La Dame aux Camélias*, or *Camille*,[26] by Dumas *fils*, could only shake their heads over it. "Why *Camille?*" asked Brooks Atkinson of *The New York Times*. ". . . it is inconceivable that anyone should have an artistic interest in the old Dumas *fils* rumpus. . . . When [Marguerite] totters and staggers and gasps in the last act one does not suffer as one should." Walter Kerr of the *Herald Tribune* finds the play worth knowing historically but no more.[27] The latter-day consensus is, in fine, that *Camille* is the threadbare romanticism of a bygone day and that any grown-up theatregoer would feel ashamed to be caught tolerating it. Consensus or no, what other dramatist's first play has attained the thousands of performances that *Camille* has been given, and has lasted over a century? Could we name one? A present-day stage historian calls it one of the two most popular plays in America in the nineteenth

---

[26] The short title "Camille" results from an erroneous christening of the heroine in 1853 by the first American translator of *La Dame aux Camélias*, John Wilkins. See A. E. Zucker and P. de F. Henderson, "*Camille* as the translation of *La Dame aux Camélias*," MLN 49:472–76 (November 1934).

[27] Both reviews September 19, 1956.

century,[28] and in the twentieth every year or so still brings
forth yet another performance of Dumas' "prodigious
moneymaker." Maybe Henry James, who had a pretty
discriminating eye for the theatre, knew what he was talking about when he called *Camille* "a singular, an aston-
ishing piece of work" and commented that "the story has
never lost its happy juvenility, a charm that nothing can
vulgarize." [29]

Not that the play is without faults in plenty. Clayton
Hamilton rightly pointed them out, and he rightly credited
a large share of the play's success to the inveterate ambition
of emotional actresses to pass the "test" [30] of *Camille*. But
the very unanimity of this ambition is no mean tribute to
the achievement of a tyro.

On February 2, 1852, at the Théâtre du Vaudeville in
Paris, the world greeted the première of Dumas' play with
mixed applause and bewilderment. *La Dame aux Camélias*
had been adapted in 1849 from his novel of the same name,
written two years before when he was only twenty-three.
The novel had been smelted out of a personal experience.
The play was first produced in sensational circumstances.
Both reasons contributed to the tremendous stir that it
made. For two and a half years it had been roughly handled
by the censors: its frank treatment of a subject previously
dealt with only in romantic drama, and thus insulated from
real life, seemed immoral. But the Duc de Morny, first minister under Louis Napoleon, foresaw that the play, precisely
because it was controversial, would helpfully divert attention from the current political agitations—this on the eve of
the *coup d'état* of 1852 that ushered in the Second Empire
—and he gave the play his support for production.

The stresses of that original production are, of course,
now long forgotten; *Camille* has become merely something
to be disparaged as a sentimental by-product of the well-
made play. Inasmuch as the French theatre in the first half
of the century had been dominated successively by two
conflicting genres, the romantic drama and the more logical
and satirical *pièce bien faite*, it is natural to see Dumas'

[28] Felheim, *Theater of Daly*, p. 204.
[29] *The Scenic Art*, p. 262.
[30] "The Career of Camille," in *The Theory of the Theatre* (New York, 1939), pp. 369–71.

first play as falling into the one category or the other. But does it?

Dumas' comment on the speed with which he converted the novel into the play reads: "I have written all my comedies with love and respect for my art, except the first [*La Dame aux Camélias*], which I brought into the world in eight days . . . without quite knowing how—thanks to the daring and luck of youth, impelled by a need for money rather than by divine inspiration.[31]

In 1844 Dumas had been captivated by Marie Duplessis, the illustrious fashion-loving courtesan adored by the most distinguished personages of her day. Her love affair with the indigent Dumas lasted until shortly before her death in 1846. The pinch that came of his reckless extravagance drove him in 1847 to the writing of his novel. Partly to ridicule a lurid melodrama concocted from it by a theatre manager, partly to capitalize on the fame that the novel had begun to bring him, he completed the play in the summer of 1849. He wrote at once impetuously and with the resolve to achieve a commercial theatrical success. For the first two acts he drew chiefly on his experience; for the remaining three, which transform and idealize his heroine, he relied on his knowledge of the contemporary stage. Bent on creating a great part for an actress, this frequenter of theatres observed and studied the tragic roles then being performed in Paris.

Rachel, the foremost actress of her time, in one of her rare departures from classical tragedy, was portraying the heroine in *Adrienne Lecouvreur*, the most sensational drama to date of Scribe and Legouvé, which had opened on April 14, 1849. In this play an ill-fated actress, poisoned by her rival for the love of a nobleman, dies in agony on the stage. Rachel amazed Paris with an interpretation so intense, it is recorded, that she frequently wept from exhaustion after performances.

Dumas was unquestionably influenced no little by *Adrienne Lecouvreur*, and the similarity of the two plays is striking. Both present the separation of lovers by a rival. In both first acts one of the lovers meets the future rival. Act II in both contains a scene of local color that halts the

[31] Foreword to *Théâtre Complet* (Paris, 1890), I, 1–2. (My translation.)

main action. In both the jealousy aroused in one of the lovers is assisted by the use of letters. Dumas' peripeteia differs superficially, but in both a separation turns on the withholding of information from one of the lovers. In Act IV each heroine makes a noble sacrifice for her lover. Both heroines faint when insulted or told of their lovers' danger. Each *scène à faire* is engineered by extreme jealousy in one of the lovers, and suspense is broken by a contrived and unexpected diversion. In each play one lover upbraids the other's (or the rival's) duplicity, real or imagined. In each the heroine dies in the last act, and the hero, having learned the truth, arrives just in time to beg forgiveness.

The truth is that both *Camille* and *Adrienne Lecouvreur* illustrate the danger of applying Scribe's methods to tragedy or to serious drama. Character and truthful values are sacrificed, as the list of resemblances shows, to theatrical manipulation. The motivations are the product of coincidence rather than of will. The technique of the well-made play wears best in light or satirical comedy, where an agile, entertaining plot implants the deeper passions or, if they are present, at least does not dissipate them.

Camille, then, has a somewhat ambiguous relation to the well-made play and cannot be said strictly to belong to the genre. It is in some ways better and in others worse constructed than *Adrienne Lecouvreur*. The main action of Dumas' play is simple, direct, and straightforward by comparison with the complex mechanism of Scribe's innumerable contrived entrances and exits, mechanical hide-and-seek claptrap for keeping characters apart, mistaken identifications, and stage business with physical objects. In *Camille* suspense is admirably sustained from the end of Act III almost to the end of Act IV by means of Marguerite's letter to Armand. The kind of theatrical legerdemain that had dominated *The Glass of Water* a decade before has noticeably diminished—a change that is to the credit of a young and inexperienced playwright.

On the other hand, the fourth and fifth acts of *Camille* (*scène à faire* and dénouement) lack the sharp focus and the economy of Scribe. The Scribean obligatory scene always discloses a new and significant truth, up to this moment withheld. Although it is a *coup de théâtre*, it seems indispensable to the action. Some moral weakness is always exposed, though generally not with too solemn an insistence. It is precisely this scene in Scribe's plays that later social dramatists—Ibsen, Shaw, and others—adapted so effectively to their own kinds of ironical revelation. The obligatory scene in *Adrienne Lecouvreur* hinges on the confrontation of women rivals hitherto kept apart and frustrated in their efforts to identify each other. The audience wants the faithful Adrienne to upbraid the calculating and unscrupulous princess for her duplicity, and in this scene Adrienne does explicitly recognize the true character of her rival, setting the record straight as between good and evil. In *Camille* the corresponding scene really adds nothing to the play's effectiveness. It seems contrived, because Armand has already learned the identity of his rival, and we have already had examples of his jealousy, his distrust of Marguerite. Despite her loyalty to Armand, she gets decidedly the worst of it. Since Armand does not learn the truth until after this scene, his contrition in the last act seems overemphasized and hence sentimentalized. And the obvious interruption two thirds of the way through the fourth act, when dinner is announced, serves merely as a device to relax the mounting tension between Armand and his rival and to bring the lovers together. Again, the death scenes of both *Camille* and *Adrienne Lecouvreur* are too long, the dialogue too rhetorical. Dumas, by weakening his *scène à faire*, deliberately played on the audience's sympathy for Marguerite and at the same time betrayed his determination to contrive, however factitiously, the redemption of the courtesan through love and suffering.

Camille, fuzzy though it may be in structure and content, belongs no more to the romantic world of Victor Hugo's dramas than to the satirical tradition of Scribe. There is a great gulf between Armand Duval's love for Marguerite Gautier and the chivalrous etiquette and daring of the three rival lovers in *Hernani* (1830) or the regenerating devotion of a swashbuckling hero to a courtesan in *Marion Delorme* (1831) and, anyway, both plays are written in a strained and elaborate verse that robs the characters of most of their humanity.

Camille, whatever its shortcomings, has probably exerted

a greater leverage on the English and American realistic social drama than any other nineteenth-century French play. The erring woman and her relation to society have held the center of the stage since 1852; and from that year can reasonably be dated the modern comedy of manners. René Doumic, a judicious French critic, was one of the first to recognize this fact. More recently a biographer of Dumas has described the singular impact of *Camille* on Paris in 1852: "Now came a young man who dared to depict not a courtesan of historical legend, not an adventuress surrounded by a halo of poetic symbolism, but a 'kept woman' of everyday contemporary life, and this author made his subject even more realistic by writing in ordinary prose." [32]

Eugénie Doche and Charles Fechter, the first artists to play *Camille*, communicated the intended spirit of the play with such subtlety and restraint that Dumas affectionately called them his collaborators. As Marguerite and Armand they commanded from spectators both pity and admiration. Marguerite, as Doche portrayed her in Paris, was "to the last breath, a courtesan," said the great critic Sarcey.[33]

Do American readers know what a courtesan is, or was? The elegant extravagances of European high society have no equivalent in this country. Dumas pointed out in his preface (1867) to the play that in 1830 a Parisian courtesan had been known as a *femme galante*—a fashionable kept woman who had acquired the education and refinement of the wellborn lady. By 1860, however, there had developed the gradations of *femme entretenue, lorette, petite dame, cocotte,* and so on. A good many aristocratic but poor daughters of officers killed in the wars of the Empire had been denied the marriages to which their background, training, and tastes entitled them. However endowed with intelligence, delicacy, and capacity for devotion, they had to exist by amorous liaisons and doubtful enterprises; but many of them had brilliant social gifts and could make their lovers grateful for far more than the pleasures of the voluptuary. For such women Dumas himself coined in 1855 the

[32] H. Stanley Schwarz, *Alexandre Dumas, fils: Dramatist* (New York, 1927), p. 33.
[33] Montrose J. Moses, "Stage History of Famous Plays," *The Theatre,* 6: 67 (March, 1906).

name that became the title of perhaps his best play, *Le Demi-Monde*.[34]

The realistic acting of Doche and Fechter in *Camille* helped Dumas give greater social meaning to French drama. In 1852 courtesans were not accepted by the middle class, even in France. But at least Marguerite (who is a courtesan, not a *demimondaine*) could be seen as her creator intended her to be. In England and America, however, the true Marguerite was travestied and obscured for years. Matilda Heron, the first famous Camille in the United States, absurdly denatured the part in conformity to squeamish Victorian tastes and in ignorance of Dumas' milieu; she concentrated her interpretation on a harrowing emotional conflict, throwing overboard analysis, suspense, and the comparatively well-ordered plot in order to exaggerate the heroine's high-minded despair and humiliation.[35]

It had been a bold undertaking to show on the stage a courtesan who had been a public celebrity and to make her capable of unselfish love. The author was censured for his idealized version of a free love that made no concession to the world. Having himself been the intemperate lover of a spectacular and wealthy *femme galante*, he now began to take refuge in masochistic apology, in overcompensation for the guilt and insecurity that his recklessness had entailed. In later plays he became more and more the preacher, less and less the man of the theatre. But, though a hint of thesis runs through the play, to the effect that a prostitute cannot be rehabilitated even if she has a regenerating love, Dumas was not yet the moralist of his later *pièces à thèse*. What he did accomplish was to bring the theatre into more direct touch with life and human problems than it had aspired to since before the Romantic Movement.[36] And it was doubtless partly to soften the impact that he resorted to the theatrical machinery of the well-made play, then at the height of its popularity. In the preface to *Camille* he

[34] Included in *World Drama*, ed. B. H. Clark (New York, 1933). Reprinted by Dover Publications, Inc., 1955 (paperback edition).
[35] Merle L. Perkins, "Matilda Heron's *Camille*," *Comparative Literature*, 7:338–43 (Fall, 1955).
[36] F. A. Taylor, *The Theatre of Alexandre Dumas Fils* (Oxford, 1937), p. 184.

disclaimed the idea of redeeming the courtesan and insisted that Marguerite's love merely illustrated the truism that an act of self-sacrifice can come from an unlikely source.

It is unquestionable that in this first play Dumas wanted to depict the life of the courtesan as it was more than he wanted to reform her. Duval *père*, the voice of respectable morality, who succeeds in separating the lovers, in the last act acknowledges that he was wrong to have done so: yet the play has a sort of implicit corrective undertone that keeps it from being an uncompromising apologia for free love. The courtesan's life is shown to be, after all, trivial and hollow; the men of this milieu are avaricious, irresponsible, and stupid; aside from Marguerite herself, the women are repellent. Several persons in the play frown on this papier-mâché world. The elder Duval is in his way likable and human; and two of the debauchees in the end see the light and marry.

But—the important point in this context—the play achieves a more concentrated dramatic conflict and greater emotional depth than most of the well-made plays of Scribe. The characters have vitality and warmth. We respect Marguerite's frankness, sacrifice, and freedom from hypocrisy. The dialogue is more outspoken and lifelike than the romantics would have ventured to make it. And, as some critics have observed, many faults of construction are atoned for by the emotional power generated through a kind of character altogether new to French drama.

Augier's Righteous Protest

Le Mariage d'Olympe (1855), *Olympe's Marriage*, one of the earliest and simplest adaptations of the satirical well-made play form to social drama, stands apart among the two dozen plays that Augier wrote; and it is a better example than *Camille* of the well-made play. Conceived as an irate reply to that drama, it failed, and it is one of Augier's plays that has never been understood in America. The reason for its Paris failure is not that Augier used the methods of the well-made play, but that he treated belatedly a theme already outworn in the Paris theatre. Moreover he applied it too didactically and uncompromisingly to please the judicious.

Three and a half years after *Camille* appeared Augier spoke out in *Olympe's Marriage*, upbraiding Dumas' apparent sanction of illicit love and attacking the assumption that a courtesan is capable of such a love as Marguerite's. This position involves some irony, for Augier had been a member of the committee that in 1849 had awarded a *brevet de moralité* to *Camille*. But by 1855 the manners of the middle class were gradually changing, and Augier, a staunch bourgeois, had become disillusioned. An age of materialism was beginning; established moral standards were being uprooted; greed, hypocrisy, and cynicism were slowly displacing the older values of honor and the family —values that Augier would defend with his last breath.

The increasing casualness with which courtesans were being received into respectable families had been exploited in *Les Filles de Marbre* (1853) by Barrière and Thiboust and by Dumas' *Le Demi-Monde*—plays that focused attention on that besetting nineteenth-century social problem, the infiltration of good society by bad women. There is a further irony in the fact that the Dumas play, which preceded *Olympe's Marriage* by only four months, is a withering indictment of immoral love; in it Marguerite Gautier is transformed into a grasping adventuress and Dumas into an implacable theatrical moralist.

The first performance of *Olympe's Marriage*, on July 17, 1855, was a tumultuous one. All Paris was by now sick of the courtesan on the stage. The spectators hissed the play, especially at the entrance of Irma, Olympe's mother. According to *Figaro*, someone shouted at the final curtain: "Voilà un coup de pistolet qui tuera la pièce!" [37] This prediction seems to have been substantially accurate. So morbid and shocking did the tone of the play seem—especially from a dramatist hitherto thought intolerant of realism— that Paris would have none of it. Even in 1863 Sarcey could write in *Opinion Nationale* that all lovers of theatre should see it if but to be convinced that in the theatre vice unrelieved by virtue can only repel.[38]

Most of Augier's plays rely less than those of Dumas on

[37] "That pistol shot will kill the play."
[38] Henri Gaillard de Champris, *Emile Augier et la Comédie Sociale* (Paris, 1910), p. 43.

the technique of Scribe, for his broad and balanced outlook, his sense of proportion, and his deeper penetration of character enabled him to dramatize his situations with a minimum of artifice. The hard, theatrical brilliance of Dumas is replaced in Augier by a softer, deeper glow. He rejected Scribe's more comic treatment of the morals of marriage, but, like Dumas, he found particular use for Scribe's way of extracting the last ounce of suspense from a situation that at the same time lent itself to a more moralizing treatment. His early plays had been rigidly classical; they had stuck to verse and the unities. When he decided to explore the possibilities of realistic drama, there was, then, a certain logic in his reliance on the proved methods of Scribe —a reliance more noticeable in *Olympe's Marriage* than elsewhere. And the two writers had a similar broad outlook. Scribe rejected the marriage of romantic passion in favor of the marriage of common sense; Dumas in his later dramas preached repentance for the Seven Deadly Sins, using the stage as his pulpit and denouncing womankind ("La Bête") as the lewdly posturing symbol of Evil; Augier struck his hardest blows at the source of decaying standards, money and avarice.

Augier also borrowed Scribe's intrusion plot, in which a virtuous but unlucky hero rights the wrongs done him by a hostile intruding force. In Augier's dramas an intruder into an established social group, such as a family, is resisted by the members until the conflict is resolved through the revelation of a suppressed truth.[39] To Scribe the defense of marriage and the solid domestic virtues meant the defense of reason and a comfortable income; to Augier it meant the defense of endogamy.

Augier resorted to various tricks of the well-made play to help him dramatize his theme in *Olympe's Marriage*. The mainspring of the action is the author's earnest moral purpose; when he calls on the technical expedients of Scribe, truth to character and general plausibility frequently yield to strained, mechanical effects. The basis of the action is a withheld secret: Pauline is the notorious "Olympe Taverny." The naïve, slightly obtuse hero has already fallen

[39] See Girdler B. Fitch, "Emile Augier and the Intrusion Plot," *PMLA* 63:274–80 (March, 1948).

prey to her scheming methods (late point of attack). The conflict resides in the familiar contention of two master wits for supremacy—here, Pauline and the Marquis. Against the Marquis the cards are stacked from the beginning. The action takes a positive step forward at the end of Act I, when Pauline lies her way into his good graces. In the greater part of this act a leisurely exposition prepares for events to come, but the pace picks up before the curtain. The question whether Pauline's campaign against the family will succeed creates a seesaw in Act II. The Scribean machinery creaks when the diamond necklace and the diary are introduced—the first to receive some rough wear before it traps the deceiver in the *scène à faire*, the second to disclose its secret contents in the recognition scene of Act III. The *scène à faire* in this play is much closer to the unmasking scenes in Scribe than the corresponding scene in *Camille* is. In it a despicable woman is exposed and the author's condemnation conclusively implied. By way of asserting his moral indignation and emphasizing the turpitude Augier inverts Scribe's favorite triangle of hero loved by two women, ingénue and *beauté passée*—the one who unwittingly destroys and the one who protects.

With this blunt expression of his conviction that courtesans do not make good wives, Augier declared his allegiance to the realistic social drama. Had he chosen a less topical subject, one of more nearly universal significance than the vindication of the domestic virtues, and had he enlivened his treatment of it with comic élan, as he did with success in *Le Gendre de Monsieur Poirier* (1855)[40] and *Le Fils de Giboyer*, or had he satirized the moral turpitude of the Second Empire without dehumanizing the protagonist, as he did in his so-called "great and terrible series," [41] he would almost certainly have given the world a more viable drama. The carousal scene of Pauline and her vulgar mother that concludes the second act seemed shocking to audiences even so recently as forty years ago. Barrett H. Clark, in the introduction to his translation, declared: "The admirable and disgusting scene . . . is one of the most

---

[40] Also included in *World Drama*, ed. B. H. Clark.
[41] *Les Lionnes Pauvres* (1858), *Les Effrontés* (1861), *Le Fils de Giboyer* (1862), *La Contagion* (1866), and *Les Lions et Renards* (1869).

trenchant and poignant which ever came from this dramatist's pen. Nowadays, even after Zola and Becque and the
Théâtre Libre dramatists, it strikes a note of horror. How
it must have shocked an audience of the 'fifties!" [42] Today
this scene strikes us as dramatically effective but quite fails
to inspire either horror or disgust.

Olympe's Marriage is by no means the best-known of
Augier's dramas, but it is his best exhibition of the characteristics of the *pièce bien faite.* Perhaps the most directly
didactic of all his works, this short play deserves attention
as one of the most vigorous adaptations of the well-made
play to social drama; and it is a memorable witness to the
dignity to which Augier elevated the drama of France.

The Well-Made Play and British Drama in the Nineteenth Century

In England Scribe's eminently translatable and actable
comedies began to appear in 1819. As the Romantic Movement declined during the first quarter of the new century,
and the poetic creators of a lofty but formless drama
stopped trying to invade the stage—which, in fact, they
had not found particularly congenial—the plays of Scribe
satisfied the demand for a robust, living theatre. The subject matter of English drama at mid-century could hardly
have been more insipid, but Scribe's inexhaustible vitality
and resourcefulness, more than any other single factor, at
least restored the compact dramatic form that had distinguished the work of the best eighteenth-century playwrights. Throughout the 1830's the famous Mathews-
Vestris management at the Olympic Theatre, London,
popularized his *comédies-vaudevilles.* Two favorites of the
Victorian era, Edward Bulwer-Lytton's *Richelieu* (1839)
and *Money* (1840), drew their inspiration from ambitious
dramas of the French master produced in Paris and London. Later still the very successful plays of Tom Taylor
were often built on Scribean models.

Even before 1830 Scribe had become an industry, a
commercial enterprise. Not only England, but also Norway
and other countries, began to import him. The young Ibsen, experimenting with various dramatic forms, could not

[42] *Four Plays by Augier* (New York, 1915), p. xiv.

avoid being impressed by Scribe's craftsmanship. During his apprenticeship as theatre poet at Bergen, 1851–56, Ibsen directed 145 plays, more than half of them adaptations of light French plays, 21 by Scribe.[43] His own *Lady Inger of Østraat* (1854) is a thoroughly Scribean drama with a tragic twist, and it was doubtless influenced, as was *The Feast at Solhaug* (1855), by various of Scribe's plays, including *The Glass of Water*, which was among those performed at Bergen.[44]

Little by little, however, Ibsen broke away from the Scribean formula in his search for a more devastating way of stripping the romantic disguises from the lives of conventional middle-class people. By opening his plays in mid-action and, while propelling the narrative to the inevitable crisis, gradually revealing past and present simultaneously in retrospective dialogue, Ibsen greatly improved Scribe's static first act. The obligatory scene he kept as the place for his iconoclastic disclosures, and in this practice he was followed by Shaw and others. In *A Doll's House* (1878) the sham of Nora's marriage is suddenly revealed to her. In *Ghosts* (1881) the depravity and hypocrisy of a son's background and upbringing in an aristocratic family are exposed beneath a lacquer of respectability. In *Hedda Gabler* (1890) the frustrated heroine's idealistic illusions are destroyed. Where Scribe traced the amusing consequences of a discovery planted early, to be disclosed through a series of logical but trivial foci of suspenses, Ibsen turned the relentless light of truth in one concentrated glare on the incrustations of falsity.

From T. W. Robertson to Shaw, many British social dramatists to whom the theatre seemed an effective pulpit made use of Scribe's dramaturgy for their own purposes. Oscar Wilde consciously modeled *Lady Windermere's Fan* (1892) on such well-made plays of adultery as Scribe's *Une Chaîne,* and he also studied Dumas and Sardou while living in Paris. To the actress Mrs. Bancroft he cheerfully admitted pilfering a whole scene from Scribe. "Why not?" Hesketh Pearson quotes him as saying. "Nobody reads

[48] Introduction to *The Works of Henrik Ibsen,* Viking Edition, ed. William Archer and C. H. Herford (New York, 1911), I, 16.
[4] Halvdan Koht, *The Life of Ibsen* (New York, 1931), I, 102–4.

nowadays." [45] Wilde's plays, however, are much more than imitative. They have a lightness and a deftness all their own, delightfully eccentric English characters, and a devastating wit. The satire surpasses Scribe's in trenchancy in such passages as that in which, ironically, Mrs. Erlynne misses social reclamation because of her compromising gesture to save her daughter.

The plot of Arthur Pinero's 1893 play, *The Second Mrs. Tanqueray*, resembles that of Augier's *Olympe's Marriage*; the structure follows that of Scribe's plays; and the thesis distinctly recalls the plays of Dumas *fils*. Augier boldly painted Pauline "Taverny" in colors too stark to be lifelike; Paula Tanqueray was sympathetically created by a writer who nevertheless accepted Dumas' verdict that the past, in Wilde's phrase, is what one is. Pinero, lacking the incisiveness of the satirist, viewed the characters in this drama largely through the prettified haze of Victorian sentimentalism.

Bernard Shaw, having endured three failures with "unpleasant" dramas, hastily wrote *Arms and the Man* in 1894. He ironically disguised his thesis by hurling at his audience the popular stagecraft that they had unthinkingly accepted for fifty years, just as they had unthinkingly accepted the glory and heroism of war and the dreamy irresponsibility of romantic love. By inverting the tricks of the well-made play he camouflaged his satire of Victorian complacency. *Arms and the Man* is an ingenious reworking of Scribe's *Bataille de Dames*, the plot of which is first sketched in *A Peculiar Position*.

Despite much that is trite, Shaw's play clearly foreshadows the genius of his best, later plays. The first act seems to plunge us into the heart of the action in the manner of Ibsen. Shaw's hero, disenchanted about war, will also have none of the posturings of romantic love; yet beneath the heroine's shallow pose he discovers the real woman, and he is capable of arousing genuine love. The obligatory scene in both Scribe and Shaw culminates in the sudden disclosure to a pursuer that a fugitive has eluded capture by a trick of disguise and with the help of two women. Shaw, however, uses the *coup de théâtre* to reveal hidden

[45] *Oscar Wilde, His Life and Wit* (New York, 1946), p. 218.

psychological truths about his protagonists. The hero who spurned the idealism of war learns that he is romantic enough to make a good husband; the heroic lover and soldier likewise recognizes that he is better qualified as a gentleman of fashion. Out of the theatrical devices that yielded the thin but amusing characterizations of Scribe the author of *Arms and the Man* developed three-dimensional persons.

The well-made play, then, was serviceable to two kinds of British dramatist: the kind that wanted nothing but to exploit the proved methods of one of the most commercially successful playwrights in history, and the kind that saw how a deadly satire of Victorian complacency could be devised from the inversion of these methods. If Wilde and Shaw wrote masterpieces whereas Pinero, except for one or two superior achievements, remained a mediocrity, the difference is a tribute to the genius of Wilde and Shaw. They borrowed their theatrical tricks, as Pinero borrowed his, from Scribe, French boulevard farce, and Adelphi melodrama; but out of them they managed to create refreshing and provocative examples of dramatic art.

STEPHEN S. STANTON

Ann Arbor, Michigan
October, 1956

NOTES

WITH the single exception of *Camille*, the French plays brought together in this volume are virtually unknown and have not been easy to obtain for many years. No English version of *A Peculiar Position* or *A Scrap of Paper* has been published since the nineteenth century. No satisfactory English translation of *The Glass of Water* has ever been available. The Clark version of *Olympe's Marriage* (the only one ever published) has been out-of-print for years, and the Reynolds-Playfair *Camille* is unfamiliar to American readers.

A Peculiar Position. Scribe and Bayard's *La Frontière de Savoie* is listed in Arvin as Scribe's 183rd *comédie-vaudeville*. Planché's adaptation was produced by Charles Mathews and Mme. Vestris at the Royal Olympic Theatre, London, in 1837, three years after the Paris première, and is probably the only version in English. The major departure from the French is the invention of new names for two characters and the deletion of Scribe's songs (which, however unfortunate from the point of view of accuracy, does not detract from the modern reader's enjoyment and is at least understandable in terms of an English production). It is reprinted from a prompter's copy published in *The Acting National Drama*, ed. Benjamin Webster (London, Chapman & Hall, 1837), vol. 1. In 1837 Charlotte Cushman played the Countess de Novara at the Park Theatre, New York. The play was included in the repertoire of Mathews and Vestris, who visited New York in 1838 with their company. Other American productions are recorded in Odell's *Annals of the New York Stage*.

The Glass of Water is an established classic of the French theatre. In 1936 an impressive revival was staged by the Comédie Française. A very free adaptation by W. E. Suter was performed at the Queen's Theatre, London, in 1863, and up to the present has furnished the only published text of the play in English (vol. 79 of *Lacy's Acting*

Edition of Plays—long out-of-print). The central action is
retained but radically condensed, a farcical subplot added,
and the names of several characters are altered. This text
well exemplifies the mutilated form in which plays of
Scribe and Sardou have been known to English and American critics. The American Laboratory Theatre staged in
1930 a version of which no script seems to have survived.
DeWitt Bodeen thus accurately restores for the benefit of
modern readers what may be the authentic prototype of
the French well-made play. His translation, given a stylized
production at the Pasadena Playhouse in 1936, transforms
long soliloquies into actable dialogue and cuts the old-
fashioned asides. But the reconciliation of Bolingbroke and
the Duchess and the last lines between Bolingbroke and
the Queen are Mr. Bodeen's. Yet these additions do not
violate the artificial formality of the play. A performance in
Russian at the Master Institute, New York City in 1953
convinced the present editor that the drama is still effective
on the stage.

Camille has been offered in English versions without
number. In this country only a few, and those of recent
date, present the drama Dumas wrote. The first adaptation
was fabricated in 1853 by John Wilkins for America's first
Marguerite Gautier, Jean Davenport; the MS. and prompt-
book are in the Theatre Collection of the New York Public Library. From the bizarre performances in the Bowery
and P. T. Barnum's "American Museum" to Laura Keene's
"pure" version, in which the drama was interpreted as a
dream, Camille enthralled New York in the 1850's. From
1855 to 1864 Matilda Heron acted her own adaptation
over 1,000 times in the major cities of the United States.
For a most amusing account of this idealized portrayal of a
French courtesan, the reader should consult Perkins', "Matilda Heron's Camille." In New York Camille was produced
38 times between 1900 and 1935. An outstanding translation by Henriette Metcalfe was performed by Eva Le Gal-
lienne and the Civic Repertory Theatre in 1931, and also
by Colleen Dewhurst at the Cherry Lane Theatre, in New
York City in 1956. The romanticized Metro-Goldwyn-
Mayer film of 1936, starring Greta Garbo and Robert Taylor, should perhaps be mentioned: The screen version by

Zoe Akins, Frances Marion, and James Hilton drew freely from the novel and the play of Dumas. In England, Sir Nigel Playfair, celebrated for tasteful revivals of great drama at the Lyric Theatre near London from 1918 to 1932, edited and translated Dumas' play for modern audiences without destroying its dramatic quality and simplicity. In 1930 Tallulah Bankhead played Marguerite in the Playfair production at the Garrick Theatre, London.

Olympe's Marriage was first produced in English in Clyde Fitch's adaptation *The Marriage Game* in 1901. After a brief run in several American cities, this melodramatic farce was withdrawn and has never been revived. Barrett H. Clark's translation first appeared in the periodical *The Drama* (Aug., 1915), and later the same year in his *Four Plays by Emile Augier*, published by Alfred A. Knopf. The restraint and dignity of Augier's play, preserved in the Clark version, are completely absent from the Fitch.

A Scrap of Paper has for nearly a century seen revivals in England and America, but only in the J. P. Simpson adaptation—still obtainable in acting editions. It was first performed in English at St. James' Theatre, London, in 1861. Our grandparents could have witnessed notable performances of it in New York by Lester Wallack, Mr. and Mrs. Kendall, E. H. Southern, John Drew and Ethel Barrymore (this last in 1914). Yet the dialogue is stilted and the characters have been tampered with. On the other hand, Léonie Gilmour's version, which is far more readable and actable, and reproduces Sardou's play as faithfully as a translation can, is practically unknown—having been accessible only in an anthology, *Dramatic Masterpieces* (New York, 1900), now out-of-print.

Camille

AND OTHER PLAYS

A PECULIAR POSITION

A Farce in One Act

by

EUGÈNE SCRIBE and J. F. A. BAYARD

English Version by

J. R. PLANCHÉ

CHARACTERS

(As they appear)

CARLO, *a soldier*
BARBARA, *Carlo's fiancée*
PEPITO, *major-domo*
COUNTESS DE NOVARA
CHAMPIGNON,[1] *an itinerant grocer and wine merchant*
MAJOR LASCARI
MME. CHAMPIGNON
SERVANTS

PLACE: *Near* CHAMBÉRY, *capital of* SAVOY.

TRANSLATOR'S PREFACE: This farce is little more than a free
translation of the *comédie-vaudeville* "La Frontière de Savoie," by Messrs. Scribe and Bayard. The only merit I can
claim is the having induced Mr. Liston to add the part of
Monsieur Champignon to the long list of characters which
owe their popularity to his inimitable acting.

J. R. P.

[1] The word means mushroom.

A PECULIAR POSITION

A large apartment in an old château. Large folding doors in center, and two doors on each side of the stage. The table is laid for dinner.

Enter CARLO *and* BARBARA.

BARBARA. Oh Carlo! My dear Carlo! How glad I am to see you. Who would have thought of you?

Carlo. Why Barbara, I hope you always thought of me.

Barbara. Dear Carlo, so I do; but I meant to say, of seeing you—I never dreamed I should whilst you were quartered at Lans-le-bourg. Have you got leave of absence?

Carlo. Only for an hour.

Barbara. For an hour! You've come six-and-thirty leagues, and have to get back in an hour!

Carlo. Silly wench! No; we had orders to march suddenly to Chambéry, where we arrived last night, and this morning a detachment was sent forward to the frontier. My company is stationed betwixt this and Les Eschelles, not half a league distance.

Barbara. Oh! I'm so glad. Then you'll stay and dine?

Carlo. No, I must be back within the hour. I have only just run here to tell you that I am in the neighbourhood, and to ask what your mother has said to my proposal.

Barbara. Won't hear of it, dear Carlo! Says I shall never marry a soldier, with her consent.

Carlo. Plague take it! Well, never mind, Barbara, I have only another year to serve, and then I'll turn my sword into a ploughshare—and—

Barbara. And by that time I shall be married to another.

Carlo. To another!

Barbara. Yes; my mother insists upon my receiving the addresses of Pepito, a nasty little mischief-making, tattling, babbling fellow; one of the new servants that the Countess hired just after I came here. He knows my mother, has saved a little money, and has managed to get into her favour, so that she will hear of nobody else.

5

Carlo. Oh, don't you be afraid! I'll settle his business for him, depend upon it. Only you be firm in your refusal for a short time, and before I quit this neighbourhood I'll find some way to send him packing. But farewell—I must be off again.

Barbara. Directly?

Carlo. This very moment—I shall barely save my distance.

Barbara. And when will you come again?

Carlo. Oh, very soon—to-morrow or next day; nay, perhaps before night again; for we are to be on the *qui vive.* The Government has received some information about the Carbonari—a movement is apprehended—and the French frontier is to be vigilantly guarded. Not a rat is to leave Savoy without a passport from the minister, properly *viséd* by the local authorities. So one kiss, dear Barbara, and—

Barbara. Hush! somebody's coming. 'Tis Pepito, I declare; I wouldn't have him see you—he'll tell mother and—

Carlo. Pepito! I'll strangle the villain!

Barbara. No—no—no—pray don't make a disturbance. My lady will be so angry—you'll ruin all.

Carlo. Well, I haven't time to strangle him comfortably, so I'll postpone the pleasure; but if ever I do lay hands on him—

Barbara. Well, but do go now, dear Carlo. Here, this is the nearest way out, and nobody will see you. Quick! quick!

[*Hurries him out.*

Enter PEPITO.

Pepito [*as he enters*]. Very pretty! very pretty, upon my word!

Barbara [*aside*]. Oh mercy! I hope he didn't see Carlo.— [*aloud*] What's very pretty, Pepito?

Pepito. What's very pretty? Why you're very pretty—my charming wife that will be soon.

Barbara. Is that all?

Pepito. No, that is not all; but I'm called a tattler—a mischief-maker—and therefore I shall keep this little secret to myself; particularly as I might get into a scrape with my lady by telling it.

Barbara. Into a scrape with my lady! [*aside*] Oh, if I could but make him tell now! [*aloud*] What is it, Pepito? you'll surely tell me.

Pepito. No, no! Women can't keep secrets. Their tongues are always running, it would get about somehow or another, that I saw a great, tall man, wrapped up very mysteriously in a blue cloak, glide into the Countess's apartment.

Barbara. You don't say so!

Pepito. No; I don't say so; but if I did say so, people might say I said so;—and then you know—

Barbara. And then you know you'd be turned out of the château as you deserve for scandalizing my lady.

Pepito. Well, but I didn't—

Barbara. But you hinted as much, and I'll just go and tell my lady, I will.

Pepito. You wouldn't be so spiteful! you don't know what mischief you might make. For it really is true—

Barbara. True! That you saw a man steal into my lady's room?

Pepito. Muffled up in a great blue cloak.

Barbara. And you didn't stop him, and question him?— Why, he may be a thief, and we may be all robbed and murdered!

Pepito. Hush! hold your tongue, don't make a noise. My lady will be very angry; she begged me not to say a word about it to anybody—

Barbara. She. Why there is the Count himself, you foolish fellow.

Pepito. Would her husband, and our master, come into his own house that way—

Barbara. That way? why the master of the house may come in any way, mayn't he? We've been expecting him now every day for more than a week—he came off a long journey—very tired, no doubt—and went straight up to his room.

Pepito. Then why shouldn't the Countess have said so, instead of desiring me not to take any notice to anybody of what I had seen?

Barbara. And you disobey her directly. Very well, sir, she shall know—

Pepito. And suppose it should not be the Count, what will she say to *you*, and what shall *I* be obliged to say to the Count when he does come?

Barbara. You're a scandalous good-for-nothing little man! I'm sure it must be he, and you can't say to the contrary, for you never saw him in your life, any more than myself. He went to Naples before I came here, and two months before you poked your ugly face into the house.

Pepito. Come, come, be civil, respect your future husband.

Barbara. You never shall be my husband.

Pepito. But your mother says I shall, the dear old soul! It's all settled, and you must have me.

Barbara. And suppose I love somebody else, better?

Pepito. I don't care, you shall marry me.

Barbara. But suppose I've promised to marry him—

Pepito. I don't care for that. If you haven't married him.

Barbara. Well then, suppose I have married him!

Pepito. Eh! oh, nonsense—you're joking.

Barbara. Am I—well—you'll see! [*aside*] Come, that's not a bad thought; and as he provoked me—

Pepito. Married!—to whom!—when!—where!—

Barbara. I sha'n't tell you any more—it's enough for you —I'm married—there. You may go and tell my mother that; it's a fine opportunity to make a little more mischief;—so good morning to you.   [*Exit* BARBARA.

Pepito. Married! I feel as if a stack of chimneys had fallen on my head! Tell her mother! Indeed I will tell her mother. The poor dear respectable old creature, to be so treated. But she shall be revenged on her undutiful daughter, I'll take care of that! She shall leave me everything she has in the world, the dear old soul, that she shall; and I won't give a crust to her unnatural child, if she comes starving to my door!—Hah!—the Countess!—

Enter the COUNTESS.

Countess. Pepito, leave the room directly.

Pepito. Yes, madam. [*aside*] What a flutter she's in! There must be something very wrong somewhere.

                                        [*Exit* PEPITO.

Countess. What's to be done? He must not remain here.

They will be sure to seek him in his own château, and search every corner! There is no chance of concealing him. He must cross the frontier—once in France, he is safe; but how?—this passport is in his own name, and by this time, orders may have reached Les Eschelles for his arrest. What shall I do—what shall I do?

Re-enter PEPITO.

Who's there? How dare you, sir—when I desired—

Pepito. Your pardon, madam; but there is a person without who would speak with you immediately.

Countess. A person!—what sort of a person? [*aside*] I tremble all over.

Pepito. Why, madam, he is a very odd sort of person; he won't be said "No" to. I told him you were particularly engaged—could see nobody.

Countess [*aside*]. How unfortunate!—such an answer will arouse or increase suspicion! [*aloud*] You did wrong, sir. Who told you to say I was engaged?

Pepito. Shall I show him in, then?

Countess. Certainly—directly—stay—did you ask his business?

Pepito. Oh dear, yes, madam! I always ask everybody's business.

Countess. And what did he say it was?

Pepito. He said it was no business of mine. Very rude, madam, don't you think?

Countess [*aside*]. Refused to answer! 'Tis an officer of the police! All is lost.

Pepito. What shall I do, madam! send him packing?

Countess. Oh, 'tis no use! he would not go; he will insist on entering.

Pepito. Oh, bless you!—yes; he does. He says he must see the Countess herself—in private.

Countess [*aside*]. Then there is no doubt. Well, let me know the worst. [*aloud*] Show him in here, Pepito.

Pepito. Yes, madam. [*aside*] Very mysterious all this! I don't like the look of it.   [*Exit* PEPITO.

Countess [*running to the door by which she entered, and half opening it*]. Bolt this door inside, and stir not, for your life! [*Shuts the door. Someone is heard to bolt it inside.*]

Kind fortune! Give me courage to support this interview.
The least agitation may betray me. He comes!

Re-enter Pepito *ushering in* Champignon.

Pepito. There's my lady.

Champignon [*aside*]. A magnificent woman upon my
word!

Countess [*aside*]. He is not in uniform—some spy—some
agent.

Champignon [*aside*]. How she looked at me! If I were a
vain man I should say she was struck by my appearance—
even in this inelegant and travelling costume.

Countess [*aside*]. There is a malicious triumph in that
smile. He knows he holds his victim in his grasp. I must
speak to him. [*aloud*] Sir, you desired to see me; may I
inquire your name and business?

Champignon. I have a thousand apologies to make for
this intrusion, madam. My name is unknown, I believe, to
you; but that, as well as my business, shall be communicated
immediately, if you will condescend to favour me with a
private,—a strictly *private* interview [*looking at* Pepito].

Countess. Leave us, Pepito. [*aside*] How alarming is this
studied civility!

Pepito [*aside*]. I wonder if I can hear through the keyhole.
[*Exit* Pepito.

Champignon. I trust, madam, you will excuse the very
great liberty I have taken in requesting a private audience;
but if I were a vain man—I might say—I have a peculiar
way of doing business; and the delicate nature of the com-
munication I am about to make—servants are such med-
dling creatures—they have always their own interests in
view—I never curry favour with them—I never attempt to
bribe them—in all important cases it is my maxim to go
direct to the person I wish to secure.

Countess [*starting*]. Secure! Oh, heavens!

Champignon. What's the matter, madam? You are disturbed?

Countess. Not at all, sir; not at all. Pray proceed, sir.

Champignon. As I was saying, madam, according to my
maxim, I should, in this case, have gone direct to the master
of the house.

Countess. The master of the house! Sir, the Count de Novara is not here.

Champignon. So I have been told, madam; and, therefore, I took the liberty of inquiring for you; and if you will do me the honour to answer me one or two questions—

Countess. Sir, I presume you have a right to interrogate me, and, therefore, I must needs reply.

Champignon. By no means, madam. If you have the slightest repugnance to answer when you hear my questions, I beg you will say so at once, and I make my bow immediately. I have a peculiar way of doing business.

Countess [aside]. If I refuse to answer, he considers it a proof of guilt, and so reports it immediately to his employers—[aloud] Sir, I await your question. If it is one I can reply to, I—

Champignon. Oh, certainly, although it more immediately concerns the Count, you, as his wife, madam, cannot be supposed to be ignorant of the fact.

Countess [aside]. Dreadful intimation!—[aloud] Speak, sir, relieve me from this suspense.

Champignon. Without further preface, then, madam, the Count de Novara has been, I am credibly informed, in the habit of purchasing cognac and liqueurs of various descriptions of an Italian of the name of Gilletti, residing at 54 Grande Rue, Chambéry.

Countess [aside]. He has been arrested, and has in some way compromised my husband.

Champignon. Am I right so far, madam?

Countess. Sir, I know not why I should deny that Signor Gilletti has occasionally supplied the château with various articles in which he deals; but, further than that, neither the Count nor myself have any knowledge of him; and, moreover, we have lately had so much occasion to complain of his charges, that the Count has signified his intention of withdrawing his custom.

Champignon. Then my information was correct, and I have no hesitation in placing this paper in your hands.

Countess. A paper—which has been found on Signor Gilletti!

Champignon. No, madam; one I have caused to be printed for general circulation.

Countess. A proclamation—a description of the person of some unfortunate—

Champignon. No, madam, no; simply a list of the articles in which I deal, and which I can with confidence recommend as unequalled, either in quality or price, by any similar establishment in civilized Europe.

Countess. Sir!

Champignon. I have a peculiar way of doing business—never interfere with a brother tradesman. Had I not been assured, by persons on whom I could confidently rely, that Monsieur the Count de Novara had positively signified to Signor Gilletti his dissatisfaction, I should never have presumed to solicit the custom of his lordship, or—

Countess. Can it be possible? You are, then—

Champignon. Pierre-Auguste-Polydore Champignon, at the Golden Pineapple, near the Promenade, Chambéry, sells all sorts of wines, liqueurs, spices, dried fruits, preserves, pickles, tea, coffee, chocolate, macaroni, vermicelli, Italian oils, French capers, and English blacking.

Countess [*aside*]. What a relief!—[*aloud*] Oh, my good friend! if you knew how happy you have made me!

Champignon. Madam! You overwhelm—you confuse—[*aside*] If I were a vain man, I should say—[*aloud*] May I then hope, madam, that you will honour me by your favours?

Countess. Sir, I am afraid that the Count has already promised; but when he returns, I will mention your name—you will call again, perhaps? [*going*]

Champignon. With the greatest pleasure, madam, on my return from France. I must pass the château—and—

Countess [*stopping suddenly*]. From France! Are you on your way there now, sir?

Champignon. That alone, madam, could excuse my presenting myself to the Countess de Novara, en voyageur—I am going to Lyons—perhaps to Paris—to make purchases. —Madame Champignon accompanies me as far as the frontier—parting with her is the only drawback to my joy at revisiting, even for one day, *ma belle France*—my native country!

Countess [*aside*]. What an idea! If I could but manage—[*aloud*] Indeed, you are not a Savoyard then?

Champignon. A Savoyard! No, madam; I am a Frenchman, nay a Parisian, by birth; my home is at present in
Savoy, but, as the song says, "Je suis Français! mon pays
avant tout."

Countess. But are they not very strict just now, respecting
anybody—and particularly a Frenchman—passing the
frontier.

Champignon. Rigorous in the extreme, madam; but I
happen to be in a peculiar position; the Golden Pineapple
being honoured by the custom of his Majesty the King of
Sardinia, I have a passport from the minister which acts
like a talisman upon all the authorities.

Countess. Indeed! Will you permit me—

Champignon. By all means, madam—[*giving passport*]
You see, madam: "Permit freely to pass, &c. &c. Pierre-Auguste-Polydore Champignon, native of France, *Epicier Dro-
guiste* to his Majesty the King of Sardinia, &c. &c. &c."

Countess. Oh, perfectly; with such a passport as this,
there can be no doubt—I beg your pardon. [*drops the list
he had previously given her*]

Champignon. Permit me, madam. [*stoops to pick it up*]

Countess [*quickly changing the passports*]. You are very
kind—thank you; it's the list of your wares, I believe; if you
will allow me, I'll keep it, and on your return, perhaps
[*offering him the other passport*]—

Champignon. I shall make a point of calling, madam.

Countess. Barbara! Barbara!

Enter Barbara.

Barbara. Yes, madam.

Countess. Take care of this paper, and when M. Champignon returns, let him know what coffee, or chocolate, or
anything else he sells, is wanted. The Count himself will
speak to you about the wines, sir; I wish you a pleasant
journey! [*aside to* Barbara] Keep him in conversation for a
few minutes—[*aloud*] Good morning, sir. [*knocks at door;
the bolt is withdrawn*]   [*Exit* Countess.

Barbara [*aside*]. Keep him in conversation! Dear! how
odd!

Champignon [*aside*]. She's a splendid woman, and a most

affable, engaging woman; upon my honour, if I were a vain man, I should say—

Barbara. Are you going, sir?

Champignon. Going, my dear! Yes, my love, I am going on a long journey.

Barbara. If you'll just stop while I look over this list, sir— perhaps I could tell you now, sir.

Champignon. An uncommonly pretty girl, I declare! [*aloud*] Stop, my love! Egad, with such a mistress, and such a maid, if it were not that Madame Champignon is not very fond of waiting, I shouldn't care if—

Barbara Madame Champignon! What, are you married then?

Champignon. Unfortunately—I mean—undoubtedly I am—to a most exemplary female—in fact a charming person—rather hasty, perhaps, and a *leetle* inclined to be jealous; but if I were a vain man, I should say—*that* can scarcely be wondered at—I confess I have been in my time a terrible fellow—when I lived in Paris—Rue des Filles, St. Thomas!—and even now—occasionally.—What's bred in the bone—eh—you little smiling, rosy rogue, you—

Barbara. Oh, sir! sir!

Champignon. Oh, sir! sir, indeed! Harkye!—a word in that pretty little white ear. I'm to have the custom of the château, you know. I shall often look in; and if you're fond of barleysugar—

Barbara. No—I don't like sweet things.

Champignon. I do. [*kissing her*].

Barbara. Be quiet—or I'll call out.

Champignon. If you do I'll never kiss you again. Like liqueurs?— Send you some "parfait amour!"

Barbara. I don't want any of your amours—get away do— here's somebody coming—and there's your wife waiting for you.

Champignon. Very true!—so she is! Poor Madame Champignon! kicking her heels in the little smoky post-house at Les Eschelles. Adieu my angel—adieu for ten long days—I must tear myself away!

[*Sings*]—"Partant pour la Syrie.
             Lejeune et beau Dunois."
                    [*Exit singing, and kissing his hand to her.*

Enter PEPITO. CHAMPIGNON *goes out.*

Pepito. Mighty gallant, indeed, whoever he is.

Barbara. Well, and what's that to you?

Pepito. A great deal—for I've seen your mother; and she says you are *not* married—she doesn't believe a word of it— and therefore you are to marry me.

Barbara. Very well; perhaps you'll believe when you see my husband.

Pepito. Yes, *when* I see him; and that'll be when I look in the glass someday shortly.

Barbara. He must be looking over your shoulders, then: for it won't be you.

Pepito. I know better, I can see by your face you're telling a story. I defy you to name your husband.

Barbara. I could if I liked! I could if I liked.

Pepito. You can't—you can't—I dare you.

Barbara. You dare me! [*aside*] I've a great mind—he won't be back for ten days, and by that time—

Pepito. There, you can't—you haven't a word to say for yourself.

Barbara. Haven't I? Do you know who that was that went out just now?

Pepito. No; he wouldn't tell me.

Barbara. Then I will. That's my husband.

Pepito. He! and I let him in!

Barbara. It was very kind of you, I'm sure.

Pepito. The devil! If this is true—

Barbara. Hadn't you better run after and ask him?

Pepito. Then that's why he was so confoundedly mysterious.

Barbara. Of course; d'ye think he'd have trusted his rival? He'll be fine and angry with me for telling you; but as you dared me—

Pepito. You've married that man?—Why he's fifty!

Barbara. He is no such thing; and if he were, he's worth fifty of you.

Pepito. Very well—very well! What did he want with my lady?

Barbara. To tell her we were married; because I was afraid to do so myself.

Pepito. Well you might be afraid, and ashamed, too. Marry such a fellow as that, when you might have had such a man as me!

Enter MAJOR LASCARI *and* CHAMPIGNON.

Champignon. But sir, I assure you—

Major. And I assure you, sir, that my duty alone—

Barbara [aside]. Oh, mercy! He's come back again!

Pepito. There's the very rascal!

Champignon. But business of the greatest importance—

Major. Sir, I will not detain you an instant longer than my orders imperatively compel me. Your name, if you please.

Champignon. Champignon.

Major. Where are you going?

Champignon. First to join my wife; and then—

Pepito. It is not true!

Champignon. What do you mean by that?

Pepito. Why that one of you must tell a story; for Barbara says *she's* your wife.

Champignon. Barbara!—No—does she though? [aside to her] Oh you little rogue! I wish you were.—Egad—if it wasn't for Madame Champignon—

Pepito. He doesn't like to admit it; she told me he wouldn't.

Major. Well, sir!

Barbara [aside]. Don't deny it. You'll oblige me.

Champignon [aside]. Oblige her! Poor little girl! Champignon! Champignon—this is the old story.

Major. Sir, I want your answer.

Champignon. My answer, sir?—My answer is that whether I am her husband or not, my name is Champignon. Pierre-Auguste-Polydore Champignon, as my passport shall convince you—and—

Major. Oh, you have a passport!—That's another affair.

Champignon. I believe it is too [producing it]. There, sir, look at that, and detain me at your peril.

Enter the COUNTESS.

Countess [aside]. A soldier!—Then 'twas but just in time.

Major. How is this?—"Champignon!" There is no such name; this passport is made out in the name of the very nobleman I have orders to arrest—the Count de Novara.

Barbara and *Pepito*. The Count de Novara!

Champignon. The Count de Novara!—Poh! poh!—you can't read—

Major. Can you? [*showing it to him*]

Champignon. To be sure—eh! why—this is not my pass-port—

Major. Then where is yours, and what business have you with this?

Champignon. Confound it! it must have been some mistake of that booby of a clerk; he knows me well enough, too, but because I told him I meant to call here, and talked about the count; the stupid fellow has written the name by mistake—

Major. And described the person by mistake, too? "aged 49."

Champignon. I'm only 47, sir.

Major. You look older; "Height 5 feet 8 inches."

Champignon. I'm 5 feet 9, sir!

Major. Bah! that's near enough; "eyes gray, hair brown, nose ordinary—"

Champignon. Ordinary!

Major. "Mouth idem, complexion idem."

Champignon. Pshaw! nonsense! But what does it signify? Here!—here's the Countess herself, she'll tell you who I am, won't you, madam?

Countess. Sir, I will say whatever you wish me to say; but I fear it is now too late.

Champignon. Too late!—Not at all.

Countess. You are recognised, and all denial would be idle.

Champignon. Recognised!—why, you don't mean to say, madam, that I am *your* husband, do you? [*aside*] The deuce is in the women!

Countess. If I could hope to deceive that gentleman, I might be tempted to deny it; but that unfortunate passport has discovered all.

Champignon. Discovered all!

Countess. But do not be alarmed, sir; I trust there is no danger, you are innocent.

Champignon. As a lamb!—ask Madame Champignon.

Countess. Nay, sir—drop all disguise, and confide at once in the honour of this gentleman, I am sure he will not exceed his orders, and obey them he must; they are, I trust, not very severe.

Champignon. I trust not, with all my soul.

Major. They are simply to detain his Lordship till the arrival of a courier from Turin; I have only to request he will not attempt to leave the château; I do not wish to deprive him of your society, Madam. He may remain perfectly unmolested in the bosom of his family.

Champignon. In the bosom of my family!

Countess. You hear, sir, you may stay with me.

Champignon. May I! [*aside*] Egad, I should like nothing better; but what does it all mean? if I were a vain man, I really should say, this is a very peculiar position. Egad, she shall have her own way; if it's a joke, I'll see how far she'll carry it. [*aloud*] Madam, to me your wishes always were commands. Sir, I am your prisoner. As you will have it, I am the Count de Novara.

Pepito. I'm stupefied! Why Barbara!

Barbara [*aside*]. What shall I say now? [*to* PEPITO] Well, if he is the Count, he is a base man, that's all I say.

[*Exit* BARBARA.

Pepito. I'm horrified!

Champignon [*aside*]. Poor Madame Champignon! Well, I can't help it; when a lovely woman insists upon anything, I never can say no—never could in my life! [*aloud to* MAJOR] May I ask your name, sir?

Major. Lascari—Major Lascari.

Champignon. And you are instructed to prevent my proceeding on my journey?

Major. I am, Count.

Champignon. You positively insist on my remaining in the château?

Major. In compliance with my orders, Count.

Champignon. Very well, Major; you will be responsible for whatever may occur in consequence.

Major. Certainly.

Champignon. Then I shall order dinner immediately, for I am getting remarkably hungry, what say you, my dear?

Countess [*to* PEPITO]. You hear your master?—obey him.

Champignon. You hear your mistress?—dinner directly!

Pepito [*aside*]. The vile seducer!—I wish it may choke him!   [*Exit.*

Champignon [*aside*]. I shall dine tête-à-tête with the Countess!—Poor Madame Champignon!

Countess [*aside*]. I must detain the Major, if possible. [*aloud*]—Major, I trust your orders will not prevent your dining with us.

Champignon. Eh!—[*aside to* COUNTESS] We don't want him.

Major. You are very kind, madam. I shall have much pleasure.

Champignon [*aside*]. Confound him!

Major. Will you not divest yourself of your disguise, Count?

Champignon. Disguise!

Major. Yes, this bourgeois-looking coat and cap, as they are now useless, will you not exchange them for a habit more befitting your rank?

Champignon. My rank? Oh—ay—but it doesn't signify. What do you say, my love?

Countess. Just as you please, sir. There are two suits, you know, in your dressing room [*pointing to door*]. Or there's your morning gown, if the Major will excuse.

Major. Oh, madam.

Champignon. Ah! I shall feel more comfortable in the morning gown, and, as we're all at home, you know, amongst ourselves, for we won't call the Major company; so if you will excuse me for a few minutes—you are not afraid of my escaping?

Major. Not in the least, Count; for, independently that I consider you upon your parole, the attempt would be fatal. There are sentries all round the château, with orders to fire upon any individual leaving it suspiciously.

Champignon. I shall not attempt it, upon my honour!
                                                                    [*Exit.*

Countess [*aside*]. Merciful powers! another instant, then, and he would have fallen!

Major. You have not long resided here, I believe, madam?

Countess. Not above three months, sir. The Count is fond of shooting, and took this place merely for the season;

but we had scarcely arrived here when some private affairs compelled him to set out for Naples. It is this unfortunate journey, taken suddenly, and for family reasons with some degree of mystery, which has drawn upon him the suspicions of the government; but he is innocent, indeed, sir, of all political intrigues, as he can prove, if they will but give him time.

Major. I trust he can, madam. You will, I am sure, believe that this is the most disagreeable duty which can devolve upon a soldier.

Re-enter PEPITO.

Pepito. I beg your pardon, my lady, but I can bear it no longer, and speak I must.

Countess. What is the matter?

Pepito. The Count may turn me away if he likes, but I don't care—it's downright treason, and I'll denounce him.

Major. Treason!

Countess. Pepito!—[*aside*] I shall sink.

Pepito. Yes, Major; yes, my lady; and it's treason as much against you, my lady, as against me.

Countess. What do you mean, sirrah?

Pepito. He has taken advantage of his being unknown to Barbara, and entrapped her affections.

Countess. Barbara!

Major [*aside to him*]. Hold your tongue; don't make mischief.

Pepito. I will—I will make mischief. He has made mischief enough. Barbara says she's married to him! married to a married man!

Countess. Impossible!

Pepito. Ah! so I said. I didn't believe it was in human nature. But Barbara vows it is; and he didn't deny it. Did he, Major, when I accused him? I ask you, upon your honour, now, as an officer and a gentleman.

Major [*aside*]. Ugh! you tattling booby; what is it to you?

Pepito. What is it to me?—There's morality!—Why she is promised to me by her mother, sir! I was to marry her myself, and have all the old woman's money.—What is it to me indeed!

Countess [*aside*]. He talked about his wife, certainly.

Did he mean Barbara? or has he really deceived the poor girl. I must see her at any rate—learn her story, and trust her with my secret. [*aloud*] Major, Excuse me for a few moments; I must speak to this girl.   [*Exit Countess.*

Major. There, you've made a fine piece of work. This may end in the separation of the Count and Countess.

Pepito. I don't care, and I don't believe *they* would much. I could tell something about the Countess if I liked. Hang me if I don't think one's as bad as t'other! Ay—you may stare, Major. But you ask her who the man in the blue cloak was? That's all.

Major. Why you scandalous little rascal! I ask her, indeed!—No; it's no business of mine. [*aside*] A precious family this.

Re-enter COUNTESS.

Countess. Pepito! Leave the room! and never let me hear you breathe about this subject again!

Pepito. Madam!

Countess. Leave the room, I say.

Pepito [*aside*]. Won't I though?   [*Exit* PEPITO.

Major. There was no foundation, I presume, for any serious charge?

Countess. None in the least, sir. The girl merely made up the story to annoy Pepito, whom she can't bear; and little thinking it was her master, whom she had never seen.

Major. Ha! ha! and he would not contradict her for fear of betraying himself to me. I see it all.

Countess. Here he comes—not a word to him, if you please.

Re-enter CHAMPIGNON *in a splendid morning gown, cap, and slippers. Servants at the same time enter with dinner.*

Champignon. I call this remarkably becoming now—really. If I were a vain man—I should say, that if I made such an impression in my common everyday dress, in this elegant dishabille, I must be irresistible! Oh, Champignon! Champignon! Thou hast been the hero of many adventures. But this, of all, is the most peculiar position!

Countess. Now, Count, are you ready for dinner?

Champignon. Ready! my dear Countess; I've the appetite

of a chamois hunter. It's past five o'clock: and, at the Golden Pineapple, we always dine at—

Major. The Golden Pineapple!

Countess. The—the hotel the Count was staying at, at Naples. Major, will you take that chair? The Count will sit here.   [*Exeunt Servants.*

Champignon [*aside*]. She places me next to herself—the dear creature! [*aloud*] Yes, yes, I sit here, next to my darling wife! In conjunction with Venus, and in opposition to Mars, as the almanac would say that hangs up in the back parlour of the Golden—

Countess [*treading on his foot*]. Do you eat macaroni, Major? [*helps him*]

Champignon [*aside*]. She trod on my toe!—She positively trod on my toe! I'll put the other foot forward though, for I've a confounded corn upon this.

Countess. Macaroni, Count?

Champignon. Macaroni! to be sure; I've the greatest possible respect for macaroni, and flatter myself I am rather a judge—[*eating some*] O dear! O dear! O dear! This won't do at all—a very inferior article, I can assure you; I suppose you had this from that Italian fellow, Gilletti. He ought to be ashamed of himself; an Italian too—to call this macaroni! Why we wouldn't give it house room at the Golden —[COUNTESS *treads on his foot.—Aside*] Confound it, she will tread on the one with a corn.

Countess. I am afraid they have made you dainty at Naples; of course, you were then in the very land of macaroni.

Champignon. At Naples—oh yes, true; oh yes, fine place —Naples; famous for soap, too, as well as macaroni—I have some very superior for shaving—if the Major—

Count. Don't you think the Major would rather judge of your wine than your soap, Count, at the present moment.

Champignon. My charming Countess, you are perfectly correct—a most deserved rebuke. What's this?—Marsala— pretty fair; and Bordeaux of the very first quality, I vow. You didn't have this from Gilletti's, I'll swear. [*drinks*]

Countess. No, sir; you know very well that was a present to you from the French minister at Turin.

Champignon. Oh, ay—to be sure; I remember—know

him very well—lives close by the Promenade—served him myself often.

Countess. Exactly; and he sent you this in acknowledgment of your services.

Champignon. True, true. [*aside*] She will tread on the wrong foot. [*aloud*] Major, you don't drink—you are dull—thoughtful; you have left some pretty girl behind you, I'll venture to say. These mushrooms have been pickled.

Major. Nay, Count, not I; I was never in love but once in my life—and that was for a very short time; and, to own the truth, I believe more because she was going to be married to another, than for any other reason.

Countess. Married to another! Poor Major; and so you lost her then?

Major. Yes, madam, if it is to be termed a loss. She was a woman of the world, and preferred a tradesman with money to a gentleman with none.

Champignon. A sensible woman! We'll drink her health if you've no objection.

Major. Not in the least. I believe she liked me better than the man she married, after all; and she always said if he behaved ill to her she'd seek me out were I at the farther end of the world.

Champignon. A woman of spirit too! Here's to the health of—

Major. Adolphine!

Champignon. Adolphine! Why that's the name of my wife!

Major. Your name, madam?

Countess [*treading violently on* CHAMPIGNON'S *foot*]. Yes, one of my names. [*aside to him*] Would you destroy me?

Champignon [*aside*]. Destroy her! Oh, murder! She's lamed me for life! It's jealousy—downright jealousy.—The mere mention of another woman!

Major. What's the matter, sir? You seem in pain.

Champignon. A twinge,—a sharpish twinge in my foot.

Major. The gout, sir?

Champignon. No, a corn. I have a very bad corn on *that* foot, my love.—Some wine, Major.—That parmesan is too dry.—Don't weep.—The true test of good Parmesan is—

Enter PEPITO.

Countess [*to* PEPITO]. Well, sir?

Pepito. There's a lady inquiring for you, madam, or the Count.

Countess. For the Count! [*aside*] Should she know him. —Who can she be? [*aloud*] Did you say we were at dinner?

Pepito. Yes, madam. She said she'd wait.

Major. Pray make no ceremony, madam, I have dined.

Champignon. Is she pretty?

Pepito. Not particularly.

Champignon. Let her wait, and tell them to take away, and bring some coffee and liqueurs, if you have any worth drinking.—Huile de Venus, or Kirchwasser, or cognac.

Pepito. Well, I'm sure!   [*Exit* PEPITO.

Champignon. I don't know but what I prefer cognac to anything else in the way of a chasse—eh, Major?

Major. Your pardon. I will do myself the pleasure to return for my coffee. I must just visit the sentries.

Champignon. Oh, by all means! [*aside*] I'm glad he's going! I long for the dénouement of this delicious adventure.

Countess [*aside*]. I hope Barbara is at hand, ready to appear, as I told her, the moment we were left together— the man might presume—

Major. I'll be back in a quarter of an hour, at furthest.
                                        [*Exit* MAJOR.

Champignon. Oh, pray don't hurry yourself! [*to* COUNTESS] At length, most charming of women—

Countess [*aside*]. Ah! here she is!

Enter BARBARA.

Champignon. What the devil do you want?

Barbara. M. Champignon! Is that the way you speak to me? I want to know, sir, if you have told my lady what you promised?

Champignon. What I promised?

Barbara. Yes. What did you come here for, pray, but to tell my lady that we were married, and to ask her to speak to my mother.

Champignon. Smother your mother! What d'ye mean, you little foolish girl—married to you—

Countess. M. Champignon! Can I believe my ears!

Champignon. There's not a word of truth in it as I live and breathe, madam!

Barbara. Oh, you base man!

Countess. Pepito told me something of this; but I refused to listen—I could not imagine that one of my own servants—

Champignon. It is not true, madam! I'm a married man, and she knows it.

Countess. More shame for you—you must have promised her marriage at least.

Champignon. I never promised her anything but some barleysugar.

Barbara. Didn't you acknowledge to the Major—

Champignon. Yes; because you asked me to oblige you— you attacked me on my weak point—I never could say no to a lady in my life. But I give you my word, madam, that you—and you alone—

Countess. Don't speak to me, sir—don't come near me. Go, faithless man—leave the château, and never let me see you more.

Champignon. Go! it's very easy to say go—how the devil am I to go? If I attempt it they'll shoot me.

Countess. Hush!—I had forgotten that.

Champignon. You're very kind—but I had not.

Countess. And I dare not yet avow—he may not yet have passed the frontier.

Madame Champignon [*without*]. I don't care!—I will see the Countess—I insist upon it!

Champignon. Eh! That voice!

Countess [*aside*]. Ah! the lady who was inquiring for me or for the Count.

Enter PEPITO *with* MADAME CHAMPIGNON.

Madame Champignon. Don't tell me! I know he must have been here! Ah! there he *is!*

Champignon. My wife, by all that's terrible!

Countess, Barbara, and *Pepito.* His wife!

Pepito. Another wife! Why he's the Grand Turk!

Madame Champignon. M. Champignon! What doe

this mean! You here in a morning gown and slippers—
quietly at your ease—while I have been in agony on your
account.

Countess. Nay, if 'tis thus—I must explain—and trust to
their kindness. [*aloud*] Madam—a few words will—

Re-enter the MAJOR.

—[*aside*] The Major!—I dare not!—

Madame Champignon. Pray speak, madam—I am on the
rack.

Champignon. So am I.

Major. What's the matter, Count?

Madame Champignon. Count!—He—

Major. To be sure; the Count de Novara!—and!—or I
am much mistaken.—Adolphine!

Madame Champignon. Antonio!—I shall faint! [*falls in
the* MAJOR's *arms*]

Champignon. Hollo! hollo! Major!—I say—do you know
—that's my wife?—

Major. Your wife?

Pepito. Yes!—The Blue Beard!—He has deceived her as
he has Barbara.

Champignon. Hold your tongue, you fool. Adolphine!—
aren't you ashamed of yourself. Wife I say—

Madame Champignon. Don't touch me.—Wretch!—
Monster!—your wife!—I am no longer your wife!—Take
me from his sight, Antonio!

Major [*to* COUNTESS]. Pray, madam, may I ask—

Countess. Question me not, sir. I cannot answer!

[*Exit* COUNTESS.

Pepito. Now, Barbara! Now, you see—

Barbara. Don't talk to me, sir.—Oh, you horrid man! [*to*
CHAMPIGNON]   [*Exit* BARBARA.

Champignon. Madame Champignon!

Madame Champignon. Antonio! Protect me from him!

Major. But pray explain—

Madame Champignon. Away—away from him, and I will
tell you all.

Major. Come, then!—Nay, sir; you do not quit this
room, till the mystery is unravelled. Pepito, bolt the doors.

[*Exeunt* MAJOR *and* MADAME CHAMPIGNON.

Pepito. That I will!—I shall be revenged on somebody.

[*Exit* PEPITO.

Champignon [*following*]. But I say!—Major!—Madame Champignon! [*The door is bolted.*] They've bolted me in! —Well, this is certainly the most peculiar way of walking off with a man's wife! But if I'm not revenged on Madame Champignon it sha'n't be my fault, that's all I know; up to this moment I but contemplated an innocent frolic—a simple flirtation—a passing gallantry—a pardonable peccadillo. I had left the follies of my youth in the Rue des Filles, St. Thomas. My constant heart would have shuddered at any serious infidelity, and flown back with unsullied pinions to connubial love and the Golden Pineapple!—But now! —O rage!—O vengeance!—There is no atrocity I am not prepared to commit; I will employ all the powers of fascination I possess to victimize the whole sex, in revenge for this heartless desertion! It's getting dark! Welcome ye shades of night—black as the deeds I contemplate. Beautiful but capricious Countess, whatever may have been thy motive for placing me in this peculiar position, thy heart shall be the first sacrifice upon the altar of revenge! [*approaches the door by which the* COUNTESS *has disappeared, and taps gently*]

Countess [*within*]. Who's there?

Champignon. Idol of my soul! 'tis I, your adoring Champignon. [*The door is bolted*] Hah! she unbolts the door— [*tries it*]—no, she's bolted it. Loveliest of your sex, you've made a mistake—you've *fastened* the door. No answer—no movement! Inexplicable woman! Hah! an excellent thought —I'll pique—I'll nettle her. That's a sure card to play with all such coquettes. I'll begin with Barbara; she shall be my first victim. [*goes to the door through which* BARBARA *went out*] Bewitching Barbara, are you there? [*The door is bolted*] Barbara, my love, you've bolted the door; 'tis I, your own Champignon! Don't be silly—my coldness was only feigned. I love—I adore you. It was only to deceive my wife that I pretended to slight you—[*sings*]

> "Ouvre moi ta porte,
> Pour l'amour de Dieu!"

[*The door is unbolted*] That's done it! She opens the door! Celestial melody, I thank thee!

Enter CARLO *with two swords under his arm, and a lighted candle in his hand.*

Who the devil are you?

Carlo. An injured man, who requires satisfaction.

Champignon. Satisfaction!

Carlo. Yes, sir; you have descended to attempt the seduction of a girl in humble life—you must not plead your rank to evade the consequences.

Champignon. I! What do you mean?

Carlo. I mean that you are, or you are not, the Count de Novara. If you are he, you have assumed the name and character of a tradesman to effect the ruin of Barbara, for which you must answer to me.

Champignon. In that case, I am not the Count de Novara.

Carlo. In that case, then, you are the tradesman you represent yourself, and, being a married man, have had the villainy to conceal that fact, and offer marriage to an innocent and unsuspecting girl, for which you shall answer to me!

Champignon. It's no such thing—she insisted herself. Let her come out and say it to my face.

Carlo. She is not there—I have not seen her; but Pepito, who was at least an honourable rival, has told me all,—therefore, Count or no Count, defend yourself! Here are two swords—choose.

Champignon. The bloodthirsty monster! Choose!—I won't choose!—I don't choose to choose! It's false altogether.

Carlo. False! Did I not hear you this moment declare your affection, and acknowledge you had deceived your wife?

Champignon. Oh, that I was in the little back parlour of the Golden Pineapple! Sir, I assure you it was a mere joke, to turn the tables on Madame Champignon, who has behaved most shamefully.

Carlo. A joke! The destruction of a poor girl's character; for such was the least evil which could arise from your conduct! This, to me, is adding insult to injury— Defend yourself.

Champignon. I won't; you shall be hanged for murder, for I won't move hand or foot. [*Sits down in a chair*]

Carlo. Coward! you cannot be the Count de Novara. Coward, I say; cannot that move you?

Champignon. Nothing can move me. I am in a peculiar position.

Carlo. Be it so. You are worthy the death that awaits you -a public execution.

Champignon. What!

Carlo. The common courage of a man might have saved you from that infamy; you had the chance of falling by the sword of a soldier in fair combat. You will now be shot like a dog.

Champignon. I tell you what. If this is a joke, it's by no means an agreeable one, and I must trouble you to explain.

Carlo. An order has arrived from Turin for the immediate execution of the Count de Novara.

Champignon. What's that to me, sir? I am not the Count de Novara, I am Pierre-Auguste-Polydore Champignon, *Épicier* to the King of Sardinia, and I should like to see anybody shoot me like a dog.

Carlo. You will not have the pleasure of *seeing* it, certainly, for your eyes will be bandaged; but shot you will be, take my word for it. If you are not the Count, you have connived at the escape of a traitor, and will be treated accordingly.

Champignon. Treated he calls it! My dear sir, you don't mean to say that they really think me guilty of such a crime as—

Carlo. There can be no doubt; you have the Count's passport, and someone has already passed the frontier with that of Monsieur Champignon.

Champignon. Then, I'm a murdered man! Robbed and murdered!

Carlo. Hark! They come. I offer you still the chance.

Champignon. Go to the devil!—I won't fight—I won't be shot. Madam! My Lady! Countess! I'm in a peculiar position. [*Knocking violently at door*]

Enter the MAJOR, MADAME CHAMPIGNON, *and* BARBARA

Major. Pierre-Auguste-Polydore Champignon.

Champignon. That's me! you hear!—I am not the Count. Oh, my dear Madame Champignon.

Major. I arrest you on the charge of having connived at the escape of the Count de Novara, a proclaimed traitor, who has crossed the frontier by means of your passport. [Countess *appears at door*]

Champignon. I'm a dead man!

Countess [*advancing*]. My husband safe! Oh, then, hear me, sir. I am the offender! It was I who, to save a husband's life, exchanged the passport without the knowledge of this person.

Champignon. Hear her! Hear her! I am innocent. There never was such an innocent!

Major. You must excuse me, madam, but I cannot believe your assertion—it does not agree with the voluntary assumption of the Count's name and dress by this individual, and I must, therefore, only consider it as a generous devotion on your part to save the accomplice of your husband.

Champignon. Me!—an accomplice!

Countess. Indeed, sir, he was ignorant of the purpose for which, at my request, he assumed this character.

Champignon. Yes—at her request—you hear, Madame Champignon.

Major. This will avail him little, unless you could prove that the Count de Novara was no traitor.

Countess. Alas! sir, though confident of his innocence, that must be the work of time, and, to gain that time, he fled—

Champignon. And left me to be shot instead of him— the unnatural monster!

Major. In that case, madam, we have only to hope that, before the execution of Monsieur Champignon, the Government may itself obtain some light upon the subject.

Champignon. To be sure—before; I don't care what they do after.

Countess. But what time, sir, will be allowed to him?

Major. A quarter of an hour.

All. A quarter of an hour!

Champignon. Madame Champignon!

Countess. Oh, sir, you have a smile upon your lips; you

would not do this for mere mockery; you must have some intelligence.

Major. You are right, madam; I have the pleasure of placing in your hands this despatch by which you will perceive that the order I have just received was to release the Count if he had been taken, as the Government had convinced itself of the unfounded nature of the charge against him. I have despatched a courier with the welcome news to the Count himself.

Countess. Oh, sir, how can I express my gratitude to you for that kindness?

Major. Nay, madam; it is in itself a sufficient recompense.

Champignon. And what's to recompense me for having my feelings trifled with in this barbarous manner?

Major. Ask Madame Champignon, if some punishment was not deserved for your professions to Barbara and to the Countess.

Champignon. My professions—

Madame Champignon. Ay, M. Champignon, I heard you, and so did the Major: "Idol of my soul!" and "bewitching Barbara, I adore you, it was only to deceive my wife that I pretended—

Ouvre moi ta porte!"

Oh, for shame, M. Champignon!

All. Oh, for shame, M. Champignon!

Champignon. For shame yourself, Madame Champignon; didn't you fling yourself into the arms of an officer, before my face, in a most peculiar position?

Countess. Come, come, no recrimination—no more misunderstanding. Both Barbara and myself have a right to answer in some degree for his conduct; neither of us could well explain to him our own, and, "if he had been a vain man" he certainly might have presumed, in his "peculiar position"—

Champignon. You hear, Madame Champignon, I *might* have presumed—while you—but I'll be generous; the Countess desires it, and I never could say "no" to a lovely woman in my life—Adolphine!

Madame Champignon. Polydore! [*they embrace*]

Champignon [aside]. I shall keep an eye on the Major, though.

Countess. Barbara, I will speak to your mother in favour of Carlo; M. Champignon, forget not you have the custom of the château.

Champignon. Forget it, madam! Impossible! but I have a peculiar way of doing business, and must first beg leave to ascertain the opinion of my other customers. Ladies and gentlemen, I feel I cannot serve this château unless I obtain your approval. If I were a vain man, I should say I have long been honoured by your favours, and therefore may indulge in the hope that you will not withdraw them from me, now that I am placed in this "PECULIAR POSITION."

THE GLASS OF WATER

A Play in Three Acts

by

EUGÈNE SCRIBE

English Version by

DeWITT BODEEN

CHARACTERS
(As they speak)

HENRY ST. JOHN, *Viscount Bolingbroke*
MARQUIS DE TORCY
ARTHUR MASHAM
ABIGAIL CHURCHILL
SARAH CHURCHILL, *Duchess of Marlborough*
ANNE, *Queen of England*
THOMPSON, *the Queen's doorkeeper*
LADIES AND GENTLEMEN OF THE COURT
MEMBERS OF PARLIAMENT

PLACE: *St. James Palace*, LONDON.
TIME: *The early eighteenth century, during the reign of Queen Anne.*

THE GLASS OF WATER

ACT ONE

SCENE I

*A reception room in St. James Palace, London. Morning.
A beautiful, regal room, done in exquisite Queen Anne
style. There is a large door to the rear, center, and a smaller
entrance on either side. A table with writing materials is on
the right; to the left is a small round table.* MASHAM *is on
the stage when the lights go up, asleep in an armchair near
the door, left. He cannot be seen by* BOLINGBROKE *and the*
MARQUIS DE TORCY, *who enter immediately from the right.*
BOLINGBROKE *is speaking; one has the idea that his reassur-
ing speech has been going on for some little time.*

BOLINGBROKE. . . . Oh, but you needn't worry, M. le
Marquis. This letter *shall* be brought to the Queen's attention. Frankly, I don't at the moment know how . . . but
I assure you I shall find the way to get it to her . . . somehow . . . and she will receive you with all the respect due
an envoy of the King of France.

De Torcy. I hope you're right, M. de Saint-Jean. Remember . . . I intrust not only my own honor, but that of my
country . . . France . . . to your loyal friendship.

Bolingbroke. I am twice honored, monsieur.

De Torcy. I am pinning on you, monsieur, my one last
hope of gaining an audience with the Queen. If you succeed,
an honorable and glorious peace between England and
France will be possible; if you fail . . . ah, well . . . God
help us! [*He places his hand in* BOLINGBROKE'S.] Au revoir,
monsieur, et bonne chance!

Bolingbroke. Au revoir. [DE TORCY *leaves.* BOLINGBROKE
shakes his head, muttering sadly.] It's plain to see that old
age is the time when a man loses his illusions.

Masham [*Stirring in his sleep, quite blissfully*]. Ah! how
beautiful she is! . .

Bolingbroke [*With a smile*]. And youth, the time when a man discovers them!

Masham [*Still dreaming*]. Yes, I love you . . . my dear, I shall always love you.

Bolingbroke. You are indeed dreaming, you lucky fellow. [*Coming down and discovering who it is.*] Ah, but it is young Masham!

Masham. Such eyes! . . . such lips! . . . such . . oh, it is too much for one man!

Bolingbroke [*Tapping him on the shoulder*]. In that case, my friend, let me share it with you.

Masham [*Awake and rubbing his eyes*]. What? . . what? . . . oh, it's you, St. John.

Bolingbroke. Disappointed?

Masham [*Stretching*]. I was dreaming of the most beautiful woman in the world.

Bolingbroke. What a youthful folly!

Masham. Ah, St. John, wait till *you* fall in love!

Bolingbroke [*Drily*]. I was in love . . . once.

Masham. Really? Tell me . . . what happened?

Bolingbroke. I married her.

Masham. Well . . . don't stop. Go on. What happened after that?

Bolingbroke. Nothing. I just married her.

Masham. What was she like?

Bolingbroke. Oh, beautiful . . . charming . . .

Masham. Ah!

Bolingbroke. But impossible to live with. Her dowry amounted to a cool million . . . and she had as many faults in her character. So I gave up the dowry and the wife . . . but still came out the winner!

Masham. How so?

Bolingbroke. My wife was one of the shining stars at court. Being on the side of the Marlboroughs, she was, of course, a Whig. I, to be contrary, enrolled myself upon the Tory lists . . . ah, I have her to thank for that. I owe to my dear wife my present happiness.

Masham. Indeed?

Bolingbroke. Yes, for from that day my life's work was revealed to me. The Tory party was the food I had been craving. In the midst of political tempests or stormy debates,

I can really breathe; I am at perfect ease . . . and, like the English sailor upon the high seas, I am absolutely at home —in my element, my empire!

Masham. But the Whigs control England. The Tory party isn't in power.

Bolingbroke. Ah, my dear boy, you don't know how the vanquished can disturb the security of the victor. In vain does the Whig ministry attempt to crush me and my party with the pseudo-glory of its war victories; in vain does it dominate at this moment England and all Europe. I, with the help of a few friends, manage to keep the Tory party uppermost in the minds of the victorious Whigs. Lord Marlborough, at the head of his army, literally trembles upon hearing of one of my speeches or upon reading an article of mine in the Tory paper. He has on his side Prince Eugene, the Netherlands, and five hundred thousand soldiers; I have on mine, Swift, Prior, and Atterbury. For him, the sword; for me, the pen! We shall see some day who has the victory!

Masham. Nevertheless, Lord Marlborough continues to be victorious upon the battlefield.

Bolingbroke. To be sure. He wants the war to go on so that he can continue to rob the public purse and to fill his own; as for myself, I want peace and industry, which, more than all of Marlborough's victorious battles, will assure the prosperity of England. It is precisely that peace with France which I must make the Queen, Parliament, and England herself to understand.

Masham. Not an easy thing to do.

Bolingbroke. No, for brute force and success gained by cannon shot will always confuse the mind of the common man to such an extent that he never even dreams that the conquering general may be a fool, a tyrant, or a scoundrel . . . and Lord Marlborough is all of that. I shall prove it. I shall catch him some day red-handed in the very act of pilfering the coffers of the state.

Masham. You wouldn't dare expose him.

Bolingbroke [*Taking out a paper*]. I have already hinted at his follies. Look . . . this article here in today's Tory paper . . . I shall repeat it tomorrow, and the day after . . . every day . . . for in the end there is one voice which makes itself understood . . . one voice which still speaks louder than all your bugles and drums . . . and that is the voice of Truth! But I beg your pardon . . . I forgot . . . for the moment I thought I was in Parliament . . . and here I am forcing you to undergo a course in politics when you were dreaming of the most beautiful woman in the world.

Masham. Ah, she is indeed.

Bolingbroke [*Touching* MASHAM's *medals*]. A great lady, I daresay she is . . . someone with influence and power.

Masham. What do you mean?

Bolingbroke. These medals! This handsome uniform! You have come up in the world, my dear boy, since I last saw you.

Masham. But not because of any great lady. I assure you. It is the strangest story in the world . . . the story of my promotion. You wouldn't believe it. . . .

Bolingbroke. On the contrary, I can believe anything that happens in the English court.

Masham. Well, milord, for many years, as you know, I had hoped for a place in the palace of the Queen. The difficulty came, of course, in presenting my petition to Her Majesty. However, on the day that Parliament opened, I forced my way through the crowd which surrounded her carriage . . . indeed, I was almost touching it when suddenly a large gentleman knocked against me, turned around, and . . . I suppose, believing me to be a student . . . snapped his fingers in my face.

Bolingbroke. Not a very courteous gentleman, I might suggest, for all his size.

Masham. Exactly, milord. Oh, I tell you I was perfectly furious. I can still see his insolent face . . . I think I could recognize that face among a thousand others, and if I ever meet him again . . .

Bolingbroke. Did you get your petition to Her Majesty?

Masham. Yes . . . for in that moment the crowd came between us and practically threw me against the carriage of the Queen, to whom I tossed my petition. For a fortnight there was no answer. Then I received a letter for an audience with Her Majesty! You can imagine how I has-

tened to present myself at the Palace, dressed in my only
silk coat and, for certain financial reasons, on foot. I was
practically within two steps of St. James Palace, when a
carriage, driving pell-mell down the street, splattered me
from head to foot with mud . . . my silken coat was
ruined . . . and to cap the climax, who should appear at
the window of the carriage but this same insolent fool . . .
the snap-finger man . . . and he was laughing again. In
my rage I tried to run after him, but the carriage soon
disappeared from sight, and I, furious and in utter despair,
was forced to return, having missed my audience.

Bolingbroke. And your good fortune!

Masham. On the contrary. The very next day I received
from an unknown person a handsome court costume, and, a
few days later, the place that I was asking for in the Queen's
house. I was there hardly three months, when I received
what I wanted more than anything else in the world . . . a
promotion to ensign in the Queen's Guards.

Bolingbroke. Really! And you have no idea who your
mysterious protector may be?

Masham. None . . . except that he assures me of his
constant protection if I continue to conduct myself in a
worthy fashion. I could ask for nothing better. There is
only one thing that puzzles me, however . . . he absolutely
forbids my getting married.

Bolingbroke. Ah-ha!

Masham. Believing, without doubt, that marriage would
hinder my chances for advancement.

Bolingbroke. So you really think that is the reason?

Masham. Why, yes. . . .

Bolingbroke. Well, well! My dear Masham, for an old
page of the Queen and for a young officer in the Guards,
you have an almost Edenlike innocence.

Masham. Why do you say that?

Bolingbroke. Has it never occurred to you that this unknown protector of yours may be a protectress?

Masham. Don't be silly.

Bolingbroke. Some great lady who is interested in
you . . .

Masham. No! No, milord, that is absolutely impossible!

Bolingbroke. Why so much astonishment? Queen Anne, our charming sovereign, is a very respectable and a very discreet woman who is also a little bored with her royal duties. All the ladies of her court are likewise bored. So they all have their young protégés . . . some very handsome, very young officer, who, without ever leaving St. James Palace, receives the most amazing military promotions.

Masham. Milord!

Bolingbroke. Fortune is never more flattering than when she is aided by personal charm.

Masham. Ah, if I thought . . .

Bolingbroke [*Sitting*]. Not so fast. After all, I may be mistaken . . . and if your protector is really some great lord . . . a friend, let us say, of your father . . . why, let these advancements help you along. Ah! but if he had ordered you to *get* married . . . that would be a different matter . . . but to *prohibit* your marrying . . . well, anyway, it's clear that this friend is not an enemy . . . quite the contrary . . . and to obey him shouldn't be so difficult.

Masham [*Sitting near* BOLINGBROKE's *armchair*]. Yes, it is . . . really, terribly difficult . . . especially since I love someone . . . and she loves me too!

Bolingbroke. Oh yes, the most beautiful woman in the world. I keep forgetting her.

Masham. Oh, she is so beautiful . . . but she is very poor. Don't you see? It is for her that I want honors and wealth. I am only waiting to make my fortune so that I can marry her.

Bolingbroke. How does this ravishing beauty earn her livelihood?

Masham. She is a jeweler's assistant . . . at Master Tomwood's. . . .

Bolingbroke. So?

Masham. But he has just gone bankrupt, and she finds herself penniless . . . without the slightest resource . . .

Bolingbroke [*Rising*]. I might have known! . . . it is the charming Abigail. . . .

Masham. Abigail? You know her then?

Bolingbroke. Great heavens, yes. During the lifetime of my wife . . . I mean, while I lived with her . . . I was a

steady customer of Master Tomwood's jewelry shop. My
wife loved diamonds a great deal . . . and I, the jewelress.
You are quite right, Masham, a charming girl, naive, but
gracious and witty. . . .

Masham. You mean you were in love with her too?

Bolingbroke. I was . . . for a week! Then I saw that I
was wasting my time . . . and I could never afford to
waste that . . . so we became good friends, Abigail and I.
This is the first time, Masham, I really regret . . . not having lost my wealth . . . but having so foolishly wasted it.
I might now have come to your aid . . . I could have seen
you married to her . . . but for the present my creditors
are hounding me on all sides . . . and, as to the future,
there is not much hope. All the family fortune reverts to
Richard Bolingbroke, my cousin, and there isn't much
chance of his dying off, for unfortunately, he is young, and,
like all fools, enjoys the best of health . . . but we could
perhaps go to court and find something for Abigail. . . .

Masham. Just what I was about to say . . . a situation
as companion to some noblewoman, who must be neither
imperious nor overbearing . . .

Bolingbroke [*Scratching his head*]. Such a noblewoman
is not easy to find.

Masham. I had thought of the old Duchess of Northumberland, who, I have heard, is looking for someone to read
to her.

Bolingbroke. Not so bad . . . one of the least deadly of
the court bores.

Masham. And I have advised Abigail to seek an audience
with her this morning; but the very idea of coming to the
palace of the Queen sends the dear girl into a fit of trembling.

Bolingbroke. No matter . . . the hope of finding you
here . . . she will come, depend upon it, and . . . but
look! . . . see there, my young officer of the guards, what
did I tell you? Here she is! [ABIGAIL CHURCHILL *has entered timidly, and runs to* MASHAM.]

Abigail. Arthur, my dear! [*They embrace; she follows*
MASHAM'S *eyes and turns to discover* BOLINGBROKE. *She
curtseys.*] Milord St. John!

Bolingbroke. None other, my dear child. Ah, you must

have been born under a very lucky star! The first time you
come to court you find two real friends here . . . not even
the Queen has that good fortune.

Abigail. Yes, you are right. I am lucky . . . especially,
today!

Masham. So you have at last got up enough courage to
present yourself to the Duchess of Northumberland?

Abigail. You don't understand. I have just found out that
the position has been taken.

Masham. And you call that luck?

Abigail. Yes, for I have found another! . . . one much
more pleasant, I think . . . and which I owe . . .

Masham [*Jealously*]. To whom?

Abigail. To chance.

Bolingbroke. Ah, Chance! The most accommodating and
the least exacting of protectresses!

Abigail. Imagine now, among all the fine ladies who fre-
quented the shop of Master Tomwood . . . ah, there was
one so lovely, so gracious, and she always asked for me. . . .

Bolingbroke. Naturally.

Abigail. It always seemed to me that this lady was not
very happy in her domestic life . . . that she was a slave
in her own home, for she often told me with a sigh . . .
"Ah, my dear Abigail, how happy you must be here, you
who can do whatever you want!" . . . How could anyone
say that? . . . I, who, chained to that counter, could never
leave it to see my dear Arthur except on Sunday after mass,
when he was not on duty at court. However, one day . . .
nearly a month ago . . . the beautiful lady took a fancy
to a little bonbon box exquisitely worked in gold. But she
had forgotten her purse . . . and so I said the box could
be sent to milady's home. But milady seemed very embarrassed and hesitated in naming her address . . . no
doubt, I thought at the time, because of her husband . . .
there are noblewomen, you know, who do not care to speak
of their husbands . . .

Bolingbroke. Naturally.

Abigail. And so I said, "Take it along, milady. I shall
assume all the responsibility. She looked at me amazed, as
if she were astonished that anyone could have faith in her.

Then she smiled charmingly. "Very well, I shall come back," she said . . . but no! She didn't come back!

Bolingbroke. Naturally.

Abigail. That is, until yesterday, when a carriage stopped at the door, and milady got out. A great many affairs too complicated to explain had detained her . . . she was not free to leave her home whenever she wished . . . and she was anxious to come in person to settle her debts. All at once she stopped speaking, having noticed that there were tears in my eyes, for I could not help being relieved at her presence. Finally, I told her everything . . . except, of course, about dear Arthur . . . and when she found out that this morning I was going to seek an audience with the Duchess of Northumberland, she said to me, "It won't do you any good to go there; the place has already been taken, . . . but I hold a rather enviable place in society and live in a house of considerable size—of which, unfortunately, I am not always the mistress. Nevertheless, I offer you a place in my household," she said; "will you take it?" I threw myself in her arms, and cried, "You are so kind." But she would have none of my gratitude, and gave me a slip of paper containing a password which would enable me to enter into the palace. And, as you see, it has . . . for here I am!

Masham. Most singular!

Bolingbroke. And that paper . . . could I see it?

Abigail [*Giving it to him*]. Certainly.

Bolingbroke. Ah-ha! This handwriting! I might have guessed it!

Abigail. Do you know who she is?

Bolingbroke [*With calm indifference*]. Yes, my dear . . . it is the Queen.

Abigail. The Queen?

Masham. The Queen gives you a place in her household . . . and her protection and friendship as well . . . oh, my darling, your fortune is assured forever!

Bolingbroke. Wait, my friends, wait . . . don't build your castle in Spain when you're still in London.

Masham. But the Queen can do anything! The Queen is mistress in her own home!

Bolingbroke. Not this Queen. Queen Anne is good and kind by nature . . . but she is also weak and indecisive . . . she does not dare take a step without first consulting those who surround her. She cannot, therefore, but be ruled by her counsellors and favorites . . . and there happens to be near her a strong-minded lady, quick to see things as they are . . . that is, Lady Churchill, Ducness of Marlborough, a greater general than her own husband, the Duke . . . as clever as he is cowardly, as ambitious as he is miserly, more Queen of England than Anne herself!

Abigail. Is the Queen fond of the Duchess?

Bolingbroke. She hates her . . . even when calling her her best friend . . . and her "best friend" returns the compliment!

Abigail. Then why doesn't she break with her? Why does she submit to such domination?

Bolingbroke. That, my dear girl, is more difficult to explain. In our country . . . here in England, as Masham will tell you, it is not the Queen, but the majority who rules; and the Whig Party, of which the Duchess' husband, Lord Marlborough, is the leader, controls not only the army, but Parliament. They have gained the majority, and Queen Anne, who is lauded everywhere as England's glorious Queen, is forced to submit to ministers who displease her, friends who do not love her, and a favorite who tyrannizes her.

Abigail. Ah, if this is the case . . . if everything depends upon the Duchess . . . I have still some hope!

Masham. How so?

Abigail. I am a kind of a relative to the Duchess.

Bolingbroke. You, Abigail?

Abigail. Truly . . . by *mésalliance* . . . a cousin of hers . . . a Churchill . . . was disowned by her noble family when he married my mother!

Masham. Is it possible? . . . you, a relative of the Duchess?

Abigail. Of course I have never presented myself to her because she had always refused to receive or to recognize my mother . . . but I . . . a poor daughter . . . who will ask nothing from her except that she not harm me . . .

why should she go out of her way to oppose the kindness
of the Queen?

Bolingbroke. That's not a good enough reason . . . you
don't know the Duchess. But this time at least I can help
you . . . and I shall do it too . . . even if I draw upon
myself her hatred!

Abigail. Ah! how kind you are!

Masham. How can we ever repay you?

Bolingbroke. With your friendship.

Abigail. That's little enough.

Bolingbroke. It is a great deal for a statesman who had
ceased to believe in such a thing. But I do believe in you,
and am relying upon you! [*Giving them his hand.*] Between
us henceforth . . . an alliance offensive and defensive!

Abigail [*Smiling*]. An alliance to be feared, milord!

Bolingbroke. More than you might believe possible, and,
God willing, the day should bring us two victories: Abigail's
situation . . . and another affair I have greatly at heart
. . . a letter that I would give anything to have placed this
morning in the hands of the Queen . . . I am only waiting
to find the means. Ah! if only Abigail were appointed! if
she were received among Her Majesty's ladies in waiting,
all my messages could reach the Queen in spite of the
Duchess.

Masham. Is that all? I can do that much for you.

Bolingbroke. So?

Masham. Every morning at ten o'clock . . . and it's
almost ten now . . . I carry to Her Majesty during her
breakfast . . . [*Picking up a paper from the table.*] . . .
the *Gazette of the Social World*, which she glances over
while drinking her tea; she looks at the pictures, and sometimes asks me to read her a review of some ball or soiree.

Bolingbroke. Good enough! How fortunate that Her
Majesty reads the *Gazette of the Social World!* . . . it is
probably the only uncensored reading material permitted
her. [*He slips a letter under the cover of the journal.*] The
Marquis' letter this morning in place of the descriptions of the newest hoopskirts and furbelows. And while
we are about it. . . . [*Taking a journal from his pocket and
slipping it also into the journal. The clock begins to strike
ten.*]

Abigail. What are you doing?

Bolingbroke. Today's copy of the Tory paper, which I slip under the cover . . . so! Her Majesty will see therein how the Duke and Duchess of Marlborough deceive her . . . ah! but that was the clock chiming ten. Go, Masham, hurry! [*He gives him the journal, and* MASHAM *exits by the door left, leaving the door open.*]

Masham. Count on me!

Bolingbroke. There, you see! The triple alliance already produces its effects . . . Masham will both protect and serve us.

Abigail. It makes me regret that I can serve only in such small ways!

Bolingbroke. Ah, but you must not despise little things; it is they which are responsible for great effects! You think perhaps, as every one else does, that political catastrophes, revolutions, and falls of empires come from serious and important causes . . . not at all! States are subjugated or controlled by heroes, by great men; but these great men are themselves slaves to their passions, their whims, their vanities . . . that is, by whatever is small and mean in this world. Perhaps you do not know that a window in the Château Trianon, criticized by Louis XIV and defended by Louvois, was responsible for the war which involves Europe at the present moment. It is to the wounded vanity of a courtesan that a kingdom owes its disasters; perhaps to so small a cause as that the king absent-mindedly failed to answer her over the breakfast table. And, without going any farther away from home, look at me, Henry St. John, who for twenty-six years was regarded as a fop, a rattle-brained gentleman incapable of any serious occupation . . . do you know how overnight I became a statesman?

Abigail. How?

Bolingbroke. I became a statesman, my dear girl, because I knew how to dance the sarabande with the right woman; and I lost my power because I caught a cold and had to stay in bed when I should have been at court.

Abigail. Is it possible? How do you hope to regain your power?

Bolingbroke. I shall return to my lodgings to wait there and hope.

Abigail. For a revolution?

Bolingbroke. No, for an accident . . . a whim of fate
. . . a grain of sand which will upset the carriage of the
victor.

Abigail. I see . . . and this grain of sand . . . you intend to stir it up?

Bolingbroke. No, but if I find it, I can perhaps push it
under the wheel. The wise man does not try to compete
with Providence . . . he does not try to make events, but
to profit from them. Great effects are produced by small
causes . . . that is my system . . . I have confidence in it.
You shall see the proofs of it.

Abigail [*Hearing someone approaching*]. Is Arthur coming back so soon?

Bolingbroke. No . . . it is Her Ladyship, the triumphant
and superb Duchess!

Abigail [*Sotto-voce, looking through the open left doorway, from which the* DUCHESS *is about to enter*]. Is *that* the
Duchess of Marlborough?

Bolingbroke [*Sotto-voce*]. None other.

Abigail. Ah, but I have already seen her somewhere . . .
yes, at the jewelers! . . . why, she came recently to buy
some tabs set with diamonds.

Bolingbroke. Sh! [*The* DUCHESS *of Marlborough enters,
reading the* Gazette of the Social World. *She sees* BOLING-
BROKE, *and smiles a sweet greeting.*]

Duchess. Ah, milord St. John!

Bolingbroke. You have not forgotten me, eh, milady?

Duchess [*Showing the paper in her hand*]. I promise
you, milord, that I shan't soon forget your article in today's
Tory paper.

Bolingbroke. You have deigned to read. . . .

Duchess. With the Queen, whom I have just left.

Bolingbroke [*Troubled*]. Ah! so that's it!

Duchess. Yes, milord . . . an officer of the guards has
just brought me this copy of the *Gazette of the Social
World.* . . .

Bolingbroke. In which I am not in the least concerned.

Duchess [*With irony*]. I well know it. You have long
since gone out of fashion, milord, . . . but in the leaves of

the *Gazette* and near your own paper was this letter from the Marquis de Torcy.

Bolingbroke. Addressed to the Queen!

Duchess. Exactly why I read it.

Bolingbroke [*Indignantly*]. Madame!

Duchess. It is the duty of my office. I am First Lady of the Queen's Household, and it is through my hands that all letters must first pass. If you didn't know that before, milord, you know it now . . . so if you ever have some little epigram written against me, some bon mot with which you wish to acquaint me . . . simply address your letter to the Queen . . . and you may rest assured that I shall receive it.

Bolingbroke. I shall remember that, madame . . . but at least I have succeeded on one point . . . Her Majesty now knows the propositions of the Marquis.

Duchess. Ah, but that is just where you are mistaken, milord. You see, I read them first . . . that was quite enough . . . the fire has done them justice by now, I dare say. [BOLINGBROKE *is beside himself with disappointment; the* DUCHESS *bows courteously before him, and starts to leave, but perceives* ABIGAIL, *who has stayed in the background.*] And who is this beautiful child? What is your name, my dear?

Abigail [*Advancing and making a full bow*]. Abigail . . .

Duchess [*Haughtily interrupting*]. Ah yes! the pretty little jewelress. Yes, I recognize you now. So you're the girl the Queen was speaking to me about!

Abigail. Ah! Her Majesty has spoken of me to you. . . .

Duchess. Leaving me mistress of admitting or refusing you . . . and since this appointment depends upon me alone . . . well, I shall see . . . I shall examine you with impartiality and justice. You are aware, of course, that a certain social rank is necessary.

Bolingbroke. She has that!

Duchess [*Looking haughtily at* BOLINGBROKE, *and then returning to* ABIGAIL]. I should have admitted you with pleasure, my dear, but in order to enter the service of the Queen, one must come from a distinguished family.

Bolingbroke. That's just her strongest point.

Duchess. We shall see . . . there are so many people

who call themselves nobles, but who really have no claim to titles.

Bolingbroke [*To* ABIGAIL]. I think the time has come, my dear girl, to tell the Duchess that you are her cousin.

Duchess [*Furious*]. Oh!

Bolingbroke. A distant relative, without doubt . . . but still, a cousin to the Duchess of Marlborough, who, in her severe impartiality, hesitates and asks if she is of good enough family to enter the service of the Queen. You understand, madame, that for me, who am only a writer gone "out of fashion," there may be in the recital of this quaint adventure just that little thing that could put me back into style again . . . and you understand, too, that my paper would have a good chance from tomorrow on to make some charming bon mots regarding the noble Duchess, cousin to a little jewelress . . . but, rest assured, madame, your friendship is too necessary to your young relative that I should wish her to lose it; and on the condition that she will this day be admitted by you into the service of Her Majesty, I swear on my honor never to reveal this anecdote, rare as it may be. I am awaiting your answer.

Duchess [*Haughtily*]. I shan't detain you long. I must present my report to the Queen regarding the admission of this young girl, and whether she be my relative or not . . . that will scarcely change my decision. I shall make her known to Her Majesty . . . to her alone! Regarding you, milord, it will suffice you to know that I have never granted anything because of threats, a powerless weapon which I thoroughly despise . . . and if I have recourse to threats today, it is only because you have forced me to them. When one is a publisher, milord St. John, and especially when one is on the opposing side, before trying to put the affairs of the state in order, it is quite necessary to straighten out one's own affairs. That's just what you've failed to do . . . you have enormous debts . . . nearly two hundred thousand francs, which your impatient creditors have sold to me for a sixth of their value paid in cash. I have bought them all . . . I, so greedy, so intent upon personal gain! You cannot accuse me this time of wishing to enrich myself . . . for these debt claims are, I am told, absolutely worthless . . . but they do have one advantage . . . that of en-

titling the holder to have his debtor placed in prison . . .
an advantage by which I cannot yet profit, since you are still
a member of the House of Commons . . . but tomorrow
the session finishes, and if this rare anecdote of which you
have just spoken appears in the morning paper, the evening
paper will announce that its witty author, milord St. John,
is composing at that moment, in Newgate, a treatise on the
art of making debts. But I doubt whether I shall be forced
to that extremity, milord . . . you are altogether too necessary to your friends on the opposition for me to wish to
deprive them of your presence, and . . . painful though it
may be for so eloquent a speaker to keep silence . . . I
think you understand even better than I the necessity of
keeping your mouth shut. [*She makes him a deep curtsey,
and leaves.*]

Abigail. Well . . . what do you say to that?

Bolingbroke [*Gaily*]. Most admirably played . . . by
God! that's legitimate warfare. I have always said that the
Duchess was not only a woman quick to think, but to act.
No, she never threatens; she simply strikes. This idea now
of acquiring my debts and thereby holding me under her
thumb . . . really, it's magnificent! . . . what my best
friends would not do for me, she has done . . . she has
settled up my accounts . . . how profound must be her
affection! Such beautiful hatred excites my emulation. [*Putting an arm around* ABIGAIL, *who has bowed her head.*]
Come, Abigail, courage!

Abigail. No, no . . . I am giving up everything. Your
liberty is at stake.

Bolingbroke. We shall see about that! [*Looking at a clock
which is on one of the panels at right.*] Good Lord, it's the
hour when Parliament convenes . . . I must not fail to be
there . . . I must speak against the Duke of Marlborough
who is asking for some subsidies . . . I shall prove to the
Duchess what I know about economy . . . I shan't vote a
shilling . . . Adieu! I am relying upon you, Masham, and
our alliance! [*He leaves by the door right.* ABIGAIL *sadly
picks up her bonnet and starts to leave by the door at back,
when* MASHAM *throws open the rear doors, and stands on
the threshold, pale and frightened. She runs to him.*]

Abigail. Arthur!

Masham [*Embracing her*]. Oh, my dear. I've been looking everywhere for you.

Abigail. What's the matter?

Masham. Everything is lost.

Abigail. Everything? . . . what has gone wrong? Tell me!

Masham. It was in St. James Park . . . I had just gone around the bend in a road, when suddenly I came face to face with him . . .

Abigail. Him? Whom do you mean?

Masham. My evil genius . . . my Nemesis . . . you know! . . . the snap-finger man. At the first glance we recognized each other . . . and he laughed . . . he laughed *again!* I didn't know what I was doing . . . without saying a word, without even asking his name, I drew my sword . . . he, his . . . and then . . . oh God! the laughter seemed to choke in his throat!

Abigail. You killed him?

Masham. I don't know . . . I don't know . . . I only saw him fall. I heard people running, and, remembering what I had heard the other day . . . these severe laws against duelling . . .

Abigail. The penalty is death!

Masham. If they want to press the charges, yes . . . it all depends upon the heirs.

Abigail. No matter. You must leave London!

Masham. I shall go tomorrow.

Abigail. No, tonight . . . now!

Masham. But what of you . . . and milord St. John? . . .

Abigail. He is going to be arrested for his debts, and I shan't secure my appointment . . . but it doesn't make any difference. You first . . . you before everything . . . you must go!

Masham. Yes! . . . [*Taking her in his arms.*] Oh, my darling, I love you so much . . . I wanted just this sight of you . . . this one moment before I left.

Abigail. Go! go, my love, go!

Masham. My dear!

Abigail [*Tearing herself from him*]. Adieu . . . adieu!

. . . and, if you truly love me, never come back to see me again. Go! . . . quickly go! [*He leaves quickly by the door right. She looks after him, and then sinks slowly into a chair, and weeps.*]

ACT ONE

SCENE II

The reception room. The following morning. QUEEN ANNE *is discovered, in a languid position on a chaise longue; she is eating bonbons.* THOMPSON, *her doorkeeper, stands near her, attentive. The* QUEEN *repeats to him wearily.*

QUEEN. And you say, Thompson, that they are members of the House of Commons?

Thompson. Yes, Your Majesty. They desire an audience.

Queen. You told them of course that I was in conference . . . that matters involving the whole of England and Europe detained me . . . [*She selects a bonbon.*] How I hate nutty sweets!

Thompson. Yes, Your Majesty, that's what I always tell them . . . about the conference, I mean.

Queen [*Munching*]. And that I never receive. . . .

Thompson. Before ten o'clock . . . exactly what I told them. So they gave me this note and said that they would be back at ten o'clock to pay their respects to Your Majesty.

Queen. Very good . . . the Duchess will be back from Windsor by that time . . . this is all her business . . . it's the least she can do for me . . . I'm so busy with other things. . . . [*She selects another sweet.*] I don't like raisins either. [*Turning to* THOMPSON.] Do you know who these gentlemen were?

Thompson. There were four of them . . . I recognized two of them, because they used to be your ministers.

Queen [*Quickly, with interest*]. Who were they?

Thompson. Sir Harley and milord St. John.

Queen. Oh! . . . and they've gone?

Thompson. Yes, Your Majesty.

Queen. Such a pity! . . . I'm sorry now I didn't receive

them . . . St. John, especially! . . . ah, when he was in power, things went so much better. My mornings were never so long . . . I was scarcely ever bored . . . and today, while the Duchess was gone, it would have been such a lucky opportunity. I could have talked to him again . . . he's such a clever man . . . really, Thompson, it was most stupid of you.

Thompson. Yes, Your Majesty . . . but I had orders from Madame, the Duchess . . . a strict rule . . . that whenever milord St. John presents himself . . .

Queen. Oh, yes, the Duchess . . . well, that's different! What a pity these aren't all peppermints! Thompson, did milord St. John say anything?

Thompson. No, Your Majesty . . . but he wrote this note for Your Majesty.

Queen. Read it to me.

Thompson [*Reading the note*]. "Madame, my colleagues and I seek an audience with Your Majesty . . ."

Queen. Yes, yes, skip the uninteresting part.

Thompson. Yes, Your Majesty. Let me see . . . [*Reading.*] . . . ah, yes. . . . "I should like to enjoy again the privilege of my sovereign's charming company . . . a pleasure too long denied me . . ."

Queen. Dear Sir Henry! Such a nice man!

Thompson [*Continuing*]. "That the Duchess alienates you from her political enemies, you probably know . . . but her defiance goes further when she rejects a young girl whose tenderness might have lightened the boredom which surrounds Your Majesty. She has refused the child a position in Your Majesty's household, a position which you yourself had promised the girl. She claims that the girl is not highly enough connected, but, madame, let me inform you that Abigail Churchill is a cousin of the Duchess of Marlborough . . ."

Queen [*Getting up*]. So! Well, this is the last straw! [*Muttering angrily to herself.*] I'll show her who is mistress in this palace. I'll show her that my desires are not to be ignored.

Thompson. Yes, Your Majesty.

Queen. Thompson, go immediately into the city to the shop of Master Tomwood, the jeweler. Ask there for Miss

Abigail Churchill, and tell her to come here at once to the palace. Don't stand there staring at me! I am commanding you . . . I, the Queen! Go!

Thompson. Yes, Your Majesty. [*He leaves.*]

Queen. We'll see who is Queen of England around here! [*The* DUCHESS *has entered in time to hear that last statement. The* QUEEN *turns and discovers her; all her bravery melts, and she immediately hides* ST. JOHN's *letter in her bosom.*] Oh!

Duchess. May I inquire after Her Majesty's health?

Queen [*Indifferently*]. I am ill . . . a stupid headache . . .

Duchess. Her Majesty must have met with some opposition . . .

Queen. A great many!

Duchess. You know then what has happened?

Queen. No, what?

Duchess. The city is in an uproar. I shouldn't have been surprised if the noise had reached here.

Queen. How frightful! Can't you quiet things down? I was to have gone this afternoon for a boating party upon the Thames.

Duchess. Your Majesty needn't worry. I shall tend to everything. We have just dispatched a regiment of dragoons to Windsor, who, at the first noise, will march into London. I have just had an agreement with the leaders, all of whom are devoted to my husband and to Your Majesty.

Queen. So that's why you went to Windsor!

Duchess. Yes, madame . . . and you were going to accuse me . . .

Queen. I, accuse?

Duchess [*Smiling*]. Ah! you were ready to receive me very badly . . . I saw that I was in disgrace.

Queen. Not at all, my dear Duchess. It's just my nerves . . and my stomach too. I don't know what's the matter with it. It must have been those strawberries this morning.

Duchess. No, I think I know why . . . Your Majesty has received some bad news . . .

Queen. Oh no . . . really I haven't.

Duchess. Why do you wish to keep me in ignorance? Are

you afraid that I too might become upset? I know your great kindness, but . . .

Queen. Oh, you are quite wrong.

Duchess. I saw you . . . upon my arrival, you quickly hid a note . . . and with such a flurry that it wasn't difficult to guess that the letter concerned me.

Queen. No, Duchess . . . I assure you . . . the matter concerns only a young girl . . . [*Taking the letter from her bosom.*] . . . who is recommended to me in this letter . . . a young girl whom I wish . . . whom I command to have placed among my ladies in waiting . . . .

Duchess [*Smiling and reaching for the letter*]. So . . . nothing could be better . . . and if Your Majesty wishes to permit . . .

Queen [*Withdrawing the letter*]. It's not necessary for you to see this . . . I have already spoken to you about her . . . It is about Abigail.

Duchess. So! And who recommends her so highly?

Queen. No one of any importance.

Duchess [*Hardly able to contain herself with anger*]. Ah! I understand now how our enemies triumph since our Queen delivers us to them, at the very moment when we are fighting for her. While we are battling tooth-and-nail for her interests, she, far from aiding us, is forever entering into secret correspondence with our declared enemies . . . it is for them that she abandons and betrays us!

Queen. No, no . . . please! . . . my poor head! . . . no, Duchess! You are imagining all this . . . why, this letter has nothing about politics in it and what it contains is of such a nature that . . .

Duchess. That Your Majesty is afraid to show it to me.

Queen [*With angry impatience*]. Out of respect to your feelings, yes! [*She gives her the letter.*] For it contains facts that you can hardly deny.

Duchess [*Reading the letter*]. Is that all? The attack is scarcely to be feared.

Queen. Are you not opposed to the admission of Abigail? Do you deny that you are?

Duchess. I do not.

Queen. Is it not true that she is your cousin?

Duchess. She is, Your Majesty . . . and that's the very reason why I don't want her in your household. For a long time now, I have been accused of giving places to my friends, my relatives . . . of surrounding Your Majesty with people devoted to me . . . and to appoint Abigail would be to give a pretext to those who wish to slander me. Your Majesty is too just, too generous not to understand what I mean.

Queen [*Embarrassed and half-convinced*]. I see . . . well, yes, certainly . . . I understand . . . but I should wish, however, that this poor Abigail . . .

Duchess. Ah! you may rest assured . . . I shall find for her . . . far from you, far from London, some brilliant and honorable position. Why, she is my own dear cousin!

Queen. Oh well, that's all right then.

Duchess. And then, furthermore, there is this other person in whom Your Majesty has taken an interest . . . oh, I am really so happy when I can serve you . . . this young man now . . . this ensign in the Guards whom Your Majesty pointed out to me the other day . . .

Queen [*With a great deal of emotion*]. Oh, yes, yes . . . the young guardsman who reads so beautifully to me every morning.

Duchess. I have found a way to advance him to a captaincy in the Guards. An occasion arose, and no one knows about his advancement . . . not even my own husband, who signed the promotion papers without knowing what they were . . . and this morning a new captain will come to pay his respects to Your Majesty.

Queen [*Joyfully*]. Ah! . . . *he* will come . . .

Duchess. I have put his name on your audience list.

Queen. Very good. I shall receive *him*.

Duchess. Now you see . . . when it's possible, I am the first person to help you.

Queen. You are so kind to me. [*The* QUEEN *sits down near the table; the* DUCHESS *is near the armchair.*]

Duchess. Heavens, no! quite the contrary . . . I merely do my duty. I love Your Majesty more than I can say. I am so devoted to her best interests.

Queen. Of course, of course.

Duchess. And queens have so few real friends . . . friends who are not afraid to oppose them. I cannot help being as I am . . . I who know nothing of flattery or deceit . . . and if I seem to hurt your feelings, it is simply because I am showing my love for you.

Queen. Yes, you are right, Duchess, real friendship is a rare thing.

Duchess. Isn't it so! What matters it if a person has fits of temper when her heart is true. [*The* QUEEN *smilingly offers her hand, which the* DUCHESS *kisses.*] Your Majesty promises me that this affair is settled . . . it came very near making me lose your good graces . . . it really made me so terribly unhappy!

Queen. I, too, was unhappy. Forgive me.

Duchess. And it's agreed then? . . . you won't see our friend Abigail again?

Queen. Of course not . . . if you don't want me to.

Thompson [*Appearing and announcing*]. Miss Abigail Churchill! [ABIGAIL *enters and bows. The* QUEEN *is embarrassed.*]

Queen. Why . . . why, we were just talking about you.

Abigail. Your Majesty commanded me to come here.

Queen. Commanded? . . . why, I merely suggested . . . I said . . . see if this young girl . . . what did I say, Duchess?

Duchess [*To* ABIGAIL]. Her Majesty merely wanted to see you, my dear girl, in order to tell you that your request for admittance into Her Majesty's service could not be granted.

Abigail. My request? I should never have dared ask anything. It was Her Majesty herself who requested . . . out of the goodness of her heart . . . that I be admitted . . .

Queen. True . . . but for important reasons . . . political considerations . . .

Abigail. Am I that important?

Queen. These . . . and other state matters . . . force me to give up a dream that would have been most pleasant. From now on it is not I, but your cousin, the Duchess, who will have charge of your future. She has promised me to secure for you . . . far from London . . . a splendid situation.

Abigail. I see.

Duchess. I shall tend to it this very day. [*The* QUEEN *has taken center-stage; the* DUCHESS *turns to* ABIGAIL.]

Duchess. Wait for me. I want to talk to you as soon as I have seen the Queen to her apartments. [*She goes toward the door at the back; the* QUEEN *turns to* ABIGAIL.]

Queen. You'll thank the dear Duchess, won't you? [*The* QUEEN *and the* DUCHESS *leave.* ABIGAIL *shakes her head sadly.*]

Abigail. You poor woman! [*She starts to go just as* BOL- INGBROKE *enters from the opposite side.*]

Bolingbroke. Abigail!

Abigail. Ah! St. John! Come here! I am so unhappy . . . everything is going wrong again.

Bolingbroke [*Comforting her*]. Come, come, my dear Abigail . . . what's the matter?

Abigail. Ah, but this good luck that was promised us . . .

Bolingbroke. Dame Fortune has kept her word . . . she has kept to every letter of her agreement.

Abigail. What do you mean?

Bolingbroke. Have you never heard of Lord Richard Bolingbroke, my cousin?

Abigail. No.

Bolingbroke. He was the most merciless of my creditors . . . it was he who sold my debts to the Duchess of Marlborough . . . he was the eldest in the family. To him went the estate, the immense Bolingbroke fortune.

Abigail. So! and this cousin? . . .

Bolingbroke [*Laughing*]. Abigail, look at me more closely. Don't you think I look like an heir?

Abigail. You mean you . . .

Bolingbroke. I am now Lord Henry St. John, Viscount Bolingbroke, only surviving member of that illustrious family, owner of a magnificent inheritance. I come to seek justice from the Queen! [*The* QUEEN *is heard offstage.*]

Abigail. The Queen is returning! [BOLINGBROKE *goes to the door and calls in his fellow members of the Tory party.*]

Bolingbroke. Come in, my friends. [*They enter, grouping themselves around him. The* QUEEN, *with the* DUCHESS *and several Lords and Ladies of the court, enters, and takes center-stage.* BOLINGBROKE *addresses her.*]

Bolingbroke. Madame, it is more as a true friend to his country than as a stricken relative that I come to ask of you justice and vengeance. The defender of our freedom, Lord Richard, Viscount Bolingbroke, my noble cousin, was yesterday . . . in your palace . . . moreover, in the very gardens at St. James . . . killed in a duel!

Abigail. Oh, God!

Bolingbroke. That is, if one could call it a duel . . . a fight unwitnessed, wherein his adversary has been protected in his flight, and is being withheld from the action of the law . . .

Duchess. Permit me . . .

Bolingbroke. Why should one not believe that those who are hiding him are those who have given him arms? . . . why should one not believe that the ministry is protecting him? [*The* Duchess *and her followers show signs of irritation and shrug their shoulders.*] Yes, madame, I accuse the present ministry . . . and the cries of your furious citizens speak even louder than I. I accuse the ministers . . . I accuse their partisans . . . their friends . . . I shall not name anyone, but I accuse everyone . . . of attempting to get rid by treasonable means of an adversary so much to be feared as Lord Richard Bolingbroke, and I come to declare to Her Majesty that for those serious riots which today shook the city, it is not us, her loyal subjects, whom she must blame . . . but those who surround her, those of whom public opinion has a long time been suspicious. I demand their recall!

Duchess [*Haughtily*]. Has milord finished?

Bolingbroke. Yes, madame.

Duchess. Now, madame, listen to the truth . . . proved by authentic reports which I received this morning. It is unfortunately too true that yesterday in St. James Park Lord Richard was killed in a duel . . .

Bolingbroke. But by whom?

Duchess. By a cavalier whose name even Lord Richard himself did not know . . .

Bolingbroke. I ask Your Majesty if that sounds reasonable.

Duchess. Nevertheless, it is true . . . those were the last words Lord Richard spoke in the presence of a few people

who ran to his aid . . . some royal servants, whom, milord,
you can see and question yourself if you wish.

Bolingbroke. They would stand by you, my dear Duchess.
The high places with which you have honored them are
sufficient guaranty for their loyalty to you. But still . . . if,
as you claim . . . the real culprit got away without being
recognized, he must still have been someone familiar with
the plan of this palace in order to have gone through it
without having been discovered.

Abigail. Milord . . .

Bolingbroke. How is it that people . . . murderers . . .
can come and go through the palace without being discovered? Is it not the duty of the First Lady of the Queen's
Household to know who enters and who leaves the palace
of the Queen? Why has she not given the strictest orders?

Duchess. I have! Her Majesty has just prescribed the most
rigorous measures in this ordinance.

Queen. And I shall see that they are carried out by madame, the Duchess . . . and by you, milord St. John. It is
the duty of you both to see that this culprit is discovered
and punished.

Duchess. I trust you won't say now, milord, that I am
keeping this unknown cavalier from the fury of your vengeance.

Queen. Milord and gentlemen, are you satisfied?

Bolingbroke. We always are, when we are able to obtain
a hearing from Your Majesty. [*The* QUEEN *gives her hand
to* BOLINGBROKE; *the members of his party bow. She goes
out with the* DUCHESS *and her court. The members of the
Tory Party crowd around* BOLINGBROKE *to congratulate
him.*]

Members. Well done, milord . . . Beautifully played
. . . Magnificent . . . We've only started, milord!

Bolingbroke. Right . . . for with this ordinance I shall,
if necessary, arrest everyone in England! [*His friends with
smiles and bravos exit; he starts to go himself, but his attention is drawn to* ABIGAIL, *who has sunk into an armchair.*] Abigail! What is the matter?

Abigail [*Taking his hand*]. Milord, we are lost!

Bolingbroke. What do you mean?

Abigail. This culprit on whom you have drawn the ven-

geance of the court . . . he whom you have sworn to track
to earth . . . to arrest . . . to condemn . . .

Bolingbroke. Yes?

Abigail. That man is Arthur.

Bolingbroke. Masham?

Abigail. Lord Bolingbroke, your cousin, is the man who
for a long time has insulted him . . . the man whose name
he did not know.

Bolingbroke. I see . . . it was my cousin who was the
cause of everything . . . a duel, a riot, this splendid speech
which I just delivered . . . and now this royal ordinance.

Abigail. Which commands you to arrest Masham.

Bolingbroke. Arrest him? Come now . . . arrest the man
to whom I owe everything . . . my rank, a title, and a
fortune? No! no! I am not such an ingrate! [*He starts to
tear the ordinance, but suddenly stops.*] Good God! my entire party is counting on me! the Whig party will be watching me! and in the eyes of the world Bolingbroke was my
relative, my cousin!

Abigail. What shall we do?

Bolingbroke. Well, I shan't do anything, other than to
make a big noise about the whole affair in articles and
speeches, until you are absolutely certain that he has left
England. I shall try to follow him then with a rage which
will hide my true feelings . . . but by that time he will
be beyond the reach of my hands and the power of the
Queen's ordinance.

Abigail. Good! Then, perhaps, there is hope after all. Let
me see . . . he left yesterday . . . thank God, by now he
must be safely out of England! [*And suddenly she sees*
MASHAM *standing in the door; she stifles a cry.*] Ah!

Bolingbroke. Masham! Why have you come back?

MASHAM [*Quietly*]. I never left.

Abigail. But yesterday you promised . . . you told me
good-bye . . .

Masham. I had barely left London when I heard a horse
galloping madly after me . . . it was an officer fast in pursuit of me. His mount was fresher than mine, and he soon
caught up with me. For a moment I was going to defend
myself, but he very smilingly presented me with a package,
in which he said I should find my new orders.

Abigail. Your new orders?

Masham. Really, I think I'm living in a madhouse. There in the package was a promotion to a captaincy in the Queen's Guard.

Bolingbroke. Well!

Masham. But that wasn't all. "Tomorrow morning," said the officer, "you are to pay your respects to Her Majesty, the Queen, but tonight we are having a regimental dinner, and I am to bring you back." What could I do?

Abigail. And so you let him bring you back.

Masham. Yes, to that confounded dinner, which lasted all last night.

Abigail. Oh, my poor darling.

Masham. Why do you say that?

Bolingbroke. We haven't time to tell you everything . . . but it will suffice you to know that the man you killed was Richard Bolingbroke, my cousin.

Masham. Good God!

Bolingbroke. The first blow of your sword has made me worth sixty thousand pounds; I might wish that the second blow would make you worth as much . . . but unfortunately it is I who have been appointed to arrest you.

Masham [*Giving* BOLINGBROKE *his sword*]. I await your orders.

Bolingbroke. What? Oh, come now . . . all I ask is that you never betray yourself . . . as for me, I shall hardly even look for you, and, if I find you, it will be your fault, not mine.

Abigail. Up to now, thank heaven! no one has the slightest suspicion that you are the culprit!

Bolingbroke. Let them continue so. Live quietly, Masham, at home. Don't go out very much!

Masham. But this morning I must pay my respects to the Queen.

Bolingbroke. Well then, do so . . . and then return home.

Masham. Furthermore, here is a letter which commands me to do the very opposite of what you advise.

Abigail. A letter?

Masham. From my unknown protector, to whom I no

doubt owe my newest promotion. I was just given this note and box as I entered the palace.

Thompson [*Appearing at the door leading to the* QUEEN'S *apartments*]. Captain Masham, Her Majesty the Queen awaits you!

Masham [*Giving* ABIGAIL *the letter and* BOLINGBROKE *the box*]. Take these . . . and see what is in them . . . [*He goes out, following* THOMPSON.]

Bolingbroke. Read your letter.

Abigail [*Reading*]. "My dear boy, You are now an officer! I have kept my word. Keep yours by continuing to obey me. Every morning you are to appear at the chapel, and every evening you must be present at the Queen's entertainments. Soon the time will come when I shall make myself known to you. Until then, keep silence and obey my orders . . . otherwise, you will regret it. . . ." What orders? Do you know, milord?

Bolingbroke. He cannot get married.

Abigail. Who is this protector of his? . . . some lordly friend of his father?

Bolingbroke. I should be more willing to wager that it was some lady.

Abigail. But Arthur . . . oh, nonsense! . . . he is too honest, too faithful . . .

Bolingbroke. He can hardly help it if he attracts a protectress who persists in remaining incognito.

Abigail. Ah, but here is a postscript. Maybe there is some clue here . . . [*Reading.*] "I am sending to you, my dear Captain Masham, the marks of your new rank."

Bolingbroke [*Opening the box*]. And here they are! . . . some magnificent tabs set with diamonds . . . well, it's just as I thought!

Abigail [*Inspecting the tabs*]. Oh, good heavens! I know! St. John, I know who this mysterious lady is!

Bolingbroke. What do you mean?

Abigail. Those diamonds . . . I remember now . . . They were bought in Master Tomwood's shop. I sold them myself just last week.

Bolingbroke. To whom? Tell me quick!

Abigail. Oh, I can't! I daren't. A great noblewoman, and I am truly lost if Arthur is loved by her!

Bolingbroke. What does it matter so long as he doesn't love her? . . . so long as he doesn't even know who she is?

Abigail. But he shall know . . . I am going to tell him.

Bolingbroke [*Taking her hand*]. No! . . . if you really want him to love you, keep him from knowing this woman's identity.

Abigail. But why?

Bolingbroke. My poor child . . . it's evident that you don't know men very well. Those who are the most modest and the least self-satisfied have their share of vanity. Arthur is very proud that he is loved by a great lady . . . and if it is true that she is also one to be feared! . . .

Abigail. More so than I dare tell you.

Bolingbroke. And who is she then? [*Seeing that the* DUCHESS *is about to enter from the door leading to the* QUEEN's *apartments,* ABIGAIL *cries.*]

Abigail. There she is!

Bolingbroke. So! The Duchess! [*Quickly taking the letter she holds*] Leave me with her . . . alone! Go quickly!

Abigail. But she asked me to wait for her.

Bolingbroke [*Pushing* ABIGAIL *out the opposite door*]. That's all right. She'll find me here instead. [ABIGAIL *has vanished. The* DUCHESS *enters, lost in thought.* BOLING-BROKE *approaches her from the rear.*] Milady!

Duchess [*Turning*]. Oh! Oh, it's you, milord . . . I was looking for your young protégée,

Bolingbroke. Might I be so bold as to request a moment of your valuable time?

Duchess. With pleasure . . . what is it? . . . have you perhaps some information regarding this culprit whom we must bring to justice?

Bolingbroke. None as yet . . . and you, madame?

Duchess. No more than you.

Bolingbroke. Good!

Duchess. Good indeed! What is it that you wish, milord?

Bolingbroke. First, madame, to tell you that I am no longer your debtor. Upon acquiring my new wealth, my first act was to place with your banker the sum of two hundred thousand francs . . .

Duchess. You are too kind, milord.

Bolingbroke. I am honored by the value at which you

place my debts. It was a great deal to do for one's dearest enemy, madame. You told me yourself that the first thing a good statesman must do is to straighten out his own affairs, and in the future I intend to profit by your instructions.

Duchess. I see. No longer having to fear for your freedom, you intend now to wage a more violent war, eh?

Bolingbroke. On the contrary, I was just going to propose peace.

Duchess. Peace between us? Rather difficult, don't you think?

Bolingbroke. Very well then . . . an armistice! . . let us say, an armistice for twenty-four hours!

Duchess. What is to be gained by that? You can commence your attack upon me whenever you wish; I myself have told, not only the Queen, but the entire court that Abigail is my cousin. My actions are beyond your slanders . . . and I was just about to tell this young girl that I was going to place her with a very noble family about thirty leagues from London.

Bolingbroke. Very kind of you . . . but I doubt if she will accept.

Duchess. And why not, pray?

Bolingbroke. She has decided to stay in London.

Duchess [*With irony*]. Because of you, perhaps?

Bolingbroke. Perhaps.

Duchess. Ah! but now I begin to see . . . to understand this interest you had in her . . . to appreciate the ardor with which you defended her. But can it be true, milord, that you really love this girl?

Bolingbroke. And what if I did?

Duchess. I should rest the easier.

Bolingbroke. Indeed?

Duchess. Yes, for when a statesman falls in love, then begins his downfall.

Bolingbroke. And when a stateswoman falls in love? . . . ah, madame, I know of a most interesting case. There is at this very court a great lady . . . whom you yourself are well acquainted with. She, however . . . poor, misguided lady . . . has become fascinated by the youth and charm of a certain gentleman, and has taken a strange delight in becoming his unknown protectress. I suppose that her in-

terest has not as yet gone further . . . but, without ever
revealing her identity to him, she has taken the advancement of his fortune into her own hands. [A *gesture of alarm
from the* DUCHESS.] Interesting case, isn't it, madame?
But that's not all. Listen now to this . . . recently, and
through her husband, who is a great general, she has had
her young protégé made an ensign in the Queen's Guards,
and this very morning she secretly sent him his promotion
to a captaincy, along with certain marks of his new rank
. . . some tabs set with diamonds, which, I am told, are
really magnificent.

Duchess [*Embarrassed*]. It's all too fanciful . . . you
might at least have better proof.

Bolingbroke. Ah, but I have . . . and here it is! the letter
which accompanied her gift. [*The* DUCHESS *starts; he lowers
his voice confidentially.*] You understand, madame, that we
two working together . . . for we two alone know this secret . . . might see the downfall of this great lady. Places
such as she has given are subject to the control of the
Houses and to the Cabinet . . . You say that some proof
is necessary . . . but such a rich present bought by her
. . . and this letter, the handwriting, which, although disguised, could easily be recognized . . . all this would create
such frightful scandal that this great lady could hardly
brave it out . . . for she has a husband . . . this same
general of whom I spoke . . . whose violent and rash temper would be excited to a veritable fury . . . for great men
. . . heroes such as he . . . expect fidelity from their
wives.

Duchess [*Pale and with anger*]. You wouldn't dare!

Bolingbroke [*Changing his tone*]. My dear Duchess . . .
let us not become melodramatic; let us rather play the
scene quietly and with finesse. You realize, of course, that
these proofs are too valuable to remain in my hands, and
that it is my intention to give them to whom they belong . . .

Duchess. If this were true!

Bolingbroke. Between us, no more promises or protesta-
tions . . . but from henceforth, actions! Abigail will be
admitted by you today into the household of the Queen,
and these things will be handed over to you.

Duchess. Now?

Bolingbroke. No . . . but as soon as Abigail enters upon her duties . . . and it will depend upon you whether that be tomorrow or tonight.

Duchess. Ah! have you no faith in me or in my word of honor?

Bolingbroke. Perhaps I know you too well, madame.

Duchess. Hatred makes you blind, milord.

Bolingbroke [*Gallantly*]. Not at all . . . for I find you most charming! and if, instead of being on opposite sides, heaven should unite us, we might rule the world together, my dear.

Duchess. You actually believe . . .

Bolingbroke. In the beauty of your face, if not the generosity of your character.

Duchess. I see. Well, milord, you have learned your lesson well.

Bolingbroke. I could not have had a more charming teacher. I may depend upon it then . . . this very evening . . . Abigail's appointment . . .

Duchess. If I may depend upon it . . . this very evening . . . that letter!

Bolingbroke. I promise.

Duchess. I swear.

Bolingbroke. For twenty-four hours then . . . a faithful armistice!

Duchess. So be it! [*She gives him her hand, which he carries to his lips. They part, and she adds with a devastating smile:*] But afterwards . . . war! [*They bow respectfully to each other. She turns to leave; he kisses his hand after her.*]

ACT TWO

SCENE I

The reception room. Late afternoon of the next day. ABIGAIL *and the* QUEEN *discovered.* ABIGAIL *has a book in her lap; the* QUEEN *is working on a piece of embroidery.*

ABIGAIL [*Looking up from her book*]. Ah, Your Majesty, even yet I can't believe in my good luck . . . that for one whole day now I have scarcely even left you. I hardly thought I should be permitted to devote my life to you . . .

Queen. Oh, it wasn't easy. You must have believed . . . when I received you so coldly . . . that all was lost. But see, my dear, one never knows . . . I have a way of yielding. Of course I never lose sight of my projects, and the first occasion that arises finds me firm and decisive.

Abigail. Then you have spoken to the Duchess like a Queen?

Queen [*Giving herself away*]. No, for I had nothing to say to her . . . but she must have seen by my coldness that I was not pleased . . . for only a few hours later she came to me, looking most shamefaced, and said that, after all, the obstacles which opposed your nomination weren't so very important, and she would yield the rules of etiquette to my own wishes . . . and then, in order to punish her, I hesitated for a few moments . . . and then I said quite decisively, "I wish it."

Abigail. How kind you are! [*She picks up her book again.*] Shall I read to Your Majesty? [*The* QUEEN *nods that she is ready to listen, and* ABIGAIL *begins to read:*] "The history of Parliament has always been . . ."

Queen [*With a gesture of boredom, putting one hand on the book*]. Do you know . . I had good reason for wanting you by me . . . for, since you have come here, my life is different! I am no longer bored. I can speak my thoughts! I am free! I can forget that I am a Queen!

Abigail. A Queen, bored?

Queen [*Taking* ABIGAIL'S *book and putting it on the table*]. More so than anyone else . . . I, especially. To occupy oneself all day with institutions like Parliament . . . to have business with no one but matter-of-fact, egotistical, dull people . . . dear me! . . . with them I must always listen . . . but with you I can talk . . . you have such young, such sparkling ideas!

Abigail. Not always. Sometimes I am very sad.

Queen. Ah! there is a kind of sadness which does not displease me . . . like yesterday . . . when we were speaking of my poor dear brother, who has been banished, and whom I can never see again unless Parliament passes a bill permitting him to return to England.

Abigail. Ah! that's terrible.

Queen. Isn't it though? . . . and even while I spoke, I saw that you were weeping, and from that moment on I knew that you were a true friend.

Abigail. They do right in calling you the good Queen Anne.

Queen. Yes, I am good . . . but everyone knows it, and they abuse my kindness. They exhaust my patience with their continual questions. They all want positions! They're all alike!

Abigail. Well, give them their honors and the offices they ask for; as for me, I desire only to share in your troubles.

Queen [*Getting up and throwing her embroidery on the table*]. Then, my dear, it is my whole life you would share . . . for it is indeed troublesome. You alone take the place of my family . . . they are exiled to France . . . and I am an exile upon this throne.

Abigail. But why do you stay alone here? . . . you who are so young, so free?

Queen. Hush, my dear. If I were to take a husband, it would be one whom I should never have chosen myself; he would be selected by Parliament, and I should have to marry him for reasons of state. No, no! I prefer my liberty . . . I prefer being a slave to loneliness and freedom.

Abigail. I see . . . when one is a princess, one cannot choose for herself . . . nor love anyone.

Queen. No, one cannot.

Abigail. But an ideal now . . . a dream lover . . . would he also be denied you?

Queen [*Smiling*]. If Parliament found out about him, yes.

Abigail. And you daren't defy Parliament? You haven't the courage . . . you, the Queen?

Queen [*Slyly*]. Who knows? I am perhaps braver than you might think.

Abigail. Well, that sounds differently.

Queen. I was only joking . . . it's only, as you say, an ideal . . . a dream . . . something to dwell upon . . . a romance which I alone am composing and which will never be read by anyone but me.

Abigail. But why not? Why shouldn't we two read it . . . sotto voce? . . .

Queen. Well, some day I may tell you about him.

Abigail. He is some great lord . . . I am sure of that.

Queen. He may be someday. Now he only speaks prosaic words to me . . . oh, life is so very futile for a Queen!

Abigail. Well, you don't have to be a Queen when you are with me.

Queen. True! Here, with you, there is nothing to fear . . . and, what is even nicer, Abigail, . . . what I love you especially for . . . is that you don't continually speak to me of affairs of state . . . you . . .

Abigail. Oh dear!

Queen. What's the matter?

Abigail. That's exactly what I was going to do . . . a very important request on the part of . . .

Queen. Whom?

Abigail. Lord Bolingbroke. You see, madame, not very long ago when Lord Bolingbroke was traveling through France, he met with a most worthy gentleman . . . a friend . . . who did him many great services . . . and he wishes, in turn, to obtain for this friend . . .

Queen. A situation? . . . a title?

Abigail. No, an audience with Your Majesty . . . or at least an invitation for this evening to your court circle . . .

Queen. The Duchess, in her position as First Lady, has charge of all invitations. I shall give her his name. [*She sits down to write.*] Who is it?

Abigail. The Marquis de Torcy.

Queen. Oh, my dear, be quiet!

Abigail. Why?

Queen. The Marquis is a gentleman whom I greatly esteem . . . but he is an envoy from the court of Louis XIV . . . and if it were even known that you had mentioned his name . . .

Abigail. What then?

Queen. Nothing more would be needed to excite suspicion . . . and if I were actually to see the Marquis . . .

Abigail. But Lord Bolingbroke is counting on you . . . it is really most important . . . he insists that everything will be lost if you refuse to see him.

Queen. Really?

Abigail. Promise me that you will see him.

Queen. Well, the fact is . . . but hush! . . . not a word! . . . the Duchess!

The DUCHESS *enters from the door rear.*

Duchess. Here, madame, are the dispatches from the general, and which, in spite of the effect produced by Bolingbroke's speech, . . . [*She stops short in perceiving* ABIGAIL.]

Queen. Yes, yes . . . go on!

Duchess. I am waiting until the young lady has left.

Abigail. Your Majesty wishes me to retire?

Queen. No . . . for I have some orders to give you presently. Read your book about Parliament, dear. [*To the* DUCHESS, *as* ABIGAIL, *amused, reads.*] You were saying, Duchess?

Duchess [*With ill humor*]. Very well . . . in spite of Bolingbroke's speech, the subsidies were voted, and the majority, up till now doubtful, has gone to us on the condition that the question be sharply defined, and that we break off all negotiations with Louis XIV.

Queen. Well . . . all right . . .

Duchess. That is why the arrival in London and the presence here of the Marquis de Torcy produces such a bad effect. You see now that I was absolutely right, while we were in session, in promising in your name that you would not see him . . . and I have promised today that he would receive his passport.

Abigail [*Dropping her book*]. Oh!

Duchess. What's the matter with you?

Abigail [*Looking at the* QUEEN, *begging her help*]. Nothing . . . this book . . . I just dropped it . . .

Queen [*To the* DUCHESS]. It seems to me, however, that without showing prejudice to anyone, we could perhaps hear what the Marquis has to say . . .

Duchess. Grant him an audience . . . receive him . . . and this uncertain majority of ours will turn against us . . . and Bolingbroke's cause will be gained.

Queen. You believe that . . .

Duchess. It would be a hundred times better to withdraw

the bill . . . not to present it at all . . . and if Your
Majesty wishes to take upon herself the consequences, . . .
to take the blame for the general collapse which will certainly follow . . .

Queen [*Frightened and in a bad humor*]. No, no! Good
heavens! let's not talk any more about this . . . there has
been too much already. [*She sits down near the table left.*]

Duchess. I'm glad you realize that. I shall write my
husband what has happened, and at the same time write for
the Marquis de Torcy his deportation papers, which I shall
submit to Your Majesty for her approval and signature.

Queen. All right.

Duchess. And here . . . at three o'clock . . . I shall
come to take you to chapel. [*The* DUCHESS, *with a curtsey,
leaves. The* QUEEN *picks up the dispatches which the* DUCH-
SEE *just gave her.*]

Queen. You see how it is . . . nothing but boredom
. . . Parliamentary bills, political discussions . . . and
these military dispatches which I simply can't make head or
tail of. [*She starts to go out with the dispatches, muttering:*]
Oh, damn! damn! damn! [*She is out.* ABIGAIL *looks after her
with a sympathetic smile.* MASHAM *enters.* ABIGAIL *is
startled.*]

Abigail. Arthur!

Masham [*Softly, taking out a letter from his uniform*].
Sh! a letter from our friend!

Abigail. From Bolingbroke! [*Taking the letter and reading quickly.*] "My dear girl . . . Since Fortune now smiles
upon you, I should advise you and Masham to speak to the
Queen about getting married. And, my dear, while you are
at the top of Fortune's wheel, I am at the very bottom.
Come to my aid. I shall be outside, waiting." [*Instinctively
she runs for the door, crying over her shoulder:*] Come,
Arthur! [*She has vanished, and* ARTHUR *is hastening to the
door, but at that moment the* QUEEN *emerges from the opposite doorway.*]

Queen. Abigail, I was . . . [*She sees* MASHAM.] Oh,
Captain Masham!

Masham. At Your Majesty's service!

Queen. Now what can I do for you?

Masham.. A favor . . . will Your Majesty grant me a favor?

Queen. You have only to mention it. Ah, that will be an occasion . . . you who never speak but prosaically . . . you who never ask for anything!

Masham. True, madame, I have never dared . . . but today! . . .

Queen. Today finds you more courageous, eh?

Masham. I find myself in an extremely delicate position . . . and if Your Majesty will deign to give me a few moments of her time . . .

Queen. At this very moment that's rather difficult . . . some dispatches of the most extreme importance . . .

Masham. I beg your pardon . . . I shall wait. [*He starts to bow himself out, but she stops him with:*]

Queen. However, the interests of my subjects must come first, and . . . since you are one of the most faithful . . . I shall this time waive these major considerations for more personal ones. Come now . . . you wish to speak of your new rank perhaps, eh?

Masham. No, madame.

Queen. It's not about your promotion?

Masham. Oh no, madame! I wasn't even thinking about that.

Queen [*Smiling into his eyes, pointedly*]. So? Then what were you thinking about?

Masham. I beg your pardon, madame. I'm afraid I must be lacking in respect to speak like this to Your Majesty.

Queen. Not at all. Don't be so backward . . . I love secrets. Go on . . . please! [*She takes his hand tenderly.*] And you may count in advance upon my royal protection.

Masham [*Not knowing what to do with her hand, raises it to his lips*]. Ah! madame!

Queen [*Flushed with emotion, taking back her hand*]. Oh! very good.

Masham. Your Majesty, you must know . . . I have already . . . although his identity is unknown to me . . . a very powerful protector.

Queen. So?

Masham. That surprises you?

Queen [*Looking at him lovingly*]. No . . . I am not surprised.

Masham. This protector forbids me . . . under the penalty of his anger . . .

Queen. Yes?

Masham. He forbids my getting married.

Queen [*Laughing coyly*]. Well, this is very interesting . . . yes indeed . . . go on, Captain. [*And then, hearing* ABIGAIL *returning, but not yet seeing her, she becomes annoyed.*] Who is it? Who gave you permission to enter?

Abigail [*Entering and bowing*]. Your Majesty.

Queen. Oh, it's you, Abigail . . . I'll talk to you a little later on . . . I'm busy now.

Abigail. No, Your Majesty . . . it must be at once. A friend who is very devoted to you beseeches an audience with Your Majesty this very moment.

Queen [*In a bad humor*]. Is it always to be like this? . . . interruptions and disturbances . . . even when I am in the midst of the most pressing affairs. What is wanted? Who is this person?

Abigail. Lord Bolingbroke.

Queen [*Rising, frightened*]. Bolingbroke!

Abigail. It is a matter, he says, of the utmost importance.

Queen [*Impatiently*]. More of these claims, these discussions, these complaints. It's getting impossible. The Duchess will tend to him.

Abigail. The Duchess is gone. Now . . . before she returns . . . is your time to see him.

Queen. I told you once I don't want to be bothered.

Abigail. Your Majesty cannot dismiss him, for I have brought him upstairs.

Queen. You dared? . . .

Abigail. Punish me, Your Majesty, for here he is! [BOLINGBROKE *has entered. The* QUEEN *turns from* ABIGAIL *in a high fury.* ABIGAIL *bows her head;* MASHAM *is backstage.* BOLINGBROKE *says quietly to* ABIGAIL *and* MASHAM:]

Bolingbroke. Leave me alone with her. [*He raises his finger to his lips with a smile, and they leave. He comes downstage to the* QUEEN, *who is sulking in an armchair; she won't even look up to him at first.*]

Queen. At any other time, Bolingbroke, I should have

received you with pleasure . . . for you know I am always glad to see you . . . but today, and for the first time . . .

Bolingbroke. I come to speak to you of England's dearest interests . . . and the departure of the Marquis de Torcy.

Queen [*Getting up*]. I might have known it. I know in advance, milord, all that you are going to tell me . . . I appreciate your motives and thank you for your interest . . . but it's all quite useless, for . . . as soon as the Duchess brings them to me . . . I shall sign the Marquis' passports.

Bolingbroke. Your Majesty, if he leaves England, it means war more terrible than you can possibly imagine . . . if you would only listen to me, madame!

Queen. Everything is arranged and provided for. The Duchess is coming back at three o'clock, and I don't want her to find you here with me.

Bolingbroke. I see.

Queen. There would only be new scenes . . . new quarrels . . . and my nerves are so ragged now that I shouldn't be able to stand it. And you, Bolingbroke, you who are a real friend to me . . .

Bolingbroke. Your Majesty makes it impossible for me to be her friend. You dismiss me in order to receive an enemy. Pardon, madame, I shall cede my place to the Duchess . . . but the hour when she is to come has not yet struck. Give me those few moments which remain. You shan't have to say a word. I don't want to tire you out; I only want you to listen to me. [*The* QUEEN *looks at him a moment, and then royally sits in the armchair; she says quietly:*]

Queen. Very well, milord, I am listening.

Bolingbroke [*Looking at his watch*]. Ten minutes! Ten minutes in which to paint the misery of this country! Look, madame, I beg you, upon England . . . her commerce ruined, her finances destroyed, her debt growing larger every day, her present devouring her future . . . and all these evils caused by war . . . a useless war defeating not only our better interests but our honor. Would you have England ruined in order that Austria might be enlarged? . . . would you pay taxes so that the Emperor could be powerful and Prince Eugene, more glorious? If so, then continue with this alliance from which they alone are profiting. Yes, Your

Majesty . . . and, if you do not believe my words . . . let me give some actual figures: do you know that the capture of Bouchain, for which our allies have usurped all the honor, has cost England seven million pounds sterling?

Queen [*Her hand to her head*]. I beg of you, milord, these figures! . . .

Bolingbroke [*Relentlessly drumming in facts*]. Do you know that at the battle of Malplaquet we lost thirty thousand men, and the French in their glorious defeat lost but eight thousand? And if Louis XIV had resisted the influence of Madame de Maintenon . . . who is his Duchess of Marlborough . . . if, instead of selecting from the salons at Versailles a duc de Villeroi to command his armies, he had gone out onto the battlefield and chosen a Vendôme or a Catinat . . . do you know then what would have happened to us and our allies? Simply that against us France would have led all Europe, and, well-commanded, she would have ended by commanding the world. You used to see things clearly, Your Majesty, and perhaps you still do. Let us not blind ourselves to the Truth!

Queen. Yes, Bolingbroke, of course I want peace . . . but I am only a weak woman . . . and it would be necessary for me to decide between you and others who also love me . . .

Bolingbroke [*Interrupting*]. No, they deceive you! . . . lie to you! I can prove that they do.

Queen. No, no! Please! I should rather go on believing that they loved me.

Bolingbroke [*Disdainfully*]. And you call yourself a Queen! Why, you don't even know how to fly into a rage. Listen to me, Your Majesty . . . if I should show you how a part of all our subsidies enter the private coffers of the Duke of Marlborough . . . if I could prove to you that that is why he wants this war to continue . . .

Queen [*Believing that she hears the* DUCHESS]. Silence! Go quickly!

Bolingbroke. No, Your Majesty, the Duchess is not coming yet. If I could show you, madame, that the Duchess herself takes a no less lively . . . but more tender . . . interest in the continuance of this war, which keeps her husband away from London and the Court . . .

Queen. I should never believe you.

Bolingbroke. It is nevertheless true! And this young officer who was just here . . . Arthur Masham . . . he could give you the exact information.

Queen [*Breathlessly*]. Masham! . . . what do you mean?

Bolingbroke. The Duchess is madly in love with him.

Queen. With Captain Masham? [*She is trembling.* BOLINGBROKE, *thinking he has failed, is about to leave.*]

Bolingbroke. Masham . . . or someone like him . . . what does it matter?

Queen [*Trembling with anger*]. But it does matter. Tell me everything. [*She gets up.*] If she has deceived me . . . lied to me . . . pretended to carry out affairs of state when her real interests lay in furthering her own intrigue . . . if she has done that, I want to know about it. I want to know the Truth, milord. Stay and tell it to me.

Bolingbroke [*Amused, seeing that the* QUEEN *loves* MASHAM]. So! Oh, England, on what does your destiny hang!

Queen. Tell me, Bolingbroke. You say that the Duchess . . .

Bolingbroke. Desires the continuance of this war.

Queen. In order to keep her husband away from London, eh?

Bolingbroke. Exactly, madame.

Queen. So that she may further her affair with Masham . . . am I right?

Bolingbroke. How quickly Her Majesty perceives the Truth!

Queen. What reasons do you have for believing this to be true?

Bolingbroke. First, it was the Duchess who secured for him a position in the court of Your Majesty.

Queen. True.

Bolingbroke. It was she who obtained for him a position as ensign.

Queen. That's true.

Bolingbroke. It was she who, only a few days later, had him made a captain.

Queen. Yes, yes . . . you are perfectly right . . . she has done all that . . . and under the pretext that I wished it . . . ah! and now, come to think of it, this unknown protector of Masham's . . .

Bolingbroke. Or perhaps this *protectress!*

Queen. Who forbids his marrying . . .

Bolingbroke [*Close to the* QUEEN, *speaking in her ear*]. Do you need more proof? Do you see now why she doesn't want her husband to come home? Why should she when this war assures her happiness? And all the while, Your Majesty, she is no doubt laughing . . . laughing at you! [*The* QUEEN *makes an angry gesture.*] Ah yes, Your Majesty, it is true.

Queen. Listen! Silence! She is coming! [*The* DUCHESS *enters haughtily. Upon seeing* BOLINGBROKE, *she stops short with a little gasp. He bows. She returns a cold curtsey. The* QUEEN, *scarcely able to conceal her anger, says:*] Yes, milady . . . what do you want?

Duchess [*Holding out the papers in her hand*]. Here, Your Majesty, are the passports for the Marquis de Torcy . . . and the letter to accompany them . . .

Queen [*Indifferently*]. All right. [*She takes the papers, and throws them on the table.*]

Duchess. Your Majesty was to sign them.

Queen. I must read them over first.

Duchess. But this morning Your Majesty had decided . . .

Queen. I know . . . but I have changed my mind.

Duchess [*Angrily, glancing at* BOLINGBROKE]. Ah! and I can guess why. It is easy for me to see who is influencing Your Majesty.

Queen [*Flying into a rage*]. What are you talking about? Who's doing any influencing around here? Answer me that. You may be able to blind me to the Truth for a time, but when it comes to affairs of state, I never hesitate!

Bolingbroke. Spoken like a Queen!

Queen [*Her voice rising*]. It is evident that the capture of Bouchain has cost England seven million pounds sterling . . .

Duchess. Your Majesty!

Queen. It is evident, too, that at the battle of Hochstett . . .

Bolingbroke. Malplaquet, Your Majesty.

Queen. Thank you. At the battle of Malplaquet we lost thirty thousand men!

Duchess. I beg of Your Majesty . . .

Queen. And you want me to sign this letter . . . this very important letter . . . without first knowing exactly what is in it! Well, madame, I don't wish to make use of such ambitious plans . . . or of others! I certainly shall not sacrifice them to the interests of the state, as other women whom I could name have done.

Duchess. One word, I beg of you . . .

Queen. I haven't time for it. It's time for me to go to chapel. [ABIGAIL *has just entered. The* QUEEN *goes up to her.*] Come, Abigail! You will go with me.

Abigail [*Softly*]. How excited Your Majesty is!

Queen [*With a look at the* DUCHESS]. I have good reason to be. [*The* DUCHESS *bows her head and goes over to one side. The* QUEEN, *noticing that* MASHAM *is about to enter, takes* ABIGAIL'S *hand and whispers tensely:*] My dear Abigail, you remember the ideal, the dream lover whom I spoke of?

Abigail. Ah, the stranger!

Queen. Yes, and if you want to know who he is . . . [MASHAM *has just entered from the rear door carrying the* QUEEN'S *Bible and her gloves; the* QUEEN *whispers to* ABIGAIL:] Look then! Here he comes!

Abigail. Oh, heavens! [*The* QUEEN *takes her Bible and gloves from* MASHAM, *looks at him tenderly, and then motions to* ABIGAIL *to follow her. She goes out, followed sadly by* ABIGAIL *and proudly by* MASHAM. *The* DUCHESS *comes into center stage, picking up the papers from the table. She looks at* BOLINGBROKE *with intense hate. He smiles charmingly. She says between her teeth.*]

Duchess. The armistice is over! On with the war! [BOLINGBROKE *bows courteously. She looks at him with angry disdain, and turns to leave; he watches her with an air of triumph.*]

ACT TWO

SCENE II

*The reception room. Later, that night. The DUCHESS is dis-
covered, pacing the floor, the MARQUIS DE TORCY'S passport
in her hand. The QUEEN enters alone, returning from chapel
service, her Bible and gloves in her hand. The Duchess
curtseys low, saying:*

DUCHESS. Your Majesty. [*The QUEEN merely looks at her,
and is about to pass on, but the DUCHESS rises, and comes
forward, the papers, relating to the MARQUIS in her hand.*]
One moment, Your Majesty . . . I must beg of you . . .

Queen. What is it?

Duchess. Your Majesty, while you were communing with
God, I was communing with Parliament, and they have
promised me this time to pass the bill recalling your brother
to England.

Queen. Really?

Duchess. Provided, however, that you sign this passport
for the Marquis de Torcy.

Queen. And is that all I must do?

Duchess. That is all.

Queen. You promise that my brother will be allowed to
come back to England?

Duchess. I promise.

Queen [*Taking the papers to the writing desk*]. Very well.
The Marquis de Torcy, then, will leave England tomorrow.

Duchess. It must be tonight!

Queen. Tomorrow, I said. [*And, with a flourish, she signs
her name.*]

Duchess. Oh well . . . what's the difference? . . .
twenty-four hours more or less . . . [*She takes the signed
papers.*] I thank Your Majesty. [*The QUEEN bows haughtily
and exits. ABIGAIL enters just as the QUEEN leaves. She sees
the papers in the DUCHESS' hand.*]

Abigail. So! . . . she signed them!

Duchess. And the Marquis must leave tomorrow!

Abigail [*At the door*]. How thoroughly you must hate Her Majesty!

Duchess. No more thoroughly than she hates me. My dear girl, favor based upon love soon burns itself out . . . but, when favor is based upon hate, fuel is only added to the flames. [ABIGAIL *looks at her with amusement.*]

Abigail. Take care that you are not consumed in the blaze, milady. [ABIGAIL *exits by the door leading to the* QUEEN's *apartments. The* DUCHESS *is about to leave by the opposite door when* MASHAM *enters. The* DUCHESS *stops short.*]

Duchess. Ah! Captain Masham! That *is* right, isn't it? . . . *Captain,* I mean.

Masham. Quite right, milady.

Duchess. And what claim did you have for this advancement?

Masham. Practically none . . . if you consider my experience; as many as anyone else, however, . . . if you consider my aptitude.

Duchess [*Looking him up and down*]. Your aptitude, eh? I see that my husband was quite right in promoting you.

Masham. Your pardon . . . but I could wish that he would add one more favor.

Duchess. He will. Just let me know what else you want.

Masham. The opportunity of justifying his choice by letting me prove my worth.

Duchess. And where would you prove your worth?

Masham. Why, upon the battlefield.

Duchess. Oh, yes, yes . . . of course . . . the battlefield. Well, his word is as good as granted.

Masham. Ah, milady . . . how good you are!

Duchess. Had you ever thought differently?

Masham. No . . . well, yes. Yes, I had . . . you must forgive me . . . but I was once told that you were an enemy.

Duchess. Indeed? . . . and who told you that?

Masham. Someone who cannot possibly know how really good you are.

Duchess. Does that mean I can count upon you for anything?

Masham. I am at your service, milady.

Duchess. Very nice indeed. Masham, you don't know how much I appreciate you. Come here. [*He goes over to her, smiling into her eyes; she looks at him significantly.*] You're listening to me, aren't you?

Masham. Yes, yes, milady. I am listening.

Duchess. The Queen has assigned me a most important mission, in which you might be able to help me. Every day you must come to me and give me a detailed account of your proceedings. You will take my orders, and perhaps, together, we may be able to discover this culprit.

Masham. Culprit?

Duchess. Yes, he committed a most unpardonable crime right here in the very palace of St. James. He killed a member of the opposing party . . . Richard Bolingbroke . . . in a most cowardly fashion.

Masham [*Drawing himself up to attention*]. Your pardon, milady, but Bolingbroke was killed loyally, sword in hand, by a gentleman whose honor he had insulted.

Duchess. So! You know this culprit, eh? Whisper his name in my ear. Remember . . . you promised that I could count upon you for anything.

Masham. Madame, you need look no further. I am the culprit.

Duchess. You . . . captain?

Masham. Shall I give you my sword?

Duchess [*Quickly, putting her hand over his mouth*]. Hush! Not another word! These walls have ears. [*She strokes his lips with her fingertips.*] There is only one way to save you.

Masham. You mean? . . .

Duchess. You . . . you must go into seclusion.

Masham. You mean then that I shall go immediately onto the battlefield?

Duchess. Oh yes . . . the battlefield . . . I keep forgetting that. Well, if you prefer to go there.

Masham. Oh, how can I ever thank you?

Duchess. There'll be time for that later. Meanwhile, you shall leave tomorrow for the wars. I shall give you some dispatches to take to my husband. You must come to my house . . . tonight . . . to get them.

Masham. At what time?

Duchess. After the Queen's entertainment . . . **and, so** that no one will suspect your departure, come secretly.

Masham. I promise you, milady.

Duchess [*Giving him her hand*]. Tonight then . . . captain. [ABIGAIL *enters from the* QUEEN'S *apartments to see* MASHAM *kissing the hand of the* DUCHESS, *who can hardly restrain catching his head to her bosom.* ABIGAIL *stops short.*]

Abigail. Oh!

Duchess [*Turning*]. Well, what do you want?

Abigail. The Queen wishes to speak to you, milady.

Duchess. I'm busy now. I shall attend Her Majesty presently.

Abigail. But she wishes to see you this very minute. She is waiting, milady.

Duchess [*Furiously*]. Go and tell Her Majesty to . . .

Abigail. Yes, milady?

Duchess [*Exiting with fury*]. Oh, damn! damn! damn!

Masham. What on earth made you act like that toward the Duchess?

Abigail. Why shouldn't I? And you, sir, pray, who has given you the right to defend her?

Masham. She is really a very friendly person.

Abigail. She is as treacherous as the devil himself. I said it once . . . and I'll say it again.

Masham. Well, you're quite wrong. I found out just now how kind she is.

Abigail. By kissing her hand, eh?

Masham. On the contrary . . . I confessed to her myself that I killed Lord Richard . . .

Abigail. You confessed?

Masham. Yes, and she has promised to help me get away . . . she is going to see that I leave tomorrow for the army.

Abigail. No! you will be killed! Oh, Arthur, how can you believe that this woman loves you . . . I mean, wants to help you?

Masham. Well, she does . . . and I have promised to come to her house tonight to get some dispatches to take to her husband.

Abigail. You promised that?

Masham. Was there anything wrong in my promising?

Abigail. Oh, Arthur! what a mess you have got yourself into!

Masham. What do you mean?

Abigail. Tonight . . . at the very same time you have promised to go to the Duchess . . . the Queen has charged me to tell you that she requests your presence in her apartments . . . that she will be waiting for you . . .

Masham. I see. Then I must go to the Queen.

Abigail. No, no! You mustn't!

Masham. Well, why not?

Abigail [*Breaking down*]. Oh, Arthur . . . I am so unhappy . . .

Masham. What's the meaning of all this? First you say I mustn't go to the Duchess, but that the Queen wishes me . . . and then you say I mustn't go to the Queen . . . and then, when I ask why, you break out into tears . . .

Abigail. Listen to me, Arthur . . . do you love me? . . . really, I mean?

Masham. You know I do.

Abigail. Very well then . . . listen to me . . . even if I seem to hurt your chances for advancement . . . no matter how absurd my advice may seem to you . . . or my orders . . . give me your word of honor to follow them without asking why!

Masham. I give you my word.

Abigail. Good . . . then, to begin with, you must never speak to the Duchess about wanting to marry me.

Masham. I see. It might be better to speak to the Queen, eh?

Abigail. Even less to her.

Masham. But that's why I asked for an audience . . . I am sure she would protect us . . . she was so kind . . .

Abigail. I dare say.

Masham [*Taking* ABIGAIL's *hand*]. And she gave me her hand . . . which I kissed . . . why, what's the matter? Your hand has gone ice-cold.

Abigail. Oh, I wish I had never come to court! So many dangers lurk here . . . intrigues . . . and seductions . . .

Masham. Abigail, has somebody tried to seduce you? I

see now . . . one of these noblemen is trying to separate us . . . to steal your love from me . . .

Abigail. Oh, Arthur . . . you silly! . . . [*A knock is heard.*] Quick! It's Bolingbroke!

Masham. Bolingbroke?

Abigail. I wrote him to come. Leave us.

Masham. Leave you?

Abigail. You promised obedience.

Masham. And I shall always keep my word. Au revoir. [*He leaves. She opens the opposite door to admit* BOLING-BROKE.]

Bolingbroke. Ah, you see how I hasten to appear at the command of the new favorite . . . for that's what everybody's calling you . . .

Abigail. Milord, something has happened . . .

Bolingbroke. The Marquis de Torcy?

Abigail. Oh, I had almost forgotten him. The Duchess has secured the Queen's signature.

Bolingbroke. On the Marquis' passport?

Abigail. Yes, but that's nothing. Masham . . .

Bolingbroke. When must the Marquis leave London?

Abigail. In twenty-four hours . . . but you must know . . .

Bolingbroke. Damn the Duchess!

Abigail. Milord, there is another obstacle more to be feared than the Duchess. Masham . . .

Bolingbroke. Don't talk to me about Masham. What nonsense to mix affairs of state with lover's quarrels! I speak to you of peace . . . of war . . . the interests of all Europe!

Abigail. And I speak to you of my interests. Europe can manage her own affairs . . . but I . . . if you abandon me now, I am lost!

Bolingbroke. Forgive me, my child, forgive me. Let us see now . . . one thing at a time. The Queen, you say, has signed. That means she is on the best of terms with the Duchess, eh?

Abigail. No, she detests her more than ever . . . but still she doesn't break with her . . .

Bolingbroke. I see . . . an explosion waiting only for the spark . . . within twenty-four hours . . . yes, it's possible!

Abigail. Milord, this morning you saw me in a hopeless

state indeed when I found that it was the Duchess who was Arthur's protectress . . . but someone else now . . . an even greater lady whose name I daren't mention . . .

Bolingbroke [*Smiling*]. You needn't, my dear. So the . . . this other great lady . . . she also has taken a fancy to Masham, eh?

Abigail. Oh, it's so unjust. They all have their princes, dukes, and lords, while I have only him. How can I . . . a poor girl . . . hope to hold him against two such great ladies?

Bolingbroke. That's easier than if there were but a single rival.

Abigail. What do you mean?

Bolingbroke. My dear girl, if a country, say, wants to acquire a little province . . . and has no rival in its desires . . . the province is indeed lost! But, suppose there is another large country that wishes to acquire this same province . . . then there is a chance for escape. The two big powers will watch each other jealously . . . each will try to check the other . . . and, in the end, the threatened province will escape its dangers, thanks to its double enemy. Do you understand?

Abigail. Quite . . . but here is this danger. The Duchess has a rendezvous with Masham this evening after the Queen's entertainment.

Bolingbroke. Good!

Abigail. No, it's most wicked of her.

Bolingbroke. That's what I meant, my dear.

Abigail. And at the same time, the . . . this other great lady . . . also has an appointment with him.

Bolingbroke. There! what did I tell you? They are already checking each other. He can't possibly go to both rendezvous.

Abigail. To neither of them, I hope. Fortunately, this other great lady does not know yet . . . and will not know until the very last moment . . . whether she will be at liberty or not to receive him . . . but if she finds herself free . . .

Bolingbroke. And she will . . . depend upon it!

Abigail. If she finds herself free, in order to inform

Arthur and me, she will at the entertainment tonight complain of the heat, and ask for a glass of water.

Bolingbroke. But what she will really be saying is, "I am expecting you tonight," eh?

Abigail. Exactly. Oh, I haven't told Arthur a word about it. I don't want him to go to this rendezvous . . . nor to the other one. I'd rather die than see him go.

Bolingbroke. Would you really?

Abigail. Oh, the more I think about it, the less I know what to do. Have I the right to destroy his future! . . .

Bolingbroke. Abigail, we can save ourselves . . . but upon one condition . . . the Marquis de Torcy must have his invitation. You must secure it from the Queen.

Abigail. I must?

Bolingbroke. If you can do that, we are saved . . . and Masham too. Without compromising him and without destroying your future, I shall prevent the two rendezvous.

Abigail. Oh, milord! If you speak the truth . . . [*The doors are opened. Chamber music is heard offstage.*] But quick! they are opening the doors for the Queen's entertainment.

The DUCHESS Enters

Bolingbroke. I can stay, my dear. I have already been seen. [*The* DUCHESS *looks at* BOLINGBROKE *coldly, and curtseys ironically to* ABIGAIL. ABIGAIL *returns the curtsey, and exits, closing the doors behind her. The music is heard faintly.*] Heaven be praised! Blood is indeed thicker than water . . . for here you are on excellent terms with your pretty cousin. There should be some hope for me.

Duchess [*With irony also*]. Indeed. If I remember correctly, you did predict that someday we should be lovers.

Bolingbroke. I have already been swept off my feet . . . and you, milady?

Duchess. So far I can only admire your tact.

Bolingbroke. You might profess some admiration for my loyalty. I have kept all the promises I made to you the other day.

Duchess. And I, mine. I have appointed this person with whom you were just talking to a place in the Queen's circle where she may spy upon my plans and report to you.

Bolingbroke. Oh, milady, you are so very clever.

Duchess. Clever enough at least to thwart your plans of securing an audience for the Marquis de Torcy.

Bolingbroke [*Smiling*]. I wonder. [*He goes to the table and takes a printed letter from it.*] Milady, here is the invitation form which you . . . as First Lady of the Queen's Court . . . have the sole right to send out. Now I am certain that you will do me this one favor.

Duchess [*Laughing*]. Really, milord . . . *I* do a favor for you?

Bolingbroke. Naturally, in exchange, I shall render you an even greater favor.

Duchess. Must I remind you, milord, that our armistice is over?

Bolingbroke. Yes, but for the moment I shall act as if it were still in force. I shall give you, for your own good, a bit of information . . .

Duchess. Which will, no doubt, be pleasant to hear.

Bolingbroke. On the contrary. That's why I'm giving it to you. Milady, you have a rival.

Duchess. What are you talking about?

Bolingbroke. There is a certain lady at court . . . a noble lady . . . who has designs on Captain Masham. I have the proofs . . . I know the hour . . . the moment . . . the very signal for their rendezvous.

Duchess. You must be wrong.

Bolingbroke. Oh no, I'm right. I am as serious as you were when you asked him to come tonight to your home after the Queen's entertainment.

Duchess. Good God!

Bolingbroke. Your rival doesn't want him to come . . . she wants him for herself . . . and she may as well carry off the honors. Good evening, milady. [*He starts to go out by the right door, but the* DUCHESS *steps in his way. She is furious.*]

Duchess. And it is true . . . what you have just said . . . you know the very signal for their rendezvous? Tell me!

Bolingbroke [*Going to the table, picking up the pen and holding it out to her*]. As soon as you have written this invitation for the Marquis de Torcy. [*The* DUCHESS *looks at him a moment with helpless rage, and then flies to the table, where she begins to write the invitation.*] An invitation in the proper form and style . . . in your own strong handwriting . . . such a beautiful flourish there, madame . . . that circle there over the "i" . . . did you know that denoted haughtiness? . . . and how exquisitely you cross your "t's"! . . . [*The* DUCHESS *has finished the invitation and put it in its proper envelope. She gives it to* BOLINGBROKE.] Thank you, milady. [*He rings. A Servant immediately opens the door.*]

Servant. Milord?

Bolingbroke [*Giving him the invitation*]. Take this letter at once . . . as fast as you can . . . to the Marquis de Torcy . . . at the Embassy opposite the Palace . . .

Servant. Yes, milord. [*The Servant bows and leaves. The* DUCHESS *rises.*]

DUCHESS. Now, milord . . . this rival of mine . . .

Bolingbroke. She will be here tonight at the Queen's entertainment.

Duchess. Lady Albemarle, perhaps . . . or Lady Elworth, eh?

Bolingbroke. Oh, let us mention no names . . . but here is the signal. If this lady knows that she will be free . . . in order to let Masham know that the rendezvous may take place . . . the signal they have agreed upon is . . .

Duchess. Yes, yes! the signal! Quick! Quick! Tell me!

Bolingbroke. This lady will complain in a loud voice of the heat . . . and ask Masham for a glass of water.

Duchess. Here in this room . . . this evening . . . she will do that?

Bolingbroke. She will . . . and afterwards you can see for yourself if my information has not been correct . . . if they do not keep their rendezvous . . .

Duchess [*Furiously*]. Just let me get my hands on her! I'll tell her a thing or two.

Bolingbroke. I hope you do.

Duchess. Before the whole court I shall unmask her!

Bolingbroke. Sh! The musicale is over. The Queen and her ladies are coming this way.

Duchess. Ah, if I only knew which one of these ladies . . . [*The* QUEEN *and her ladies in waiting enter. Members of Parliament and gentlemen of the court also enter. There*

is ad lib gay talk and chatter. The QUEEN *seats herself,* ABI-
GAIL *and the ladies in waiting stand near her.* MASHAM *has
entered, and is standing in the rear. The Tories group themselves near* BOLINGBROKE. *The* DUCHESS *is inspecting the
face of each lady, her suspicions running rampant.*]

Queen [*Who has not seen* MASHAM, *turns to* ABIGAIL].
I don't see the dear Captain. Where is he?

Duchess. Your Majesty, so many people requested it that,
only for form's sake, I have sent an invitation to the Marquis
de Torcy.

Queen [*Absently*]. So sweet of you, my dear. [MASHAM
has come forward. The QUEEN *sees him, blushes, and
nudges* ABIGAIL.] Do you see? . . . he has come!

Duchess. Would Your Majesty like to play whist? Shall
I have the cards dealt?

Queen. Yes, go ahead . . . let's play. [*The Servant enters and announces in a loud voice:*]

Servant. The Ambassador from France . . . His Excel-
lency, the Marquis de Torcy. [*The* MARQUIS *enters. Buzz of
ad lib conversation.* BOLINGBROKE *takes the* MARQUIS *by the
hand and presents him to the* QUEEN.]

Bolingbroke. Your Majesty!

Queen [*Graciously*]. Ah, Monsieur l'Ambassadeur, it is an
honor to receive you.

Duchess [*Whispering to her*]. Don't be too nice to him
now.

Queen [*In a loud voice*]. Oh, but it is so awfully nice
having the Marquis with us.

De Torcy. The pleasure is all mine. [*He bows, and retires
with* BOLINGBROKE *to one side. The cards are dealt. The*
MARQUIS *says in a whisper:*] I was all packed . . . ready to
sail . . . when I received this invitation.

Bolingbroke. I know.

De Torcy. Things are going well, eh?

Bolingbroke. They're going to go even better.

Duchess. Whom would Her Majesty like for her partners?

Queen. Whom would you suggest?

Duchess. Lady Albemarle. [*It is obvious the* DUCHESS
suspects LADY ALBEMARLE.]

Queen. Very good

Lady Albemarle. I thank Your Majesty.

Duchess. And for the other player? . . .

Queen. Dear me . . . ah! . . . [*Perceiving the* MAR-QUIS DE TORCY] Of course! Monsieur l'Ambassadeur! [*General movement of astonishment;* BOLINGBROKE *is overjoyed.*]

Duchess [*Whispering*]. Choose someone else.

Queen. Oh, what does it matter?

Duchess. You see what an effect your choice produces?

Queen. Well, I told you to suggest somebody. Ah, Monsieur! [*The* MARQUIS *takes the* QUEEN'S *hand and conducts her to a whist table; he seats himself between her and* LADY ALBEMARLE. *The* DUCHESS *is in a bad humor;* BOLINGBROKE *says to her:*]

Bolingbroke. You are too generous, Duchess . . . you are doing so many nice things for me . . . really, it's much more than I asked for.

Duchess. A great deal more than I wanted, milord.

Bolingbroke. And the Marquis is a man to make the most of his opportunities. He is a very clever talker . . . look how pleased Her Majesty is with what he is saying. [*For Her Majesty is laughing charmingly.*]

Duchess. Indeed . . . well, I'll soon fix that. [*She starts toward the table.*]

Bolingbroke. Just a minute . . . don't break up the game . . . for your moment is coming, my dear Duchess. I think . . . [*With a look at the* QUEEN, *who has now raised her hand to her head.*] . . . yes, the signal is about to be given!

Duchess. Which one?

Bolingbroke. Listen!

Queen [*Pretending to answer the* MARQUIS]. Yes, you're right, Monsieur le Marquis, there is in this room . . . an almost insufferable heat. Captain Masham!

Masham [*Stepping before her*]. Your Majesty?

Queen. Captain Masham, I should like a glass of water.

Duchess. So! [*She has taken a step toward the* QUEEN.]

Queen. What's the matter, Duchess?

Duchess. I . . . I . . . what I was . . . oh, Your Majesty, can it be possible?

Queen. What on earth are you spluttering about?

Duchess. Can it be possible that Your Majesty . . . has forgotten? . . .

Bolingbroke. Milady!

Marquis. My dear Duchess!

Lady Albemarle. After all, the Queen!

Queen. Well, what's the matter, Duchess? What have I forgotten?

Duchess [*Trying desperately to collect her wits*]. The rights . . . the etiquette . . . the proper duties of the court . . . it is only one of your ladies who has the right of serving Your Majesty.

Queen. So much ado over such a little thing? [*Returning to her cards.*] Well, Duchess, suppose you give me the glass of water.

Duchess. Yes, Your Majesty.

Bolingbroke [*To the* DUCHESS, *to whom* MASHAM *has given the tray with the glass of water*]. Must I remind you, Duchess, that you were going to unmask your rival . . . tell her a thing or two? . . .

Duchess [*Taking the glass of water*]. Ohh!

Queen [*Impatiently*]. Well, milady . . . I am dying of thirst . . . and since you . . . [*The* DUCHESS, *whose hand is trembling with anger, in presenting the glass of water to Her Majesty, upsets it, and the water spills over the* QUEEN's *gown. The* QUEEN *leaps to her feet.*] God in heaven! You are as clumsy as a cow! [*Everyone rises.*]

Duchess. That's the first time Your Majesty has ever spoken like that to me.

Queen. That shows how indulgent I am.

Duchess. And after all the services I have heaped upon you! . . .

Queen. Spilled down my front, you mean.

Duchess. I see. I shan't impose myself upon Your Majesty. I tender her my resignation.

Queen. I accept it . . . with pleasure.

Duchess. Oh!

Queen. Milords and ladies, let us retire!

Bolingbroke [*To the* DUCHESS]. Well, milady, you must give up your position.

Duchess. And let her keep her rendezvous with Masham? Never! [*To the* QUEEN.] Your Majesty! One word more! In giving up my place in Your Majesty's service, I must carry out the last order with which she commissioned me.

Abigail. No!

Queen. What do you mean?

Duchess. On the complaint of milord and his Tory colleagues, Your Majesty commanded me to discover Richard Bolingbroke's murderer . . .

Abigail. Oh, God!

Duchess [*To* BOLINGBROKE]. It is you now, milord, who must answer for his safety, for I deliver him into your hands. I demand the arrest of Captain Masham!

Queen. Masham? Impossible!

Masham [*Bowing before the* QUEEN]. Yes, Your Majesty . . . it was I.

Duchess [*Smiling at the* QUEEN'S *grief, and saying to* BOLINGBROKE]. I am revenged!

Bolingbroke. And I have won!

Duchess. Oh, not yet, milord, not yet! [*At a gesture from the* QUEEN, BOLINGBROKE *accepts* MASHAM'S *sword. The* QUEEN, *overcome, is helped by* ABIGAIL *to her chambers. The courtiers leave.* MASHAM *is led away. The* DUCHESS *stands alone on the stage, smiling triumphantly.*]

ACT THREE

The QUEEN'S *boudoir. The following night. There is a large door at the rear leading out onto a balcony. At the right is a door leading to the* QUEEN'S *bedchamber, while at the left is the entrance door. The room is simply but exquisitely furnished . . . an escritoire, a table, a lounge, chairs.* ABIGAIL *is discovered waiting, looking out the balcony window, the curtains of which are drawn apart. The entrance door opens immediately, and* BOLINGBROKE *enters.*

ABIGAIL [*Turning*]. Oh, milord!

  Bolingbroke. You sent for me?

  Abigail. Yes, I . . .

  Bolingbroke. I was busy with the ministry . . .

  Abigail. With the what?

  Bolingbroke. The Tory ministry. Oh, it won't be long now.

Abigail. On the contrary . . . it's a great deal further off than you think.

Bolingbroke. What's the matter?

Abigail. Listen . . . I was here in the Queen's boudoir . . . just about to speak to her of Arthur . . .

Bolingbroke. Masham is a prisoner on his word of honor in my apartments. Go on.

Abigail. Well . . . a noblewoman whom Her Majesty respects requested an audience . . .

Bolingbroke. Lady Abercrombie?

Abigail. None other . . . and, with her, Lord Devonshire and Mr. Walpole . . . well, they came to tell her that the Whig Party was furious at her behavior with the Duchess, and at their meeting this very evening the bill for the recall of her Stuart brother would be rejected.

Bolingbroke. What did the Queen say?

Abigail. Nothing . . . she stammered about . . . and then Lady Abercrombie whispered something in her ear . . .

Bolingbroke. Did you hear it?

Abigail. I heard only one name . . . that of Masham's. They were blackmailing Her Majesty . . . for the Queen turned very pale, and said, "Very well, tell the Duchess to come back. I shall see her."

Bolingbroke. The Duchess . . . returning?

Abigail. This very hour . . . that's why I wrote you to come at once. The Queen has made an agreement with these gentlemen regarding a reconciliation.

Bolingbroke. What do you mean . . . reconciliation?

Abigail. Her Majesty has agreed to a little scheme . . . the Duchess will come this evening to hand in her official resignation . . .

Bolingbroke. I see.

Abigail. The Queen will refuse to speak to her . . . the Duchess will then fall down before Her Majesty, who will then raise her up . . . they will embrace each other . . . the bill will be passed . . . and the Marquis de Torcy given his passport.

Bolingbroke. I must speak to the Queen . . . at once!

Abigail. Her ladies in waiting are dressing her for this evening.

Bolingbroke. Good God! I must find something to re-kindle this spark of hatred between them!

Abigail [*Hearing the* QUEEN *coming*]. What good luck! It's the Queen!

Bolingbroke. Good! Abigail, leave me with her. Watch for the arrival of the Duchess. The moment you see her coming, warn me.

Abigail. Yes, milord. God help you. [*She leaves by the entrance door. The* QUEEN *enters from her bedchamber; she is wearing an attractive negligee.*]

Queen. If they'd only leave me alone, I'd . . . [*Discovering* BOLINGBROKE.] Oh, it's you, Bolingbroke. I'm awfully glad to see you. I've just passed the most frightful day.

Bolingbroke. I understand that the latest generosity of Your Majesty is to overlook last night's scandal.

Queen. Overlook? How can I do anything else? If you knew what I have gone through since that unfortunate accident . . . I am completely worn out . . . and besides I'm not even supposed to be talking to you.

Bolingbroke. You're going to take the Duchess back, eh?

Queen. In spite of myself. yes . . . for, since the poor Duchess . . .

Bolingbroke. Poor?

Queen. Oh, I'm not defending her . . . heaven forbid! . . . but I've accused her so unjustly . . . and you wouldn't want me to do that now, would you? Of course I didn't speak of the last subsidies . . . or of the capture of Bouchain . . . I haven't had time to verify them . . . ah! and milord, in regard to Captain Masham . . . remember what you told me about him and the Duchess?

Bolingbroke. Yes.

Queen. An absolute error.

Bolingbroke. What's that you say?

Queen. The Duchess thinks constantly of someone else.

Bolingbroke. Whom?

Queen. Lady Abercrombie informed me just this morning that it's Lord Evandale whom the Duchess adores.

Bolingbroke. And Your Majesty believed that?

Queen. Why shouldn't I? After all, milord, think now! Why should the poor Duchess . . . if she really loved

Masham . . . why should she accuse him before the whole court and make you arrest him?

Bolingbroke. Has it not occurred to Your Majesty that the Duchess may have yielded to a momentary fit of anger and jealousy . . . of which she now repents.

Queen. What do you mean?

Bolingbroke. What if the Duchess had found out that last night . . . after your entertainment . . . Masham was going to keep a most mysterious rendezvous.

Queen. Oh, my God!

Bolingbroke. Who the mysterious lady was I don't know . . . it may not even be true . . . but if Your Majesty wants, I could find out . . .

Queen. Oh, no, no! That wouldn't do any good.

Bolingbroke. What I do know, however, is that last night . . . after Your Majesty's entertainment . . . the Duchess herself had made arrangements for a rendezvous with Masham.

Queen. What?

Bolingbroke. Oh yes, Your Majesty.

Queen. Last night . . . and with him . . . she had a rendezvous?

Bolingbroke. Precisely, Your Majesty.

Queen. Why, the dirty little cheat.

Bolingbroke. Exactly, Your Majesty. Imagine now her despair upon having so hastily turned in her resignation . . . deprived of her office, she can no longer promote Masham . . . who is my prisoner . . . deprived of her entrance into the palace . . . a way of coming and going whenever she pleases . . . she can no longer see him under your very eyes. That's why she sent this reconciliation party to you . . . that's why she wants to return to court.

Queen. Never!

ABIGAIL *enters.*

Abigail. Milord . . . milord . . .

Queen. What is it?

Abigail. Your Majesty, the Duchess' carriage has just entered the palace grounds.

Queen. I won't see her. Abigail, you go see her . . . tell her I can't receive her . . . that we have filled the place she occupied . . .

Abigail. What, Your Majesty?

Bolingbroke. Come, come, Miss Abigail. You heard the Queen's orders. Run along.

Abigail [*Smiling*]. Yes, milord. [*She goes out. The* QUEEN *has thrown herself upon her lounge.* BOLINGBROKE *comes down to her.*]

Bolingbroke. Bravo, my Queen, very handsomely done!

Queen. Wasn't it though! Everybody thinks I'm weak, but I'm really not.

Bolingbroke. I've always said you had great strength of character.

Queen. Really, this whole affair has been enough to wear out my patience . . . [*Leaning forward.*] . . . but tell me, milord, how is poor Captain Masham?

Bolingbroke. Still my prisoner, and I suppose he will be until a new ministry has been formed, the House dissolved, and the Duke of Marlborough recalled.

Queen. Very good . . . then that must be done at once . . . and the dear Captain . . .

Bolingbroke. Yes?

Queen. Of course he must be punished . . . made to see the error of his ways . . . I daresay if he were court-martialed, that would make the Duchess very angry, eh?

Bolingbroke. On the contrary, she would be delighted. She is disappointed with Masham.

Queen. Really?

Bolingbroke. She has discovered beyond the possibility of a doubt that Masham doesn't love her . . . that he never loved her . . . but that he does love someone else!

Queen. Are you sure? Who told you?

Bolingbroke. Why, Masham himself . . . he admitted everything . . . a mysterious sweetheart . . . someone at court whom he secretly adores . . .

Queen [*Beaming with contentment*]. Really? Well, that's quite different then . . . I mean, it's very singular. [*Laughing to cover her confusion.*] Well, we'll talk about this later on.

Bolingbroke. Yes, Your Majesty. This same hour Your

Majesty will have the list of my new colleagues . . . along with the ordinance for the dissolution of Parliament . .

Queen. Good!

Bolingbroke. The preliminaries for the conference to open with the Marquis de Torcy's triumphant instatement.

Queen. Splendid! Such a nice man!

Bolingbroke. Your Majesty will sign these papers?

Queen. Of course . . . but wouldn't it be better to find out and spoil the plans of the Duchess? . . . don't you think we'd better question Masham?

Bolingbroke. Yes, of course . . . provided that it be absolutely in secret.

Queen. Why?

Bolingbroke. Because he is my prisoner, and isn't supposed to talk to anyone . . . but perhaps this evening . . . tonight . . . there won't be so great a danger of his being seen. [*The* DUCHESS *angrily enters by the entrance door, but, upon seeing* BOLINGBROKE, *stops short.*]

Queen. Yes . . . tonight . . . at once . . . much, much better.

Bolingbroke. Then I shall deliver my prisoner for Your Majesty to question at her leisure.

Queen. Very good indeed. [*The* DUCHESS, *with an evil smile, retires, closing the door. As it clicks, the* QUEEN *starts.*] What was that?

Bolingbroke. What's the matter?

Queen. I thought I heard someone. Very well then . . . this evening . . . just as soon as he can . . .

Bolingbroke. Masham will be here . . . [*Starting out.*] . . . at once! [*He goes out by the entrance door, but, as he opens it,* ABIGAIL *re-enters the room. He bows to her smilingly, and, pressing her hand, exits hastily. The* QUEEN *turns.*]

Queen. Ah, it's you, my dear! Is the Duchess angry?

Abigail. Perfectly furious. She even broke away from me and started for your apartments. She got the door open, but closed it almost immediately, and went away with the wickedest smile on her face.

Queen. Fancy that now!

Abigail. And, as she passed me, she said to Lady Abercrombie, "I have just received some information from which I shall most certainly profit."

Queen. What could she have meant? Do you suppose she could have heard of the interview I was supposed to have had last night?

Abigail. Where's the wrong there? After all, you weren't able to see him . . . and, even now, while he is a prisoner, it would be impossible.

Queen. Suppose I *were* to see him?

Abigail. You mean? . . .

Queen. Yes, Abigail. He is coming here . . . I am waiting for him now.

Abigail. Oh!

Queen [*Taking her hand*]. What's the matter with you? . . . why, you're trembling . . . ah! for me, eh? There's no danger, my child.

Abigail. Suppose the Duchess were to find out that he was here . . . in your boudoir . . . at this hour . . . [*A knock is heard at the door.*]

Queen. Hush! It is Masham! Don't leave me.

Abigail. Don't worry, Your Majesty. I shan't. [*She opens the door, and* MASHAM *enters, bowing to the* QUEEN. ABIGAIL *closes the door, and returns to her place by the* QUEEN.]

Masham. Lord Bolingbroke has sent me with these papers for Your Majesty.

Queen [*Taking the papers but looking into his eyes*]. Very nice of you. Thank you.

Masham. I must carry them back . . . with Your Majesty's signature.

Queen. Of course . . . I was forgetting . . . [*She takes the papers and goes to the table where she sits and riffles the papers.*] Dear me! Dear me! So many of them! [*She picks up a pen, and, without reading the contents, hurriedly signs the various ordinances. During that time* ARTHUR *and* ABIGAIL *have come together downstage.*]

Abigail. Arthur, my dear, I've just been given the Duchess' place.

Masham. Marvelous!

Abigail. But I'm not going to take it. I'm going to give up everything.

Masham. But why?

Abigail. So that you can rise in power.

Masham. What are you talking about?

Abigail. Arthur, you are loved by a noblewoman . . . the noblest in the entire kingdom . . .

Masham. Who?

Abigail. Hush! The Queen has finished.

Queen [*Coming toward them*]. Here are the ordinances.

Masham [*Taking the papers*]. I thank Your Majesty, and shall take them at once to milord.

Queen. I'm afraid, dear Captain, that he's going to have to prosecute you. You've been very naughty.

Masham. I'm not afraid, Your Majesty.

Queen. Of course you do have the Duchess' protection.

Masham. Your Majesty!

Queen. Oh, come, come, Captain! You won't admit it because you're very discreet . . . but I'm afraid you have been too, too naughty!

Masham. Your Majesty, I assure you I don't know what you're talking about. The Duchess means nothing in my life.

Queen. No?

Masham. And besides I'm very much in love with someone else.

Queen [*Lowering her eyes, blushing*]. So? And your sweetheart . . . is she beautiful and charming?

Masham [*Unable to take his eyes off* ABIGAIL]. More than I could possibly say. Oh! to hell with discretion! I'm going to tell Your Majesty whom I love!

Queen. Oh, Captain!

Masham. Yes, why I'm so happy . . . so faithful in my love!

Queen. Faithful? Oh, my dear boy!

Masham. And you may punish me, madame, if here before you, at your feet, I dare avow my love for . . . [*There is a noise of women approaching the entrance door. The* QUEEN *rises.*]

Queen. Good God! Someone is coming this way! [MASHAM *starts for the door leading to the bedchamber.*]

Abigail. No! no! there are ladies in waiting there!

Queen. Heavens above! if you should be found here now!
[*A knock comes to the door.*]

Abigail. Quick! On the balcony! [MASHAM *hides on the balcony;* ABIGAIL *closes the windows and draws the drapes. She goes up to the Queen.*] Calm yourself, madame. I must open the doors.

Queen. I shall die. I know it! [ABIGAIL *opens the doors. The* DUCHESS *enters, followed by her cohorts.* BOLINGBROKE *enters after them. From the opposite door, several ladies in waiting enter. The* QUEEN *rises in anger.*] How do you dare!

Duchess [*Trying to discover* MASHAM]. My audacity will be pardoned, I know, when I give Your Majesty my important message.

Queen. What has happened?

Duchess. Prince Eugene's forces have attacked the French army at Denain and been defeated. [*She sees the balcony drawn.*] Hm! [*She starts for the doors.*]

Abigail [*Stepping in her way*]. Milady!

Duchess. Let me by! [*Faintly in the distance a mob roar is heard.*] Do you hear the furious cries of the people?

Bolingbroke. They demand peace!

Duchess [*Pushing* ABIGAIL *aside*]. Let me by! [*She throws open the balcony doors, disclosing* MASHAM. *There is general surprise from the courtiers.*] Ah! Captain Masham!
. . . and in the Queen's boudoir! Well, well, well!

Queen [*Collapsing in her chair*]. My God!

Abigail [*Running forward*]. No! I was waiting for him. [*Falling on her knees before the* QUEEN] Your Majesty, forgive me . . . I am the guilty one.

Duchess. You! You dare admit . . .

Abigail. Yes! . . . the Truth!

Masham [*Bowing at* ABIGAIL's *side*]. Punish us both, Your Majesty.

Queen [*To* BOLINGBROKE]. Help me, milord . . . save me!

Bolingbroke [*Addressing the courtiers*]. Your pardon, milords and ladies! I must tell you all . . .

Duchess. And I . . . I should like to be told one thing: How a prisoner confided to milord's keeping can at this moment be free? What reason can milord give for that?

Bolingbroke [*To the crowd*]. A reason which you would have yielded to . . . just as I did, milords. Captain Masham begged me, on his word of honor as a gentleman, for permission to say his farewells to Abigail Churchill, his sweetheart.

Duchess. Abigail!

Queen. His sweetheart?

Bolingbroke. And so I granted him permission. Could you, milords and ladies, have done otherwise?

Ad Lib. Of course not . . . no! no! . . . we would have done the same!

Queen. I think I'm going to faint.

Bolingbroke. Leave us! [*The courtiers bow out.* ABIGAIL *and* MASHAM *tend to the* QUEEN, *reviving her with smelling salts. The* DUCHESS *and* BOLINGBROKE *face each other.*]

Duchess. Well, milord, at last you have won! You are the first man who has ever defeated me . . . and, if I were not already married, you would know no peace until I had wed with you.

Bolingbroke. You honor me, madame . . . especially since you don't even know my best qualities.

Duchess. But I have an excellent imagination. However, milord, let me claim the first privilege of a wife . . . [*She kisses him.*]

Bolingbroke. And let me likewise claim the first privilege of a husband . . . [*He kisses her.*]

Duchess. And now, milord, let me also claim the second privilege of a wife . . . [*She slaps him smartly on the cheek.*]

Bolingbroke. And, milady, let me likewise claim the second privilege of a husband . . . [*He slaps her smartly on the cheek.*]

Duchess [*Smiling graciously and bowing*]. My deepest respects, milord.

Bolingbroke [*A full, sweeping bow*]. My fondest regards, milady. [*She bows out. The* QUEEN *has recovered and looks at* BOLINGBROKE, *moaning:*]

Queen. Oh, Bolingbroke! what has happened? What have you done to me?

Bolingbroke. You asked me to help you . . . to save you.

Now surely, you wouldn't have this young girl who so dearly loves you dishonored before all the court.

Queen. No, no . . . tell them to come closer. [*He signals* MASHAM *and* ABIGAIL *to approach. They come forward timidly. The* QUEEN *extends her hand over them.*] Your Queen blesses you, my children.

Abigail. We thank Your Majesty.

Queen. As for you, Captain . . .

Masham. Yes, Your Majesty?

Queen. Your Queen commands you to marry this girl.

Abigail. Oh, Your Majesty!

Masham. How can we ever thank you?

Queen. Go! Leave me! I am still faint [ABIGAIL *and* MASHAM *start out; as they pass* BOLINGBROKE, *he takes* ABIGAIL's *hand and presses it reassuringly.*]

Bolingbroke. Good luck, Abigail! You see . . . my system does work . . . Lord Marlborough overthrown . . . Europe at peace!

Masham [*Giving him the papers which the* QUEEN *has signed*]. Bolingbroke, minister!

Bolingbroke. And all, thanks to a glass of water! [*They smile and leave.* BOLINGBROKE *returns to the table. The* QUEEN *gets up wearily.*]

Queen. Ah, what does life hold for a Queen? . . . boring days . . . boring nights . . . a lifetime of boredom!

Bolingbroke [*At the table*]. Yes, Your Majesty.

Queen [*At the open balcony*]. The nights are the worst! Look, milord . . . a harvest moon! . . . and what good does it do me? . . . I who am just a Queen?

Bolingbroke. Yes, Your Majesty.

Queen. I might just as well be a nun. I might just as well . . . [*Her attention is caught by something outside her balcony; her eyes brighten with new interest.*]

Bolingbroke. What is it? Your Majesty was saying? . . .

Queen [*Absently*]. Yes, I . . . [*And then with great interest:*] Who's that guardsman down there?

Bolingbroke. What? . . . oh, that's the new ensign . . . Masham's successor!

Queen. Very nice . . .

Bolingbroke. Yes, Your Majesty.

Queen. Handsome . . .

Bolingbroke. Yes, Your Majesty.

Queen. A credit to an ensign's uniform . . .

Bolingbroke. Yes, Your Majesty.

Queen. Hmm!

Bolingbroke. Your Majesty was saying? . . .

Queen. What? . . . oh, yes! . . . yes, I was just about to say, "Isn't it a lovely night!" [*Bolingbroke nods with a smile. The* QUEEN *sighs happily . . . quite beatifically . . . and, as her eyes once more roam outside the balcony, the curtain falls.*]

CAMILLE

(La Dame aux Camélias)

A Play in Five Acts

by

ALEXANDRE DUMAS *fils*

English Version by

EDITH REYNOLDS and NIGEL PLAYFAIR

CHARACTERS

(*In order of appearance*)

BARON DE VARVILLE, *Armand's rival*
NANINE, *maid*
NICHETTE, *Gustave's fiancée*
MARGUERITE GAUTIER, *a courtesan*
OLYMPE, *Saint-Gaudens' mistress*
SAINT-GAUDENS, *a roué*
PRUDENCE, *a milliner*
GASTON, *a playboy*
ARMAND DUVAL, *Marguerite's lover*
COUNT DE GIRAY, *Marguerite's friend*
SERVANT
GUSTAVE, *another friend*
DUVAL, SR., *Armand's father*
ARTHUR
A MESSENGER
DOCTOR
ANAIS
ESTHER

PLACE: PARIS *and* AUTEUIL.
TIME: 1848.

TRANSLATOR'S PREFACE: This is a translation, not an adaptation, and as careful a translation as Miss Reynolds and I know how to make, not such an easy task as we began by hoping it would be.

After it was completed we pruned it of some sentences, and even passages which seemed to have merely a topical and local interest, such as a discussion on the ethics of advocacy in the Paris law courts, and others that sounded, in English, priggish or long-winded.

Otherwise the words and the directions of Dumas have been followed perhaps more faithfully than in any recent production, even in his own country.

N. P.

CAMILLE

ACT ONE

MARGUERITE'S *drawing room, Paris.* NANINE *sewing:* DE
VARVILLE *sitting by fireplace. The bells rings.*

VARVILLE. That was the bell.
  Nanine. Valentine will open the door.
  Varville. Are you sure it's not Marguerite?
  Nanine. Yes, she won't be home before half-past ten.

Enter NICHETTE.

Oh! it is Mademoiselle Nichette!
  Nichette. Isn't Marguerite here?
  Nanine. No, my dear. Did you wish to speak to her?
  Nichette. Yes, but I can't stay now, Gustave is down-
stairs. How is she?
  Nanine. Just about the same.
  Nichette. Tell her that I'll come to see her in a day or
two. Good-bye, Nanine. Good-bye.   [*Exit* NICHETTE.
  Varville. Who was that?
  Nanine. That was Mademoiselle Nichette.
  Varville. Nichette? Sounds more like the name of a cat
than a woman.
  Nanine. Yes, it is a nickname they gave her because she
does look rather like a kitten. She once worked in the same
shop with Madame.
  Varville. Was Marguerite in a shop?
  Nanine. She was an embroideress.
  Varville. Amazing!
  Nanine. Didn't you know that? It is no secret.
  Varville. Nichette is quite a pretty girl.
  Nanine. She's a good girl.
  Varville. But this M. Gustave?
  Nanine. Which M. Gustave?
  Varville. The one who is "waiting below."

Nanine. That is her husband.

Varville. Mr. Nichette.

Nanine. That is—he is not her husband yet, but he will be.

Varville. In other words, he is her lover. Well, well! She is a good little girl, but she has a lover.

Nanine. Yes, but they love each other and nobody else, and he'll marry her before very long, see if he doesn't!

Varville. Well, it is no affair of mine. . . . I don't seem to be making much progress here.

Nanine. None whatever.

Varville. I must say that Marguerite . . .

Nanine. Well?

Varville. Well, it is a queer idea to give up everybody else for the Duc de Mauriac, who can't be very amusing.

Nanine. It is the only happiness he has, poor man. He is like a father to her.

Varville. Ah! Yes! There is quite a pathetic story about that, only, unfortunately——

Nanine. Unfortunately——

Varville. I don't believe it.

Nanine. M. de Varville, there are plenty of true things that can be said about Madame, which is all the more reason for not saying things that are untrue. If you wish to know the truth, it is this. Two years ago, after a long illness, Madame went away to recover her strength. I went with her. At the same spa there was a young girl about the same age, suffering from the same illness, who was as like her as a twin sister. That was Mademoiselle de Mauriac.

Varville. Mademoiselle de Mauriac died.

Nanine. Yes.

Varville. And the Duke, in his grief, finding Marguerite so like his lost daughter, begged her to receive him and let him love her as a father. Whereupon, Marguerite confessed to him the life she had been living.

Nanine. Because Madame never tells lies.

Varville. Of course not. And as Marguerite was not so much like his daughter morally as physically, the Duke offered to give her whatever she wished, if she would change her manner of living, which Marguerite promised to do. This promise, on her return to Paris, she naturally refrained

from keeping, and the Duke, with only a portion of his
happiness, withheld a portion of her income. The result is
that Marguerite has fifty thousand francs' worth of debts.

Nanine. Which you are offering to pay. But it may be
better to owe money to some people than gratitude to
others.

Varville. Especially with the Comte de Giray always on
hand.

Nanine. All I can say is that the story of the Duke is true,
and the Comte is only a friend.

Varville. A friend—did you say?

Nanine. Yes, a friend. What a wicked tongue you have!
There's the bell. That's Madame now. Shall I tell her all
you've been saying to me?

Varville. As you please.

Enter MARGUERITE.

Marguerite [*to* NANINE]. Tell them we shall want supper.
Olympe and Saint-Gaudens are coming; I met them at the
opera. [*To* VARVILLE.] Oh! you here?

Varville. Is it not my fate to be always waiting for you?

Marguerite. Is it my fate never to come in without finding
you here?

Varville. Is it my fault that I love you?

Marguerite. My dear friend, if I were to listen to all the
people who are in love with me, I should have no time for
dinner. I allow you to come here at any hour when I am
at home and to wait for me whenever I am out, but if you
will persist in talking of nothing but your love, I must withdraw my friendship.

Varville. And yet, Marguerite, last year at Bagnères, you
did give me a little hope.

Marguerite. My dear, that was at Bagnères, when I was
ill and bored; this is Paris—I am much better and not at all
bored.

Varville. I imagine not, when one is beloved by the Duc
de Mauriac.

Marguerite. Idiot!

Varville. And in love with the Comte de Giray.

Marguerite. I am free to love whom I choose. It concerns
no one but me, and you least of all. So if you have nothing

better to say, perhaps you will be kind enough to go. [VAR-
VILLE *walks up and down.*] Aren't you going?

Varville. No.

Marguerite. Then go to the piano. Your music is your one
redeeming quality.

Varville. What shall I play?

Marguerite. Whatever you like.

Enter NANINE.

Did you order supper?

Nanine. Yes, madame.

Marguerite [*going over to* VARVILLE]. What is that
you are playing?

Varville. A Reverie by Rosellen.

Marguerite. It's charming.

Varville. Listen! Marguerite, I have eighty thousand
francs a year.

Marguerite. How nice! I have a hundred thousand. [*To*
NANINE.] Have you seen Prudence?

Nanine. Yes, madame.

Marguerite. Is she coming this evening?

Nanine. Yes, madame. Mademoiselle Nichette called for
a moment.

Marguerite. Why didn't she stay?

Nanine. M. Gustave was waiting downstairs for her.

Marguerite. Dear little girl!

Nanine. The doctor called.

Marguerite. What did he say?

Nanine. He advised you to rest as much as possible,
madame.

Marguerite. Dear Doctor! Is that all?

Nanine. No, madame. This bouquet came for you.

Marguerite [*taking the bouquet*]. Roses and white lilac.
Put these flowers in your room, Nanine.

Varville [*ceases playing*]. Don't you care for them?

Marguerite. What do they call me?

Varville. Marguerite Gautier.

Marguerite. What other name have they given me?

Varville. The Lady of the Camellias.

Marguerite. Why?

Varville. Because you wear no other flowers.

Marguerite. And I care for no others. Their scent makes me ill.

Varville. I have no luck. Good-bye, Marguerite.

Marguerite. Good-bye!

NANINE *enters again with* OLYMPE *and* SAINT-GAUDENS.

Nanine. Here are Mlle. Olympe and M. Saint-Gaudens.

Marguerite. At last, Olympe! I thought you were not coming!

Olympe. You must blame Saint-Gaudens, it is his fault.

St. Gaudens. It is always my fault. Good evening, Varville.

Varville. Good evening.

St. Gaudens. Are you having supper here?

Marguerite. No, he is not.

St. Gaudens. And how are you, my dear girl?

Marguerite. Quite well.

St. Gaudens. I am delighted to hear it. We shall be quite a merry party.

Olympe. It is sure to be a merry party with you in it!

St. Gaudens. Naughty girl! But what about our poor dear Varville, who isn't to have any supper? I feel quite anxious about him.

Olympe [*aside to* MARGUERITE]. Why didn't you invite Edmond?

Marguerite. Why didn't you bring him?

Olympe. With Saint-Gaudens?

Marguerite. Isn't he used to it?

Olympe. Not yet, my dear. It's so difficult for a man of his age to acquire new habits, especially if they're good ones.

Marguerite [*calling* NANINE]. Isn't supper ready?

Nanine. In five minutes, madame.

Marguerite. Well, Varville, haven't you gone yet?

Varville. I am going.

Marguerite [*at the window calling*]. Prudence!

Prudence. Here I am!

Marguerite. Aren't you coming, Prudence?

Prudence. I can't.

Marguerite. Why not?

Prudence. I have two young gentlemen here who have asked me out to supper.

Marguerite. Well, bring them over here to supper. Who
are they?

Prudence. You know one of them. Gaston Rieux.

Marguerite. Of course I know him! Who is the other?

Prudence. A friend of his.

Marguerite. Come along, then, all of you.

Olympe. Does Prudence live opposite to you?

Marguerite. Just across the courtyard. It is quite convenient when I need her.

St. Gaudens. Who is Prudence?

Olympe. She is a milliner.

Marguerite. And nobody buys her hats but me.

Olympe. And you never wear them.

Marguerite. They are too dreadful! But I like her and she
is hard up. It's cold this evening. [*She coughs a little.*]
Varville, put some wood on the fire; make yourself useful
if you can't be agreeable. [VARVILLE *obeys.*]

Enter PRUDENCE, *followed by* GASTON *and* ARMAND.

Butler. Madame Duvernoy, M. Gaston Rieux, and M.
Armand Duval.

Olympe. The stylish way they announce people here!

Prudence. Well, I knew it was a swell party!

St. Gaudens. Madame Duvernoy knows society when she
sees it.

Gaston [*ceremoniously to* MARGUERITE]. I trust you are
quite well, madame.

Marguerite [*in the same manner*]. Quite, I thank you.
And you?

Prudence. The stylish way they talk here! Marguerite,
I want to present to you M. Armand Duval, the man who
is more in love with you than anyone in Paris.

Marguerite [*to* PRUDENCE]. Ask them to lay two more
places. His great passion hasn't destroyed M. Duval's appetite, I hope. [*Holds out her hand to* ARMAND, *who kisses
it.*]

St. Gaudens. My dear Gaston, I am delighted to see you.

Gaston. Saint-Gaudens as young as ever?

St. Gaudens. Younger.

Gaston. And your love affairs—prospering?

St. Gaudens [*pointing to* OLYMPE]. As you see, my dear fellow.

Gaston. Congratulations.

St. Gaudens. I was terribly afraid of finding Germaine here.

Gaston. Poor Germaine. She was very fond of you.

St. Gaudens. Too fond. Besides, there was a young man that she wouldn't give up seeing. He was her banker, you understand. She loved me for myself alone. But I very nearly cut him out! Very nearly! But it meant a great deal of hiding in cupboards, prowling about on the stairs, and waiting in the street——

Gaston. Which gave you rheumatism.

St. Gaudens. Not a bit, but times change, times change. We none of us grow younger!—But poor old Varville— no supper!

Gaston [*going to* MARGUERITE]. Isn't he wonderful!

Marguerite. It is only the old who grow no older.

St. Gaudens [*to* ARMAND, *whom* OLYMPE *introduces to him*]. Are you related to M. Duval, the Receiver General?

Armand. Yes, sir, he is my father. Do you know him?

St. Gaudens. I met him years ago at the Baroness de Mersay's with your mother, whom I remember as a very beautiful and charming woman.

Armand. My mother died three years ago.

St. Gaudens. Forgive me.

Armand. I am always glad to be reminded of my mother.

St. Gaudens. Are you an only son?

Armand. I have one sister . . . [*They walk away talking together.*]

Marguerite [*aside to* GASTON]. I think your friend is charming.

Gaston. He is. And what is more, he adores you. Doesn't he, Prudence?

Prudence. What?

Gaston. I was telling Marguerite that Armand is madly in love with her.

Prudence. Oh, there's no doubt of it.

Gaston. He loves you so much, my dear, that he doesn't dare to tell you so.

Marguerite [*to* VARVILLE, *who has been playing the piano*]. Varville—please, please.

Varville. You told me to keep on playing the piano.

Marguerite. When I am alone with you. Not when I have friends!

Prudence. He's loved you for two years.

Marguerite. Quite an old story, then.

Prudence. Armand simply lives at Gustave's and Nichette's to hear them talk about you.

Gaston. When you were ill, a year ago, do you remember that they told you of a young man who called to enquire after you every day, but who wouldn't leave his name?

Marguerite. I remember.

Gaston. That was Armand.

Marguerite. How nice of him. [*Calling.*] M. Duval, do you know what I have just been hearing? That you called to enquire after me every day when I was ill.

Armand. It is quite true.

Marguerite. Then the least I can do is to thank you. Did you hear that, Varville? You never did that for me, did you?

Varville. I've only known you for a year.

Marguerite. Don't be silly. This young gentleman has only known me five minutes.

Enter NANINE, *followed by Servants carrying table.*

Prudence. Here is the supper! I am famished.

Varville. Good-bye, Marguerite.

Marguerite. When shall we see you again?

Varville. Whenever you wish.

Marguerite. Good-bye, then.

Varville [*bowing*]. Gentlemen——

St. Gaudens. Good-bye, Varville, good-bye, old boy. [*They sit down at the table.*]

Prudence. You are really very hard on the Baron, my dear.

Marguerite. He bores me with his eighty thousand francs.

Olympe. Fancy complaining about that! I wish someone would offer to keep me.

St. Gaudens. I like that!

Marguerite. Now, children, help yourselves, but don't quarrel.

Olympe. Do you know what he gave me for my birthday?

Marguerite. Who?

Olympe. Saint-Gaudens.

Marguerite. No.

Olympe. He gave a coupé.

St. Gaudens. From Binder's.

Olympe. But I can't get him to give me any horses for it.

Prudence. All the same, a coupé is a coupé.

St. Gaudens. I am ruined. Why can't I be loved for myself alone?

Olympe. The idea!

Prudence [*pointing to a plate*]. What are these little creatures?

Gaston. Partridges.

Prudence. You can give me one.

Gaston. She only wants one at a time! What a bird-like appetite! Now we know who it was that ruined Saint-Gaudens—she did!

Prudence. She! She! Is that the way to talk of a lady? In my day——

Gaston. We needn't go back to Louis the Fifteenth. Marguerite, fill Armand's glass. He's looking sad.

Marguerite. Come, M. Duval, you must drink my health.

Prudence. And somebody must give us a song.

Olympe. You, Gaston!

Gaston. How can I sing while I'm having supper?

Marguerite. Song first, supper afterwards. That's the right way.

Gaston [*sings*].

Monsieur le Comte de Blazinot,
   De Chateau-Blanc-sur-Loire,
He followed at the Casino
   The colours rouge et noir.
      Blanche the gay, charming grisette,
      Said "You may" first time he met her,
        Then Jeanne—
        Suzanne,
      Blonde et rouge et noir.

Monsieur le Comte so debonnair,
   Gallant in thought and deed,

He sought the path that seemed most fair,
 Wherever that might lead.
   Blanche, the gay, charming grisette,
   Led the way, no one knew better,
    Then Jeanne—
    Suzanne,
   Blonde et rouge et noir.

Despite the Comte's nobility,
 His savoir-faire and pluck,
With damnéd incivility,
 Old Satan changed his luck.
   Blanche the gay, charming grisette,
   Said next day she could do better,
    Then Jeanne—
    Suzanne,
   Blonde et rouge et noir.

All. Bravo! Bravo!

Gaston [*sitting down again*]. Ah, well! Life is short and sweet and Prudence is short and fat.

Olympe. Fat, fair and forty.

Prudence. You are all very brilliant. How old do you think I am? Just thirty-five last birthday.

Gaston. But you don't look more than forty, I give you my word.

Marguerite. Talking of youth, I heard a story about you the other day, Saint-Gaudens.

Olympe. So did I.

St. Gaudens. Which story?

Marguerite. The story of the yellow hackney-carriage.

Olympe. It is perfectly true.

Gaston. Yes, but let me go and sit next to Marguerite first. I am getting dreadfully tired of Prudence.

Prudence. There's a nicely-brought-up young man!

St. Gaudens. This is a most delicious supper!

Prudence. Let us have the story of the yellow hackney-carriage.

Olympe. He is only trying to wriggle out of the story of the hackney-carriage . . .

Marguerite. The yellow one.

St. Gaudens. You can tell it if you like, I don't care.

Olympe. Well, you must all know that once upon a time Saint-Gaudens was in love with Germaine.

Gaston. This is too touching! Kiss me, Marguerite!

Olympe. You are really very trying! Don't interrupt!

Marguerite. Olympe is quite right. Gaston can be as tiresome as Varville. We shall put you in the corner like a naughty child, if you can't behave.

Olympe. Put him there now.

Gaston. On condition that I am kissed by all the ladies.

Marguerite. Prudence will oblige you and you can consider yourself kissed by all of us.

Gaston. No, that isn't fair. I am to be kissed by everybody.

Olympe. Very well, then, you shall be kissed, only sit down and stop talking.

Gaston [*sits down to the piano, plays Malbrouck on the piano*]. This piano is out of tune.

Marguerite. Don't answer him.

Gaston. It's a very dull story.

St. Gaudens. Gaston is quite right.

Gaston. Anyway, what is the point of a story that is as old as Prudence? The story is that Saint-Gaudens followed on foot a certain hackney-carriage that deposited Agénor at the door of Germaine, thereby proving that Germaine was deceiving Saint-Gaudens. As if there were anything new or original in that! Who hasn't been deceived? One's friends and one's mistresses are always deceiving one. And so ends the story to the tune of the Carillon de Dunkerque. [*Plays the Carillon on the piano.*]

St. Gaudens. I knew quite well that Germaine was deceiving me with Agénor, just as I am perfectly aware that Olympe is deceiving me with Edmond.

Marguerite. Bravo, Saint-Gaudens! You are a hero and we are all in love with you! Those who are madly in love with Saint-Gaudens hold up their hands! Unanimous! Saint-Gaudens for ever! Gaston, play something for Saint-Gaudens to dance to!

Gaston. I don't know anything but a polka.

Marguerite. Then we'll have a polka. Come, Saint-Gaudens, and Armand move the table.

Prudence. But I haven't finished.

Olympe. Do I have to dance with Saint-Gaudens?

Marguerite. No, I am going to dance with him. Come along, little Saint-Gaudens!

Olympe. Come, Armand! [MARGUERITE *polkas for a moment, then stops suddenly.*]

St. Gaudens. What is the matter?

Marguerite. Nothing. I lost my breath.

Armand [*goes up to her*]. I am afraid you are ill?

Marguerite. No, it is nothing. Don't stop. [GASTON *plays loudly and* MARGUERITE *tries again to dance and stops again.*]

Armand. Stop, Gaston.

Prudence. Marguerite is ill.

Marguerite. Get me a glass of water.

Prudence. What is the matter?

Marguerite. But it is nothing, really. Please go into the other room and smoke. I'll be with you directly.

Prudence. We had better leave her. She always wants to be alone when she feels like that.

Marguerite. Do go. I shall come presently.

Prudence. Yes, come. [*Aside.*] You never can have any fun here. *She follows the others.* MARGUERITE, *alone, trying to get her breath.*]

Marguerite. Ah! [*She looks in the glass.*] How wretched I look! [*She drops her head in her hands and rests her elbows on the mantelpiece.*]

Enter ARMAND.

Armand. Are you feeling better?

Marguerite. Much better, thank you. Besides, it is nothing new.

Armand. You are killing yourself! I wish I were your friend, your brother, even, to prevent you from hurting yourself like this.

Marguerite. And even then you wouldn't succeed. Let us go. What is the matter?

Armand. I cannot help seeing——

Marguerite. How kind you are! Look at the others, they don't trouble about me.

Armand. The others don't love you as I do.

Marguerite. Ah, yes, I had forgotten that great love of yours.

Armand. You laugh at it!

Marguerite. Heaven forbid! I hear the same thing every day. It doesn't make me laugh any more.

Armand. Promise.

Marguerite. What?

Armand. To take care of yourself.

Marguerite. If I were to begin to take care of myself, my dear man, I should die. Don't you see that it is only the feverish life I live that keeps me alive? And then, it is easy enough for women who have friends and a family to take care of themselves; but for the rest of us, the moment that we are no longer amusing to people they leave us, and the long days are followed by longer evenings. I know all about it. I was in bed for two months and after three weeks no one came near me.

Armand. I know that I am nothing to you, but if you would let me, Marguerite, I would take care of you like a brother. I would never leave you and I would cure you. And then when you were strong again, you could return to this life if you wished. But I don't think you would want to.

Marguerite. How depressing.

Armand. Have you no heart, Marguerite?

Marguerite. It's dangerous for the sort of excursionist that I am to travel with a heart. [*A pause.*] Are you really serious?

Armand. Perfectly serious.

Marguerite. Prudence was right, then, when she said that you were sentimental? And so you would like to take care of me?

Armand. Yes.

Marguerite. You would stay with me all day long?

Armand. As long as I did not weary you.

Marguerite. How long have you felt this devotion?

Armand. For two years. Ever since the day when I first saw you, beautiful, and proud. From that day I have watched you from a distance and in silence.

Marguerite. Why do you tell me this for the first time today?

Armand. I did not know you, Marguerite.

Marguerite. You should have tried to know me. When I was ill and you called so regularly to enquire after me, why didn't you come up?

Armand. What right had I?

Marguerite. Is one usually so considerate with a woman like me?

Armand. One is always considerate with a woman. And then . . .

Marguerite. And then?

Armand. I was afraid.

Marguerite. Afraid?

Armand. Afraid of the influence that you might have over my whole life.

Marguerite. You love me as much as that?

Armand [*seeing that she is laughing*]. If I were ever to tell you how much, it would not be today.

Marguerite. Never tell me.

Armand. Why not?

Marguerite. Because a woman who spends a hundred thousand francs a year may suit a rich old man like the Duke, but not a young man like you. There, we have been talking nonsense! Give me your hand and let us go back to the dining room.

Armand. If you wish it; but I'll stay here, if I may.

Marguerite. Shall I give you a piece of good advice?

Armand. Yes.

Marguerite. Go away at once, if what you say is true. Or else, love me as a friend, and in no other way. Come and talk to me sometimes, but have no illusions about me, for I'm not worth much. You are too young and have too much feeling to live in this world of ours. Love some other woman and marry. I'm trying to be honest with you. [PRU-DENCE *opens the door.*]

Prudence. What in the world are you two doing in here?

Marguerite. Being wise. We'll be with you in a moment.

Prudence. Prattle away, children.   [*Exit.*

Marguerite. It is agreed, then, that you are not to love me any more.

Armand. I shall take your advice and go.

Marguerite. Is it like that?

Armand. Yes.

Marguerite. How many others have said the same thing to me, but they did not go.

Armand. Because you held them back.

Marguerite. Indeed, I didn't.

Armand. Have you never been in love with anyone?

Marguerite. Never!

Armand. Thank God!

Marguerite. You're a strange boy!

Armand. If I were to tell you that I have passed whole nights beneath your windows and that for two months I have treasured a glove that you dropped . . .

Marguerite. I should not believe you.

Armand. You are right to laugh at me, I am a fool. The only thing to do is laugh at me. . . . Good-bye.

Marguerite. Armand!

Armand. You called me?

Marguerite. I don't want you to go away angry.

Armand. Angry? How could I be angry with you?

Marguerite. Come to see me sometimes, often; we will speak of this again.

Armand. It is too much, and it is not enough.

Marguerite. Then ask what you will of me for it seems that I am in your debt.

Armand. Don't talk like that. I can't bear to hear you laugh at what is serious.

Marguerite. I am not laughing now.

Armand. Tell me.

Marguerite. What?

Armand. Would you like someone to be in love with you?

Marguerite. That depends.

Armand. To love you deeply and for ever.

Marguerite. For ever?

Armand. Yes.

Marguerite. And if I were to believe you, what would you say? What does it matter? If I am to live a shorter time than most people, I must live more quickly, that is all. But be sure of this, however eternal your love may be and however short a time I have to live, I shall yet live longer than your love.

Armand. Marguerite!

Marguerite. In the meantime, you feel what you say

and are sincere, and that deserves something. Take this
flower. [*She gives him a camellia.* ARMAND *kisses it.*] Bring
it back to me.

Armand. When?

Marguerite. When it is faded.

Armand. How long will that take?

Marguerite. Just the little time that it takes for any flower
to fade, a morning or an evening.

Armand. Oh, Marguerite!

Marguerite. Tell me again that you love me.

Armand. I love you.

Marguerite. And now go. [ARMAND *goes, looking back.
He comes back and kisses her hand once more—then goes.
Laughter and singing in the corridor.*]

Marguerite [*alone, looking at the closed door*]. Why not?
And yet, why? That's the way life passes, trying to answer
these two questions. [GASTON *appears at the door followed
by the others. He goes to the piano.*]

Gaston [*singing and playing*]. "Chorus of villagers!"

St. Gaudens. Long live M. and Madame Armand Duval!

Olympe. On with the wedding dance!

Marguerite. You shall dance with me!

St. Gaudens. Delighted! Delighted! [PRUDENCE *puts on
a man's hat,* GASTON *a woman's. They dance.*]

ACT TWO

MARGUERITE'S *dressing room, Paris.*

MARGUERITE [*before a dressing table, to* PRUDENCE, *who
enters*]. Have you seen the Duke?

Prudence. Yes. [*Giving* MARGUERITE *bank notes.*] Can
you lend me three or four hundred francs?

Marguerite. Help yourself. Did you tell the Duke that I
was thinking of going away into the country?

Prudence. Yes.

Marguerite. What did he say?

Prudence. That you were quite right to go and that it
would do you good. Are you going?

Marguerite. I hope so. I went again today to look at the house.

Prudence. What rent are they asking for it?

Marguerite. Four thousand francs.

Prudence. Four thousand! That's what I call love.

Marguerite. Perhaps.

Prudence. Has he been here today?

Marguerite. Need you ask?

Prudence. And he is coming again this evening.

Marguerite. Yes.

Prudence. I know. He came to my place and stayed for hours.

Marguerite. Did he speak of me at all?

Prudence. What else would he talk to me about?

Marguerite. What did he say?

Prudence. Oh, my goodness! that he loved you.

Marguerite. Have you seen him in love before?

Prudence. No, never.

Marguerite. Is that really true?

Prudence. Gospel. What a shame it is that men like him haven't got a hundred thousand a year!

Marguerite. No, no, it isn't! [*Takes* PRUDENCE's *hand and holds it against her heart.*] Feel!

Prudence. What?

Marguerite. My heart beating.

Prudence. What's it doing that for?

Marguerite. Because it is ten o'clock and he is coming.

Prudence. Dear me! is it as bad as all that? I'm off!

Marguerite [*to* NANINE, *who is putting the room in order*]. Open the door, Nanine.

Nanine. I don't think anyone rang, Madame.

Marguerite. Yes, yes, I tell you!   [*Exit* NANINE.

Prudence. My dear, I shall pray for you.

Marguerite. Why?

Prudence. Because you are in danger.

Marguerite. Perhaps.

Enter ARMAND.

Armand [*running to* MARGUERITE]. Marguerite!

Prudence. You haven't said good evening to me yet, bad boy!

Armand. I beg your pardon, Prudence. How are you?

Prudence. About time! Well, children, I will leave you. There is someone waiting for me at home. Good-bye.

[*Exit* PRUDENCE.

Marguerite. Here, sir.

Armand [*kneeling at her feet*]. Well?

Marguerite. Do you love me as much as ever?

Armand. No.

Marguerite. What?

Armand. I love you a thousand times more.

Marguerite. What have you been doing today?

Armand. I have been to see Prudence and Gustave and Nichette and anyone else who could talk to me of you. I had a letter from my father, saying he was expecting me to join him at Tours, and I've written to tell him that he needn't wait for me any longer. As if I could go to Tours!

Marguerite. But you mustn't quarrel with your father.

Armand. There is no danger of that. And you?—what have you been doing? Tell me.

Marguerite. I have been thinking of you.

Armand. Really and truly?

Marguerite. Really and truly, and I have been making some splendid plans.

Armand. Have you? Tell me about them.

Marguerite. Later.

Armand. Why not now?

Marguerite. Perhaps because you don't love me enough yet. When there's a chance of their being realised, it will be time enough to tell you. All that you need know now is that I'm thinking about you.

Armand. About me?

Marguerite. Yes.

Armand. Won't you tell me what they are? Please!

Marguerite [*after a little hesitation*]. How can I hide anything from you?

Armand. Go on, I am listening.

Marguerite. Would it make you happy if you were to spend the summer in the country with me?

Armand. How can you ask?

Marguerite. Well, I've thought of a scheme

Armand. A scheme? What is it?

Marguerite. I can only tell you what the result will be.

Armand. Well?

Marguerite. If it's successful and it will be, I shall be free in a fortnight from now, my debts will be paid, and we can go and spend the summer together in the country.

Armand. And you can't tell me how you are going to manage it?

Marguerite. No.

Armand. Is it your own idea, Marguerite?

Marguerite. Why do you ask?

Armand. Tell me.

Marguerite. Yes, of course.

Armand. And you will carry it out, alone?

Marguerite [*hesitating*]. Yes, alone.

Armand [*rising*]. Have you ever read "Manon Lescaut," Marguerite?

Marguerite. Yes, the book is in the other room.

Armand. What do you think of des Grieux? Have you any respect for him?

Marguerite. What makes you ask that?

Armand. Because there is a moment when Manon, too, thinks of a scheme, which is to get money from another man and spend it with des Grieux. Marguerite, I know that you have more heart than Manon, and I have more honour than des Grieux.

Marguerite. What do you mean?

Armand. I mean that if your idea is anything of that kind, I can't have anything to do with it.

Marguerite. Very well, then, we will say no more about it. It's been a lovely day, hasn't it?

Armand. Very.

Marguerite. Were there many people in the Champs Elysées?

Armand. A great many.

Marguerite. I have no doubt that it will stay like this until the moon changes.

Armand. What do I care about the moon?

Marguerite. Well, what do you want me to talk about? If I tell you that I love you and wish to give you some proof of it, you are vexed; therefore, I talked about the moon.

Armand. How can I help it, Marguerite? I am jealous of

every thought of yours, even the smallest. What you proposed just now——

Marguerite. Oh! Are we going back to that?

Armand. Of course we are going back to it . . . what you proposed would make me wild with joy, but all this mystery——

Marguerite. Wait, let us talk reasonably for a moment. You love me and would like to spend a little time with me away from this awful Paris.

Armand. You know I should.

Marguerite. Well, I love you and should like the same thing. But in order to do this, I must have something that I haven't got now. You are not jealous of the Duke, you know that it is merely sentiment that makes us friends; leave me to arrange things.

Armand. And yet——

Marguerite. I love you. There! Is it settled?

Armand. But——

Marguerite [*coaxing*]. Is it settled?

Armand. Not yet.

Marguerite. Then come to see me tomorrow, and we will talk of it then.

Armand. Tomorrow? Are you sending me away already?

Marguerite. I am not sending you away. You may stay for a little while longer.

Armand. Only a little while? Do you expect anyone?

Marguerite. There, you're beginning again!

Armand. Marguerite, you are deceiving me!

Marguerite. How long have I known you?

Armand. Four days.

Marguerite. Am I obliged to see you?

Armand. No.

Marguerite. If I did not love you, should I have the right to show you the door as I do de Varville and so many others?

Armand. Every right.

Marguerite. Then, my dear, be satisfied.

Armand. Forgive me, forgive me!

Marguerite. Yes, but if this goes on, I shall spend the rest of my life forgiving you.

Armand. This is the very last time. I am going now.

Marguerite. Come again tomorrow, at twelve. Lunch with me.

Armand. Until tomorrow, then?

Marguerite. Until tomorrow.

Armand. At twelve?

Marguerite. At twelve.

Armand. Will you swear to me?

Marguerite. What?

Armand. That you are not expecting anyone.

Marguerite. Again! I swear to you that I love you and no one else in the world.

Armand. Good-bye.

Marguerite. Good-bye, you foolish boy. [*He hesitates a moment and then goes.*] Does he love me, I wonder? Am I even sure that I love him, I who have never loved?

Enter NANINE.

Nanine. The Comte de Giray.

Marguerite. Show him in.

NANINE *enters, followed by the* COMTE DE GIRAY.

[*Without getting up.*] Good evening. [*Exit* NANINE.

Comte [*kissing her hand*]. Good evening, my dear. How are you this evening?

Marguerite. Quite well.

Comte. It is devilish cold outside. You asked me in your letter to be here at half-past ten. As you see, I am punctual.

Marguerite. Thank you. There is something I wish to say to you.

Comte. Have you had supper?

Marguerite. Why?

Comte. I thought we might have gone somewhere for supper and talked there.

Marguerite. Are you hungry?

Comte. One can usually discover an appetite for supper. Besides I dined badly at the club.

Marguerite. What were they doing there?

Comte. Gambling, when I left.

Marguerite. Was Saint-Gaudens losing?

Comte. He had lost twenty-five louis and was squealing as if it were a thousand!

Marguerite. He was here to supper the other evening with Olympe.

Comte. Who else?

Marguerite. Gaston Rieux, you know him?

Comte. Yes. Charming fellow!

Marguerite. M. Armand Duval.

Comte. And who is M. Armand Duval?

Marguerite. A friend of Gaston's. And Prudence and I. That's all. We all laughed a good deal.

Comte. I should have come too, if I had known. By the way, did anyone leave here, a moment ago, just as I came in?

Marguerite. No, no one.

Comte. Because as I was getting out of the carriage, it seemed to me that someone ran up to see who I was and, having seen me, went away again. Very possibly he didn't like the look of me.

Marguerite. That's curious.

Comte. Have you heard the news?

Marguerite. What?

Comte. Our Polish Prince is going to be married.

Marguerite. To whom?

Comte. Guess.

Marguerite. How should I know?

Comte. He is going to marry little Adele.

Marguerite. Then she is making a great mistake.

Comte. On the contrary, it is he who——

Marguerite. My dear friend, when a man of the world marries a girl like Adele, it is not he who is making the mistake, but she. Now let us talk of something serious.

Comte. I should much prefer to talk of something pleasant.

Marguerite. We shall soon see whether you consider it pleasant or not.

Comte. Well, what is it?

Marguerite. Have you any ready money?

Comte. I never have any ready money.

Marguerite. Then you must write me an order on your steward.

Comte. Are you really poverty-stricken?

Marguerite. Very! I need exactly fifteen thousand francs.

Comte. The devil you do! That's a nice little sum! And why precisely fifteen thousand francs, if I may ask?

Marguerite. Because I owe it.

Comte. You don't mean to say that you pay your creditors?

Marguerite. They seem to like it.

Comte. Is it really urgent?

Marguerite. It is.

Comte. Very well, then I will write one.

Enter NANINE.

Nanine. This letter has just come, Madame, and it was to be given to you immediately.

Marguerite [*opens letter*]. Armand! What does this mean? [*Reading.*] "I do not choose to be made ridiculous."

Nanine. Is there any answer, Madame?

Marguerite. No, there is no answer.   [*Exit* NANINE. So ends a dream. I have a piece of good news for you, my friend.

Comte. Indeed!

Marguerite. You make exactly fifteen thousand francs by it.

Comte. You don't say so—an unique experience!

Marguerite. I no longer need the money I asked for.

Comte. And so your creditors return their bills to you marked paid, do they? It is really very nice of them!

Marguerite. No, my dear. I was in love, that's all.

Comte. By all that's wonderful, with whom?

Marguerite. With someone who didn't love me, as it often happens, and with someone without any money, as it always happens. And this is what he writes [*gives* COMTE *letter*].

Comte [*reading*]. I see, I see, it is from M. Duval. He seems very jealous, this young gentleman. That was a neat little scheme of yours! [*Gives back letter.*]

Marguerite. You asked me to supper just now.

Comte. The invitation is still open. You will never honour me by eating fifteen thousand francs worth of supper, so I shall still save something.

Marguerite. Very well, then. Let us go. . . . It is stifling

in here! [*To* NANINE, *who enters.*] Nanine, bring me my
bonnet and shawl.

Nanine. Which, Madame?

Marguerite. Any bonnet you like and a light shawl. [*To*
COMTE.] You must take us as we are, my poor friend.

Comte. My dear girl, you are upset.

Marguerite. It is nothing.

Nanine. Madame will be cold. [*Gives shawl.*]

Marguerite. No.

Nanine. Shall I wait up for you, madame?

Marguerite. No, Nanine. Go to bed. It may be late when
I come home. Are you ready, Comte?   [*They go.*

Nanine [*alone*]. She's upset. As I thought. [*Takes letter.*]
Poor M. Armand! He manages his affairs badly, this young
man.

Enter PRUDENCE.

Prudence. Where's Marguerite?

Nanine. Gone out.

Prudence. With the Comte de Giray?

Nanine. Yes.

Prudence. Did she get a letter just now?

Nanine. From M. Armand.

Prudence. What did she say about it?

Nanine. Nothing.

Prudence. When will she be home?

Nanine. Not until late, I think. I thought you were in
bed long ago.

Prudence. I was, and fast asleep when I heard a knocking at the door—— [*A knock.*]

Nanine. Come in!

Enter Servant.

Servant. Madame is cold and has asked for her pelisse.

Prudence. Is your mistress downstairs?

Servant. Yes, Madame is in the carriage.

Prudence. Ask her to come up for a moment. Tell her
that I asked for her.

Servant. But Madame is not alone in the carriage.

Prudence. Never mind. Do as I tell you!   [*Exit Servant.*
Oh, these lovers!

Armand [*calling from outside*]. Prudence!

Prudence [*opening the window*]. There's the other one getting impatient.

Armand [*from outside*]. Well?

Prudence. Wait, can't you? I will call you presently.

Enter MARGUERITE.

Marguerite. Prudence, what is it?

Prudence. Armand is in my house.

Marguerite. What has that to do with me?

Prudence. He wants to speak to you.

Marguerite. I do not wish to see him. Besides, I cannot. There is someone waiting for me. You can tell him so.

Prudence. I shall do nothing of the kind. He would only go and challenge the Comte.

Marguerite. Well, what does he want?

Prudence. How do I know? Does he know himself? But he is desperately in love.

Nanine [*entering with fur on her arm*]. Madame wished for her pelisse?

Marguerite. No, not yet.

Prudence. Well, what are you going to do?

Marguerite. That boy will make me unhappy.

Prudence. Then don't see him any more, my dear.

Marguerite. Is that your advice?

Prudence. Of course it is.

Marguerite [*after a pause*]. What else did he say to you?

Prudence. I see, you want him to come. I'll go and bring him. What about the Comte?

Marguerite. The Comte? He will wait.

Prudence. Wouldn't it be wiser to send him away now?

Marguerite. You are right. Nanine, go down and tell the Comte that I feel ill and shall not be able to get out to supper. Beg him to excuse me.

Nanine. Yes, madame. [*Exit.*

Prudence [*at the window*]. You can come in, Armand. He didn't need to be told twice.

Marguerite. Stay here, when he comes.

Prudence. Not me! I am sure to be asked to leave later on, and so I may just as well go at once.

Nanine [*entering*]. The Comte has gone, madame.

Marguerite. Did he say anything?

Nanine. No.   [*Exit.*

Enter ARMAND.

Armand. Marguerite! At last!

Prudence. This is where I leave you, children.

[*Exit* PRUDENCE.

Armand [*on his knees at* MARGUERITE's *feet*]. Marguerite?

Marguerite. Well?

Armand. I want you to forgive me.

Marguerite. You don't deserve it. You gave me a great deal of pain.

Armand. And you, Marguerite? Did you give me no pain? When I saw the Comte and realised that it was for him that you had sent me away, I lost my head—went mad, I think—and wrote to you as I did. But when, instead of defending yourself you told Nanine that there was no answer, I began to wonder what would become of me, if I were never to see you again. Don't forget, Marguerite, that if I have only known you for a few days, I have loved you for two whole years.

Marguerite. Well, you came to a wise decision.

Armand. What?

Marguerite. To go away. Didn't you tell me that you were going away?

Armand. How could I?

Marguerite. You must.

Armand. Must?

Marguerite. Yes, not only for your sake, but for mine.

Armand. You do love me a little, Marguerite?

Marguerite. I did love you.

Armand. And now?

Marguerite. Now I have been thinking it over and what I hoped for is impossible.

Armand. If you had really loved me, you wouldn't have seen the Comte tonight.

Marguerite. Armand, I am young, I am pretty and I pleased you. That was something—forget the rest.

Armand. You did not speak like that of those months that we were to spend together far away from Paris and from everyone.

Marguerite [*sadly*]. It is true. I said to myself, "A little rest would do me good. I could pass the summer quietly with him in some country place, among the woods and the hills." In three or four months we should have returned to Paris, we should have shaken hands and built up a friendship out of the remains of our love. But you did not wish it. Let us say no more about it. You have been coming to see me for four days and you have been here to supper. Send me a ring with your card and we will consider the account settled.

Armand. Marguerite, you are mad! I love you! That does not mean that you are pretty and might please me for three or four months. It means that you are everything to me. I love you. What more can I say?

Marguerite. Then you are right and it would be better for us not to see each other any more.

Armand. Of course, if you don't love me.

Marguerite. You don't know what you're saying!

Armand. Then, why would it be better?

Marguerite. Why? Because there have been hours when I have followed this dream to the end; because there have been days when I have wearied of the life I lead and longed for something different; because in the midst of this restless existence of ours, our senses live but our hearts are stifled. We seem happy and we are envied. We have lovers who ruin themselves, not for us as they say, but for their own vanity. We have friends like Prudence, who pander to us, but always remain selfish. They care little enough what we do as long as the world sees them in our box at the theatre, in our carriage in the Bois. Then I met you. For a moment I built a whole future on your love. I longed for the country. I remembered my childhood—one has always a childhood to remember whatever one may have become since; but it was nothing but a dream.

Armand. And do you think that I could ever leave you after what you've just told me? When happiness comes so near to us, are we to run away from it? No, Marguerite, no! Your dream shall come true, I swear it to you. Don't let us quarrel any more, we are young, we love each other, let us follow our happiness.

Marguerite. Don't deceive me, Armand! Don't deceive yourself! Think what I am and who I am.

Armand. You are an angel and I love you! [*Knock.*]

Nanine [*outside the door*]. Madame.

Marguerite. Yes?

Nanine [*outside the door*]. A letter has just come for you, Madame.

Marguerite [*laughing*]. This is a night for letters! Whom is it from?

Nanine. From the Comte de Giray.

Marguerite. Is the messenger waiting?

Nanine. Yes, madame.

Marguerite [*hanging round* ARMAND'S *neck*]. Tell him there is no answer!

ACT THREE

At Auteuil. A room looking out onto a garden. NANINE *is carrying out a tea tray after lunch.*

PRUDENCE [*entering*]. Where is Marguerite?

Nanine. In the garden with Mlle. Nichette and M. Gustave. They came to lunch and are spending the day with her.

Prudence. I'll go to them. [ARMAND, *who has been reading, calls to* PRUDENCE *as she is going out.*]

Armand. One moment, Prudence. There is something I want to say to you. A week ago Marguerite gave you some bracelets and diamonds that she said were to be reset. What has become of them?

Prudence. Do you want me to tell you—truly?

Armand. I am asking you for the truth.

Prudence. Madame told me to pawn them.

Armand. Why?

Prudence. To pay for things, of course! My dear boy, you seem to think that all you need do is to fall in love with each other and then glide blissfully out of Paris to some pleasant spot like this and live on air! I've seen the Duke and he absolutely refuses to give Marguerite anything more

unless she leaves you. And we all know she doesn't want to
do that! Goodness only knows where all this is going to end!

Armand. How much money is needed?

Prudence. Fifty thousand francs at the very least.

Armand. Ask her creditors for a fortnight's grace. I will
pay.

Prudence. Are you going to borrow the money?

Armand. Yes.

Prudence. Nonsense! You'll only quarrel with your father
and ruin your whole future.

Armand. I suspected something of the kind and have
written to my solicitor. Hush! She's coming.

Enter MARGUERITE, NICHETTE *and* GUSTAVE.

Armand. I want you to scold Prudence for me, dearest!

Marguerite. Why?

Armand. I haven't been to Paris for a fortnight, and
I asked her to call at my rooms and bring me any letters that
might be there. She forgot all about it, and so I shall have
to go into Paris myself. It means leaving you for an hour or
two. No one knows my address here, not even my valet,
because I wished to be left in peace. I'll jump into a carriage
and drive straight there and back.

Marguerite. Yes, go dear, but come back quickly.

Armand. I shall be back in an hour. [MARGUERITE *goes
with him to the door.*]

Marguerite [*to* PRUDENCE *as she comes back*]. Have you
arranged everything for me?

Prudence. Yes. The lawyer is coming here to talk things
over with you. And now what I want is lunch. I'm hungry.

Marguerite. Yes, go. Nanine will see that you have everything you want.   [*Exit* PRUDENCE.
[*To* NICHETTE *and* GUSTAVE.] You see, this is where we
have been living for three months.

Nichette. Are you happy?

Marguerite. Very happy.

Nichette. I always told you, Marguerite, that this was
the way to be happy. Many a time Gustave and I have said
to each other, "When will Marguerite really love someone
and take things more quietly?"

Marguerite. Well, your wish is fulfilled. I am really in

love. I think it was watching you two that first made me envious.

Gustave. And we are happy, aren't we?

Nichette. You are such a great lady that you never come to see us, or you would be content to live as we do. We have two dear little rooms in the Rue Blanche. And Gustave says that I am not to work and that he is going to buy me a carriage, one of these days.

Gustave. That will come in due course.

Marguerite. Listen to the advocate! And we shall soon be asked to the wedding, I suppose.

Gustave. If I get·married.

Nichette. What do you mean, sir, *if* you get married? Of course you'll get married, and to me, too.

Marguerite. Well, when is it to be?

Nichette. Soon.

Marguerite. You will be very happy.

Nichette. But aren't you going to do as we do?

Marguerite. Whom should I marry?

Nichette. Armand.

Marguerite. If I wished it Armand would marry me tomorrow, but I love him far too well to ask such a thing. You think I am right, don't you, Gustave?

Nichette. Gustave would marry you, if he were in Armand's place, wouldn't you, Gustave?

Gustave. Perhaps I should.

Nichette. But so long as you are happy, what does it matter?

Marguerite. I am happy. I can speak freely to you two, because you understand. There are moments when I forget the past and when the Marguerite that used to be and the Marguerite of today are two different beings. I used to spend enough money on flowers to keep a poor family for a year, but now a flower like this that Armand gave me this morning is enough to fill my whole day with perfume. Yes, I am happy, but I should like to be happier still. I haven't said anything about it to Armand yet, but I'm going to have a sale at my house in Paris. After I've paid all my debts I shall take rooms near yours, furnish them very simply, and we shall live there, forgotten by the world. In the summer we shall come back again to the country, but to a much smaller house than this one. There are still those who ask what happiness is; it was you who first taught it to me, and now I myself could teach others.

Nanine [*enters*]. There's a gentleman here, who wishes to speak to you, madame.

Marguerite. That will be my lawyer; I was expecting him. I will join you later. Ask him to come in here, Nanine.

[*Exit* NANINE.

[NICHETTE *and* GUSTAVE *go out.* M. DUVAL *appears at the door.*]

Duval. Mademoiselle Marguerite Gautier?

Marguerite. That is my name. To whom have I the honour of speaking?

Duval. To M. Duval.

Marguerite. M. Duval?

Duval. Yes, madame, to Armand's father.

Marguerite [*troubled*]. Armand is not here, sir.

Duval. I know. It is to you that I wish to speak. Be good enough to listen to what I have to say. My son is ruining himself for you.

Marguerite. You are mistaken, sir. I accept nothing from Armand.

Duval. Am I to understand, then, as your habits of luxury are well known, that my son is mean enough to help you to spend what you receive from others?

Marguerite. You must excuse me, sir. I am a woman and in my own house, two reasons which should appeal to your courtesy; your manner of addressing me is not what I should have expected from a gentleman whom I have the honour to see for the first time, and——

Duval. And——

Marguerite. I must ask your permission to withdraw, more for your sake than for my own.

Duval. Your indignation is cleverly assumed, madame. They were right when they told me that you were dangerous.

Marguerite. Dangerous to myself, perhaps, but not to others.

Duval. But it is none the less true that my son is ruining himself for you.

Marguerite. I repeat to you, with all the respect that I owe to the father of Armand, that you are mistaken.

Duval. Then will you explain to me the meaning of this letter? It is from my lawyer informing me that my son wishes to make a settlement on you.

Marguerite. I assure you that if Armand has done such a thing, it is entirely without my knowledge. He knew that if he had offered it to me I should have refused it.

Duval. This was not always your method, I think.

Marguerite. It is true. Now——

Duval. Now?

Marguerite. Now I have learned what true love means.

Duval. Fine phrases, madame.

Marguerite. Listen. . . . I know well enough that the word of a woman like me is rarely believed, but by all that I hold most sacred and most dear, by my love for Armand, I swear to you that I knew nothing of this settlement.

Duval. And yet you are living here, you must have some means of——

Marguerite. You force me to disclose to you what I should have preferred to keep secret. Ever since I first knew and loved your son, I have been pawning and selling my carriages, my horses, and my jewels. A moment ago, when I was told that someone wished to speak to me, I concluded that it was in connection with the sale of furniture, pictures and all the rest of the luxury, with which you have reproached me. I was not expecting you, sir, so you may be quite sure that this paper was not prepared specially for you, but if you doubt what I say, read this. . . . [*Gives him bill of sale that* PRUDENCE *has brought from drawer.*]

Duval [*reading*]. A bill of sale on your furniture, the purchaser to pay your creditors, the balance to be given to you? [*Looking at her in astonishment.*] Have I been mistaken?

Marguerite. You have. It is Armand who has changed me. He loved me so much—he loves me now. You are his father, you must be kind and good as he is. Don't speak ill of me to him! He would believe you because he loves you, and I honour and respect you because you are his father.

Duval. Forgive me, madame, for my discourtesy a moment ago. I was not acquainted with you and quite unprepared for what I was to find. I was deeply hurt and irritated by my son's silence and ingratitude, of which I judged you to be the cause. I beg your pardon.

Marguerite. Thank you. [*Pause.*]

Duval. And what if I ask you to give Armand a greater proof of your love?

Marguerite. No! No! You are going to ask something terrible of me. Something I have always dreaded. I was too happy.

Duval. Let us speak together now like two friends.

Marguerite. Yes—friends.

Duval. You are capable of a generosity to which few women could rise, and I speak to you as a father, who asks you for the happiness of his two children.

Marguerite. His two children?

Duval. Yes, Marguerite, of his two children. I have a daughter, young, beautiful, pure. She is to be married and she, too, has made her love the dream of her life. I had written to Armand of this marriage, but absorbed as he is in you, he has never even received my letters. I might have died and he would never have known. Society is exacting in certain respects, especially provincial society. However purified your love for Armand may make you in his eyes and in mine, you are not so in the eyes of the world, which will see in you nothing but your past, and which will close its doors relentlessly against you. The family of my future son-in-law have learned of the manner in which Armand is living; they have given me to understand that the marriage cannot take place if it continues. Marguerite, in the name of your love, grant me the happiness of my child.

Marguerite. How can I refuse what you ask with so much gentleness and consideration? I understand. You are right. I will go back to Paris. I will leave Armand for a while. It will be painful for me, but I am glad to do this for you, so that you will have nothing with which to reproach me later. Besides, the joy of our reunion will help us to forget the pain of parting. You will allow him to write sometimes, and then, later, when his sister is married——

Duval. Thank you, Marguerite, thank you, but there is still something that I must ask of you.

Marguerite. Can you ask anything more of me?

Duval. A temporary parting is not enough.

Marguerite. You mean you want me to leave Armand altogether?

Duval. You must.

Marguerite. Never! You don't know how we love each other! I have neither friends nor family, nor anyone in the world belonging to me. You don't know perhaps that I have only a few years to live. To leave Armand would kill me.

Duval. Come, come, let us be calm for a moment and not exaggerate. You are young and beautiful. You mistake for a dangerous illness what may be nothing more than the fatigue of a more or less restless life. You are not going to die. I am asking you to make a great sacrifice I know. You have known Armand for three months and you love him, but are you so sure that this love will last for ever? He will take the best years of your life and then what will happen? Either he will leave you or he will act honourably and marry you. This marriage, which will not have chastity for its foundation, nor religion for its support, could lead to nothing but disaster. What career would remain open to him? What will be left to you both when you are old? Who can promise you that he will not be less dazzled when time casts the first shadow over your beauty? That the passing of your youth will not also mean the passing of his illusion?——

Marguerite. My God!

Duval. Cannot you see what your old age will be, doubly deserted, doubly desolate? What memories will you leave behind you? What good will you ever have accomplished? You and my son have two very different roads to follow; chance has brought them together for a moment. You have been happy for three months; do not sully that happiness; keep the memory of it always in your heart. Let it strengthen you; it is all you have the right to ask of it. One day you will be proud of what you have done, and all your life you will respect yourself for it. It is as a man of the world that I am speaking to you, it is as a father that I am pleading with you. Come, Marguerite, prove to me that you really love my son, and take courage.

Marguerite [*to herself*]. And so, whatever she may do,

the woman, once she has fallen can never rise again. God may forgive her, perhaps, the world never. What man would wish to make her his wife, what child to call her mother? It is all true, what you have told me. I have said the same thing to myself many times, but I never understood it until now. You speak to me in the name of your son and daughter; it is good of you to use those names. One day, sir, you will tell this beautiful and pure young girl, for it is for her sake that I am willing to sacrifice my happiness, that somewhere in the world there was a woman who had only one thought, one hope, one dream in life, and that for her sake she renounced them all, and that she died of it. Because I shall die of it and then, perhaps, God will forgive me.

Duval [*moved in spite of himself*]. Poor girl!

Marguerite. You ask me to leave Armand for his future, for his peace and for his honour. What must I do? Tell me. I am ready.

Duval. You must tell him that you no longer love him.

Marguerite. He will not believe me.

Duval. You must leave him.

Marguerite. He will follow me.

Duval. In that case. . . .

Marguerite. Do you believe that I love Armand with a love that is truly unselfish?

Duval. Yes, Marguerite.

Marguerite. Then, sir, will you kiss me just once, as you would your own daughter, and I swear to you that this kiss, the only really pure one that I have ever received, will help me in what I must do. Within a week, your son will have returned to you, saddened for a while, perhaps, but cured for ever. Also, I swear to you that he shall never know what has passed between us.

Duval [*kissing* MARGUERITE]. You are a noble girl, Marguerite, but I fear——

Marguerite. Fear nothing, sir, he shall hate me. [*Rings bell*—*to* NANINE.] Ask Madame Duvernoy to come here.

Nanine. Yes, madame.   [*Exit.*

Marguerite [*to Duval*]. One last favour——

Duval. Ask it.

Marguerite. Within a few hours Armand will experience

one of the greatest sorrows that he has ever known, or perhaps ever will know. He will need someone who loves him. Will you be here, sir, at his side?

Duval. What are you going to do?

Marguerite. If I told you, it would be your duty to prevent it.

Duval. Is there nothing I can do for you in acknowledgment of the debt that I shall owe you?

Marguerite. When I am dead and Armand curses my memory, tell him that I loved him and that I proved it. We shall never meet again. Good-bye.   [*Exit* Duval.

Marguerite [*alone*]. God give me strength. [*Writes a letter.*]

Enter Prudence.

Prudence. You sent for me, Marguerite——

Marguerite. Yes, there is something I want you to do for me.

Prudence. What is it?

Marguerite. Take this letter.

Prudence. To whom?

Marguerite. Read the address. [*Amazement of* Prudence *on reading it.*]

Prudence. M. de Var——

Marguerite. Hush! Go at once.   [*Exit* Prudence.

Marguerite. Now Armand——

Enter Armand *and goes towards* Marguerite.

Armand. What are you doing there, Marguerite?

Marguerite [*rising and crumpling letter in her hand*]. Armand! . . . nothing, dear.

Armand. Were you writing to someone?

Marguerite. No . . . yes.

Armand. Is anything the matter? You look pale! To whom were you writing, Marguerite? Give me that letter.

Marguerite. The letter was for you, Armand, but I implore you not to take it.

Armand. I thought we had done for ever with mysteries and secrets.

Marguerite. But not with suspicions, it seems.

Armand. Forgive me, I was worried.

Marguerite. About what?

Armand. My father is here.

Marguerite. Have you seen him?

Armand. No, but he left a letter for me. He has learned where I am and of my life here with you. He is coming tonight. He will see you, and having seen you, he will love you.

Marguerite. He is coming here, you say? Very well then, I will go away for a while, so that he won't see me just at first. But I shall come back later and ask him to forgive me and not part us.

Armand. How strangely you say that! There is something the matter . . . that letter. [*Holds out his hand for letter.*]

Marguerite. The letter is a proof of my love for you, dear Armand, I swear it. Don't ask me any more.

Armand. Keep the letter, Marguerite. I know all about your secret. Prudence told me this morning. That is what took me to Paris. While you were busy planning our happiness, I was doing the same. It is all settled now. That was your secret, wasn't it? How can I ever be grateful enough for all your love for me, Marguerite?

Marguerite. Now that you know all, let me go.

Armand. Go!

Marguerite. Only for a little while. I shall be in the garden with Gustave and Nichette. How could I go far away from you? You must be patient with your father, if he is angry, and then afterwards, we can go on with our plans just as we meant to, can't we? We shall always be together, you and I, and we shall be as happy as we have been during these three months. Because you have been happy, haven't you? You have nothing to reproach me with, have you?

Armand. Marguerite, you are crying!

Marguerite. I had to cry a little. There! I am quite calm again. I'll go to Gustave and Nichette, but I shall be very near you, always yours, always yours, always ready to come back to you, and to love you. Look! now I am laughing. We shall meet again soon, never to part any more.

[*Exit* MARGUERITE, *throwing kisses.*

Armand [*alone*]. Dear Marguerite! [*He rings and* NANINE *appears.*] Nanine, if a gentleman—my father—should come and ask for me, show him in here at once.

Nanine. Yes, sir.   [*Exit* NANINE.

Armand. What is this book? . . . "Manon Lescaut!" The woman who really loves is not like you, Manon! But she didn't know what it is to love. Love cannot reason like that . . . [*Walks over to window.*] This book hurts me . . . it isn't true. [*Rings.*] Seven o'clock. My father is not coming . . . [*Calls.*] Marguerite! Marguerite! [*Goes out and calls again.*] Nanine! Nanine! There—[*Comes in and rings again.*]—is no one there? Why did I let Marguerite go? She was hiding something from me . . . and she was crying! Would she deceive me? *She* deceive me! just when she was thinking of giving up everything she had for me! But something might have happened! . . . She may be hurt . . . dead! [*Goes towards door. He is met there by a Messenger.*] Marguerite! Marguerite!

Messenger. M. Armand Duval?

Armand. That is my name.

Messenger. I have a letter for you.

Armand. Who gave it to you?

Messenger. A lady—she is on the way to Paris!

Armand. How did you get in here?

Messenger. The garden gate was open. There was no one about, and as I saw a light in this room——

Armand. Very well; you can go.   [*Exit Messenger.*
This letter is from Marguerite . . . what is there to be afraid of? . . . She wants me to join her somewhere, no doubt, and has written to—tell me so . . . [*He begins to open the letter. In the meantime M. DUVAL has entered and is standing behind his son. Begins to read.*] "When you receive this, Armand, I shall . . ." [*He utters a cry of anger, turns, sees his father and falls into his arms, sobbing.*] Father!

ACT FOUR

An elegantly furnished room in OLYMPE'S *house, Paris.
Orchestra in the distance; dancing; movement; laughter.*

GASTON [*acting as banker at a game of baccarat*]. Now then,
gentlemen.

Arthur. How much in the bank?

Gaston. A hundred louis.

Arthur. Five francs on the left.

Gaston. Aren't you a little reckless?

Arthur. Ten louis, on credit, if you prefer it.

Gaston. No, thank you very much. [*To* DOCTOR.] Aren't
you playing, Doctor?

Doctor. No.

Gaston. What are you doing over there?

Doctor. Talking to some very charming ladies.

Gaston. Do you find that more profitable?

Doctor. Much. [*Laughter and talking all round the table.*]

Gaston. Well, if this is your idea of playing, someone else
can take the bank.

Prudence. Wait! I'll stake ten francs.

Gaston. Where are they?

Prudence. They are in my pocket.

Gaston. I'll give you fifteen francs if you can show them
to me!

Prudence. Dear me! I've forgotten my purse!

Gaston [*laughing*]. That's a purse that knows its business.
Here! You can have twenty francs.

Prudence. I'll pay you back.

Gaston. Don't be silly. [*Dealing out cards.*]

Enter OLYMPE *with* SAINT-GAUDENS.

Olympe. Are they still at it?

Arthur. Yes, they've never stopped.

Olympe. Give me ten louis, Saint-Gaudens, I want to
play.

Gaston. A delightful party, Olympe.

Arthur. Yes, Saint-Gaudens alone knows what it is costing him.

Olympe. He doesn't, but his wife does.

St. Gaudens. Very witty, my dear. Ah! there you are, Doctor! There is something that I should like to ask you. I suffer at times from giddiness.

Doctor. Dear me!

Olympe. What's he asking?

Doctor. He fancies that there is something the matter with his brain.

Olympe. There is. There! I've lost! You play for me, Saint-Gaudens, and try to win.

Prudence. Saint-Gaudens, lend me three louis. [*He gives them to her.*]

Anais. Saint-Gaudens, go and get me an ice.

St. Gaudens. In a minute or two.

Anais. No, stay and tell us the story of the yellow hackney-carriage.

St. Gaudens. Oh, very well, very well, I'll go.

Prudence [*to* GASTON]. Do you remember the story of the yellow hackney-carriage?

Gaston. Of course I do. Olympe wanted to tell it us that night at Marguerite's. By the way, is Marguerite here?

Prudence. She is coming.

Gaston. And Armand?

Prudence. Armand is not in Paris. . . . Didn't you hear what happened?

Gaston. No.

Prudence. They've separated.

Gaston. Never.

Prudence. Yes, Marguerite left him.

Gaston. When?

Anais. A month ago, and quite right, too.

Gaston. Why?

Anais. One should always leave men before they leave you.

Arthur. Are you playing, gentlemen, or are you not?

Gaston. If you think I am going to go on dealing cards all night for stakes like yours, you are mistaken.

St. Gaudens. Here is the ice that somebody wanted.

Anais. What a time you've been! Dear old fellow, you are not quite as brisk as you were, are you?

Gaston. Gentlemen, the bank is broken. Do you know, it is the most extraordinary thing, if anyone had offered to give me five hundred francs to deal cards for a whole evening, I should have refused, but here have I been dealing steadily for two hours and paid two thousand francs for the pleasure of it! Queer way of enjoying oneself, gambling!

St. Gaudens. You're not going to play any more?

Gaston. No.

Enter ARMAND.

Prudence. There's Armand!

Gaston. We were just speaking about you.

Armand. Were you?

Prudence. We were saying that we didn't think you would be coming tonight, because you were at Tours.

Armand. You were mistaken, you see.

Gaston. When did you get here?

Armand. An hour ago.

Prudence. Have you any news?

Armand. None whatever. Have you?

Prudence. Have you seen Marguerite?

Armand. No.

Prudence. She is coming here tonight.

Armand. Then I *shall* see her.

Prudence. What a funny way you're saying that.

Armand. How would you wish me to say it?

Prudence. You are cured then?

Armand. Perfectly. Her debts are all paid now, I suppose?

Prudence. Yes, all.

Armand. By the Baron de Varville?

Prudence. Yes.

Armand. Everything was for the best, then.

Prudence. Well, there are some men who seem born for that kind of thing. He got what he wanted, and he gave her back her horses and carriages and her jewels and all the rest of the beautiful things that she was used to. For what happiness is worth in this world, she is happy.

Armand. She came back to Paris?

Prudence. Oh yes. She never wanted to go back to Auteuil after you left. I have never known her so restless as she is now. She is out every night and hardly ever seems to sleep. She can't go on long at this rate.

Enter GUSTAVE.

Armand [*seeing* GUSTAVE *enter*]. Excuse me a moment, Prudence. I see a friend of mine and there is something that I should like to say to him.

Prudence. Certainly, my dear. [*Goes to gaming table.*] Ten francs!

Armand [*to* GUSTAVE]. At last! You had my letter?

Gustave. Yes, and I'm here to answer it.

Armand. You are probably surprised at my asking you to come here tonight?

Gustave. Well, yes, I was.

Armand. You haven't seen Marguerite, for some time, have you?

Gustave. Not since I last saw you.

Armand. Then you know nothing of what has happened?

Gustave. No.

Armand. You believed that Marguerite loved me, didn't you?

Gustave. I still believe it.

Armand [*giving* GUSTAVE *the letter from* MARGUERITE]. Read that!

Gustave. Do you mean to say that Marguerite wrote that?

Armand. Yes.

Gustave. When?

Armand. A month ago.

Gustave. And what did you say in answer to it?

Armand. What could I say? These women are all alike, all utterly heartless. I went away with my father. We went to Tours. I thought I should be able to stay there for a while. But it was impossible. I couldn't sleep, I couldn't breathe. At last, I felt that if I did not see her once again, and learn from her own lips that what she had written to me was true, I should die. I came here tonight because I knew that she would be here. I don't know what is going to happen, but I wanted you here, because I may need a friend.

Gustave. I am quite at your service, my dear Armand,

but in heaven's name, don't forget that your quarrel is with a woman and that any act of revenge, on your part, will look like cowardice.

Armand. What of that? She has a lover to defend her. Let him challenge me, if I am a coward!

Servant [announcing]. Mlle. Marguerite Gautier! The Baron de Varville!

Olympe [going to MARGUERITE]. How late you are!

Varville. We have been to the Opera. [*He goes about shaking hands with some of the men.*]

Prudence [to MARGUERITE]. How are you tonight?

Marguerite. Quite well.

Prudence [aside to MARGUERITE]. Armand is here.

Marguerite. Armand!

Prudence. Yes. [*At the same moment,* ARMAND, *who has gone over to the gaming table, looks at* MARGUERITE. *She smiles timidly; he bows distantly and coldly.*]

Marguerite. It was a mistake to come here.

Prudence. Not at all. You would have had to meet Armand sooner or later.

Marguerite. Has he been speaking to you?

Prudence. Yes.

Marguerite. About me?

Prudence. Yes.

Marguerite. What did he say?

Prudence. That he didn't bear you any ill will, and that you were quite right.

Marguerite. So much the better, if that is so. But I don't think it is.

Varville [aside to MARGUERITE]. M. Duval is here, Marguerite.

Marguerite. I know.

Varville. Will you swear to me that you did not know that he was to be here, before we came tonight?

Marguerite. I swear it.

Varville. Will you give me your word that you will not speak to him?

Marguerite. Yes, but I cannot promise not to answer if he should speak to me. Prudence, don't go away, stay here beside me.

Doctor. Good evening.

Marguerite. Good evening, Doctor. Why do you look at me like that?

Doctor. To look at you is quite the most delightful thing that any man can do.

Marguerite. You think me changed, don't you?

Doctor. I shall come and tell you what I think, tomorrow. In the meantime I can only beg you to take care of yourself! I shall scold you at my leisure.

Marguerite. Yes, do come. I shall love your scolding. [DOCTOR *presses her hand and moves away.*]

Gustave [*coming up to* MARGUERITE]. Good evening, Marguerite.

Marguerite. Dear Gustave! How nice to see you again. Is Nichette with you?

Gustave. No.

Marguerite. Of course not. My love to her. [*Dries her eyes.*]

Gustave. What is the matter?

Marguerite. Nothing! I am very unhappy, that's all.

Gustave. Don't cry! Why did you come here?

Marguerite. I am not my own mistress. Besides, I do all I can to forget.

Gustave. If you take my advice, you'll go away from here at once.

Marguerite. Why?

Gustave. Because you never know what may happen. . . . Armand. . . .

Marguerite. Armand hates and despises me.

Gustave. No, he doesn't; he loves you. Look at him now! How wildly he is playing! He hardly knows what he is doing. There will be some trouble between him and the Baron, perhaps a duel. Make some excuse, say that you are ill, and leave here as soon as possible.

Marguerite. A duel between Armand and de Varville! . . . on my account! You are right! I will go at once. [*Rises.*]

Varville [*approaching, aside to her*]. Where are you going?

Marguerite. I am tired and feel ill. I should like to go home.

Varville. No, you are not ill, Marguerite. You want to

go home merely because M. Duval is here and is paying you
no attention. Please understand that I do not choose to
leave any place where I may happen to be just because M.
Armand Duval is there. We came to this hall and shall
remain here.

Olympe [*across the room*]. What were they doing tonight at the Opera?

Varville. "La Favorita."

Armand. It is the story of a woman who betrayed her
lover.

Prudence. How very unoriginal!

Anais. And most untrue! Women never betray their
lovers.

Armand. Some do.

Anais. Of course, there are lovers and lovers.

Armand. Just as there are women and women.

Gaston. High stakes! You are playing a reckless game,
tonight, Armand.

Armand. It is to test the truth of the old saying, "Lucky
at cards, unlucky in love."

Gaston. Well, you must be unhappy enough in love to
judge from your extraordinary luck at cards!

Armand. I intend to make my fortune tonight, my friend,
and then when I am really rich, I hope to go and live in
the country.

Olympe. Alone?

Armand. No, with someone who went with me once
before, and who left me. It all depends on how much I win.
Perhaps, if I am wealthy——

Gustave. Be quiet, can't you, Armand! Look at that poor
girl!

Armand. It is really quite an amusing story, you would
enjoy it. And there is a gentleman in it who makes his
appearance right at the very end, a sort of Deus ex machina
—a charming person!

Varville. Sir!

Marguerite [*aside to* VARVILLE]. If you challenge M.
Duval, you shall never see me again as long as you live!

Armand [*to* VARVILLE]. You addressed yourself to me,
sir?

Varville. I did. Your luck tonight tempts me to try

my own. I understand perfectly the manner in which you propose to employ your winnings, and I should be happy to help you to increase them. I therefore propose to bet against you.

Armand. I accept with all my heart, sir.

Varville [*passing in front of* ARMAND]. I stake a hundred louis!

Armand [*haughtily*]. A hundred louis! Good! Which side do you take, sir?

Varville. The one opposite to yours!

Armand. A hundred louis on the left!

Varville. A hundred on the right!

Gaston. Right, four; left, nine. Armand wins!

Varville. Two hundred louis, then!

Armand. Two hundred louis! Be careful, sir, if the proverb says, "Unlucky in love, lucky at cards," it also says, "Lucky in love, unlucky at cards!"

Gaston. Six! Eight! Armand wins again!

Olympe. It looks as though it is the Baron who will pay for M. Duval's visit to the country!

Marguerite [*to* OLYMPE]. My God! What are they doing?

Olympe [*to make a diversion*]. Supper is in the next room, gentlemen.

Armand. Shall we continue the game, sir?

Varville. No, not now.

Armand. You are entitled to your revenge. You shall have it in whatever way you wish.

Varville. You need have no fear, sir. I shall take full advantage of your offer.

Olympe [*taking* ARMAND'S *arm*]. You have been having really wonderful luck tonight, Armand, my dear.

Armand. You like me better when I'm winning, don't you?

Varville. Are you coming, Marguerite?

Marguerite. Not just yet; there is something that I want to say to Prudence.

Varville. I warn you that if you have not joined me in ten minutes, I shall return here for you.

Marguerite. Very well. [*Alone with* PRUDENCE.] Find Armand for me and beg him, for God's sake, to come here and speak to me!

Prudence. What if he should refuse?

Marguerite. He won't refuse. He hates me too much not to wish to tell me so. Go at once.

Marguerite [alone]. Let me try to think! I must keep my promise to his father! He must go on despising me if this duel is to be avoided!

Enter ARMAND.

Armand. You sent for me.

Marguerite. Yes, Armand, I want to speak to you.

Armand. Go on. I am listening. Do you wish to excuse yourself?

Marguerite. No, it has nothing to do with that. I have no wish to go over the past again.

Armand. You are right. Your part in it was too shameful.

Marguerite. Don't, Armand. Try to listen to me without hatred and without bitterness. Give me your hand——

Armand. Never! If you have nothing further to ask of me——

Marguerite. Who would have thought that you would ever have refused my hand, when I offered it to you? But it is not that that I wished to say. Armand, you must leave here at once.

Armand. Leave here?

Marguerite. Yes, immediately.

Armand. Why?

Marguerite. Because, if you don't, the Baron de Varville will challenge you to a duel.

Armand. And you suggest that I should run away?

Marguerite. Armand, I have suffered so deeply in the past month that I can scarcely find strength to say what must be said. There is a burning pain here that takes away my breath. For the sake of our past love, for the sake of anything that you have ever held dear or sacred in your life, return to your father and forget that you have ever known me.

Armand. I understand. You are afraid for your lover. It would be a thousand pities if a pistol shot or a sword thrust were to put an end to your present good fortune.

Marguerite. You yourself might be killed, Armand. That is the danger.

Armand. And what difference would that make to you? Did you care whether I lived or died, when you wrote to me that you were the mistress of another? If that letter did not kill me, it was only that I might live to be revenged. You thought that you could arrange everything very simply, and that I should take no further notice of you and your accomplice. But I tell you that between de Varville and me there is a quarrel to the death. For I shall kill him.

Marguerite. The Baron de Varville is not to blame for this.

Armand. You love him! That is reason enough for me to hate him.

Marguerite. You know that I don't love this man, that I never could love him.

Armand. And yet you left me and went to him. Why?

Marguerite. Don't ask me, Armand, I can't tell you.

Armand. Then I will tell *you.* You gave yourself to him because you don't understand the meaning of loyalty and honour; because your love belongs to the highest bidder and your heart is a thing that can be bought and sold; because when you found yourself face to face with the sacrifice that you were going to make for me, your courage failed you, and you went back to the past; because I, who would have devoted my life to you and my honour, too, meant less to you than your horses and carriages and the jewels around your neck.

Marguerite. Yes, it is all true. I am a worthless and ungrateful creature, who has cruelly betrayed you, and who never loved you. But the more degraded you know me to be, the less you ought to endanger your life for my sake, and trouble the peace of those you love. Armand, on my knees, I implore you, before it is too late, to leave Paris.

Armand. I will, on one condition.

Marguerite. I agree to it, whatever it is.

Armand. That you come with me.

Marguerite. Never! [*shrinking back*].

Armand. Never!

Marguerite. Oh, my God, help me!

Armand. Listen, Marguerite, there is madness in me tonight. I am capable of anything, even a crime. I thought that it was hatred that was driving me back to you, but it was love, Marguerite, angry, remorseful, torturing love, love that despised itself and was ashamed, for there is shame in my loving you after all that has happened. Say just one word, and I will forget everything. What do I care for this man? Only tell me that you love me and I will forgive you, Marguerite. We will leave Paris and the past behind us, find some solitude and be alone with our love.

Marguerite. I would give my life for one hour of such happiness, but it is impossible. Go, forget me. You must. I have sworn it.

Armand. To whom?

Marguerite. To one who had a right to ask such a thing.

Armand [*with growing anger*]. To the Baron de Varville?

Marguerite. Yes.

Armand [*seizing her arm*]. Because you love him! Tell me that you love him and I will go.

Marguerite. Then, yes, I love him. [ARMAND *throws her to the ground, raises his hands and then hurries to the door. He sees the guests in the other room.*]

Armand. Come in, everybody, I have something to say to you.

Marguerite. What are you doing?

Armand. Do you see this woman?

All. Marguerite Gautier?

Armand. Yes, Marguerite Gautier. Do you know what she did? She sold all that she had to live with me because she loved me so much. It was noble and generous, wasn't it? You shall all hear how vilely I treated her! I accepted this sacrifice and gave her nothing in return. But it is not too late. I know now that I was wrong and I wish to settle the account between us. I call upon you all to witness that I owe this woman nothing! [*Throws bank notes over her.*]

Marguerite. Ah! [*Gives a cry and falls to the ground.*]

Varville [*with scorn, to* ARMAND]. And I say to you, sir, that you are a coward. [GUESTS *rush in between them.*]

ACT FIVE

MARGUERITE'S *bedroom, Paris. Six months later.* MAR-
GUERITE *in bed asleep.* GASTON *enters.*

GASTON. She is still asleep. . . . What time is it? Seven
o'clock. . . . Not yet daylight. . . . I'll make up the fire
again. [*Mends fire.*]

Marguerite [*waking*]. I am thirsty, Nanine.

Gaston. Here you are, dear girl.

Marguerite [*raising her head*]. Who is it?

Gaston [*preparing a cup of tisane*]. Gaston

Marguerite. What are you doing here?

Gaston. Drink this first and then I'll tell you. I am a
born nurse.

Marguerite. But where is Nanine?

Gaston. Asleep. How do you feel this morning?

Marguerite. Better, Gaston dear. But why should you tire
yourself like this?

Gaston. Tire myself? I never go to bed before this. Besides, there is something I want to say to you.

Marguerite. What?

Gaston. Are you worried?

Marguerite. Worried?

Gaston. I mean about money? When I came I found a
bailiff in your drawing room. I paid him and showed him
the door, but you will want money to go on with. I haven't
much myself; I have been losing pretty heavily at cards, and,
besides, I have bought a heap of silly presents for New
Year's Day [*kissing her*]. By the way, same to you, my dear,
and many of them—but here are twenty-five louis. I'll put
them here in this drawer, and when they are gone, we'll find
some more.

Marguerite. How kind you are! Isn't it strange that you,
whom everyone thought such a scatter-brain, should come
here to look after me.

Gaston. That's always the way. . . . Now, I'll tell you
what we'll do.

Marguerite. What?

Gaston. It is going to be fine today. You slept well, last night, but you must try to sleep a little longer. There will be plenty of sunshine in the early part of the afternoon, wrap yourself up well, and I will come back here and take you for a drive. And then, who'll sleep tonight? . . . Marguerite! Now I must go and call on my mother, and God knows what sort of a reception I'll get. I haven't been to see her for over a fortnight. I shall lunch with her and then call for you at one o'clock. How will that suit you?

Marguerite. I shall try to have enough strength.

Gaston. You will! Of course you will.

Enter NANINE.

Marguerite is awake.

Marguerite. Are you very tired, my poor Nanine?

Nanine. A little, madame.

Marguerite. Open the window, Nanine, and let in the morning air. I should like to get up.

Nanine [*opening window and looking out into the street*]. Here is the doctor, madame.

Marguerite. Dear Doctor! His first visit is always for me. Open the door for him, as you go, will you, Gaston? Nanine, come and help me to get up.

Nanine. But——

Marguerite. Yes, I want to.

Gaston. Good-bye until this afternoon, then.

Marguerite. Until this afternoon. [*She rises and then falls again. At last, supported by NANINE, she walks over to the sofa, the DOCTOR entering in time to help her.*] Good morning, Doctor. How kind of you to think of me so early in the morning. Nanine, go and see if there are any letters.

Doctor. Give me your hand. How do you feel?

Marguerite. Ill and yet better. Better because I slept last night and have only just woken up.

Doctor. Good! We shall have you as well as ever again in the spring.

Marguerite. Thank you, Doctor. It is your duty to say that. When God said that it was a sin to tell lies, he must have made an exception for doctors. I suppose they have a special dispensation every time they visit a patient. [*To* NANINE.] What have you got there, Nanine?

Nanine. Presents, madame.

Marguerite. Oh, yes, it is New Year's Day. How much can happen in a year! . . . A year ago today at this time we were still sitting round the table singing and laughing . . . Where are the days, Doctor, when we still laughed? . . . [*Opens parcels.*] A ring with a card from Saint-Gaudens—a bracelet from the Comte de Giray. He has sent it from London; how kind of him! What would he say if he could see me in this state! . . . And chocolates. Well, men are not so forgetful after all. You have a little niece, haven't you, Doctor?

Doctor. Yes.

Marguerite. Take these chocolates and give them to the little girl, will you? It is a long time since I wanted any. [*To* NANINE.] Is that all?

Nanine. There is a letter.

Marguerite. Who could have written to me? [*Takes letter and opens it.*] Take that box and put it in the Doctor's carriage. [*Reads.*] "My dearest Marguerite. I have called again and again, but was not allowed to see you. I cannot bear the thought that you should have no share in the happiest day of my life. I am to be married on the first of January. It is the New Year's gift that Gustave was keeping as a surprise for me. I do hope that you will be able to come to my wedding—such a quiet, simple little wedding, in the Chapel of Sainte Therese, in the Madeleine. I kiss you, dear, with all the fervour of my most happy heart, Nichette." And so there is happiness for everyone in the world, it seems, except for me. But there! I am ungrateful. Please shut the window, Doctor. I am cold. Give me a pen and paper. I want to write. [*Lets her head fall into her hands. The* DOCTOR *takes writing materials from mantelpiece and gives them to her.*]

Nanine [*to* DOCTOR *as he withdraws from* MARGUERITE]. How is she, Doctor?

Doctor [*shaking his head*]. Very ill, I am afraid.

Marguerite. Doctor, will you be so kind as to take this letter and leave it at the church where Nichette is to be married? Ask them not to give it to her until after the wedding. [*Writes and folds letter.*] Here it is, and thank you. Don't forget, will you? Come back again soon.

[*Exit* DOCTOR.

Marguerite. Now, tidy this room a little, Nanine. There is the bell. See who it is.

Nanine [*coming back*]. Madame Duvernoy would like to see you.

Marguerite. Let her come in.

Enter PRUDENCE.

Prudence. Well, my dear Marguerite, and how are you this morning?

Marguerite. Better, thank you, Prudence.

Prudence. Send Nanine away for a moment. I want to speak to you alone.

Marguerite. You can finish the other room first, Nanine. I will call you if I need you. [*Exit* NANINE.

Prudence. I wonder if you would do me a favour, Marguerite.

Marguerite. What is it?

Prudence. You have money in hand, haven't you?

Marguerite. You know that I have been very short of money for some time—but what were you going to say?

Prudence. It is New Year's Day and I have some presents to buy. I'm badly in need of two hundred francs. Do you think you could lend it to me until the end of the month?

Marguerite. Until the end of the month!

Prudence. Of course, if it is not inconvenient——

Marguerite. Well, I do rather need what money I have left——

Prudence. Very well, then, we'll say no more about it.

Marguerite. Wait! What does it matter? Open that drawer——

Prudence. Which? [*Opens several drawers.*] Oh! this one in the middle.

Marguerite. How much is there?

Prudence. Five hundred francs.

Marguerite. Then take the two hundred that you need.

Prudence. Are you sure that the rest will be enough for you?

Marguerite. I shall have all I need. Don't worry about me.

Prudence [*taking some money*]. You have done me a very great service.

Marguerite. I am glad, Prudence dear.

Prudence. I will leave you now, and come back again later. You are looking better this morning.

Marguerite. I feel better.

Prudence. It won't be long now before the fine weather is here and a little country air will soon put you right.

Marguerite. Yes, that is what I need.

Prudence [*going out*]. Well, good-bye, my dear, and thank you again.

Marguerite. Send Nanine to me.

Enter NANINE.

Nanine. Has she been asking you again for money?

Marguerite. Yes.

Nanine. Did you give it to her?

Marguerite. Money is such a little thing to give, and she needed it badly, she said. But we need some, too, don't we? We must buy some New Year's presents. Take this bracelet that has just come. Sell it and come back again as quickly as you can.

Nanine. But what about you?

Marguerite. I shall not need anything. You will not be gone very long. You know the way to the pawnbroker's. He has bought enough from me during the last three months.   [*Exit* NANINE.

[*Reading letter that she takes from her breast.*] "Madam, I have learnt of the duel between Armand and the Baron de Varville, but not from my son who left the country without saying good-bye to me. I must confess that for a time I thought that you were to blame for the duel and for my son's departure. I am thankful to say that the Baron de Varville is now out of danger and I know all that has happened. You have kept your word to me to the utmost limit of your strength, and I fear that recent events have injured your health. I have written to Armand, telling him the whole truth. He is far away, but he will return to ask your forgiveness, not only for himself, but for me, too. I was obliged to do you a wrong, and I wish to set it right. Take care of yourself and hope. Your courage and self-denial are worthy of a better future. You shall have it, I promise you. In the meantime, allow me to assure you of my sympathy and of my highest esteem and regard . . . Georges Duval." . . . It is six weeks now since I received this letter, and I have read it again and again to find courage. If I only had some word from Armand! [*Raises herself and looks in the glass.*] How changed I am! But the doctor promised that he would cure me and I must try to be patient. But that is not what he said to Nanine . . . He said that I was very ill. Very ill! But one may still be very ill and yet have a few more months to live, and if only Armand would come it would save me. The first day in the New Year! It is a day to hope and to look forward in. I think clearly. What happiness there is everywhere today! There is a pretty child showing off his new toys. I should like to kiss him, but he is too far away.

Nanine [*coming to* MARGUERITE, *after putting down the money that she has brought*]. Madame——

Marguerite. Yes, Nanine?

Nanine. You feel better today, don't you?

Marguerite. Why?

Nanine. If I tell you something, will you promise to keep quite calm and quiet?

Marguerite. What is it?

Nanine. I want to prepare you, a sudden joy might be too much for you——

Marguerite. Did you say a joy, Nanine?

Nanine. Yes.

Marguerite. Armand! You have seen Armand? He is coming to see me? [NANINE *nods.* MARGUERITE *rushes to the door. He appears, looking ill. She clings to him.*] At last! Armand? It is not possible that you have come back, that God could be so good to me!

Armand. If I had not seen Nanine, I should have remained outside and never dared to come near you. Have pity, Marguerite! Don't curse me! My father has written and told me all. I was far away from you—if I had not found you again, I should have died, because it would have been I who had killed you. I have not seen my father yet, Marguerite. Tell me that you forgive us both. Oh! how good it is to see you again!

Marguerite. Forgive you, my darling! It was all my fault!

But what could I do? I wanted your happiness so much more than my own. But your father will not part us again now, will he? You do not see the Marguerite that you used to know, dear, but I am still young. I shall grow beautiful again now that I am happy.

Armand. I will never leave you again, Marguerite. We will go away from this house at once and never come back to Paris any more. My father knows what you are now, and will love you as the good angel of his son. My sister is married. The future is ours.

Marguerite. Armand! I said this morning that only one thing could save me. I had given up hoping for it—and then you came. We must lose no time, beloved. Life was slipping away from me, but you came and it stayed. You haven't heard, have you? Nichette is to be married this morning, to Gustave. Let us go to see her married. It would be so good to go to church, to pray to God, and to look on a little at the happiness of others. There was a surprise for me, too, on this first day of the New Year. Tell me again that you love me.

Armand. I love you, Marguerite. All my life is yours.

Marguerite [to NANINE, *who enters*]. Bring my outdoor things, Nanine, I want to go out.

Armand. You are a good girl, Nanine! You have taken faithful care of her. Thank you.

Marguerite. We used to speak of you every day. No one else dared to mention your name. It was she who used to comfort me and tell me that I should see you again. And she was right. You have travelled a long way and seen many beautiful countries. You must tell me about them and perhaps take me there one day. [*She sways.*]

Armand. What is it, Marguerite? You are ill!

Marguerite [*with an effort*]. No, it is nothing. Happiness hurts a little at first and my heart has been desolate for so long. [*She sits down and throws back her head.*]

Armand. Marguerite! Speak to me! Marguerite!

Marguerite [*coming to herself*]. Don't be afraid, dear. I always used to have these moments of faintness, don't you remember?

Armand [*taking her hand*]. You are trembling!

Marguerite. It is nothing. Come, Nanine, give me my shawl and bonnet.

Armand [in terror]. Oh God! Oh, my God!

Marguerite [having tried to walk, throws down her shawl in anger]. I can't. *[Falls on to the sofa.]*

Armand. Run for the doctor, Nanine! At once!

Marguerite. Yes, yes! Tell him that Armand has come back, that I want to live, that I must live . . .

[NANINE *goes.*

But if your coming has not saved me, nothing will. I have lived for love, now I am dying of it.

Armand. Hush, Marguerite! You will live, you must!

Marguerite. Sit down here beside me, as close as you can, Armand. Just for a moment I was angry with death, but I know, now, that it had to come. . . . I am not angry any more, because it has waited long enough for me to see you again. If I had not been going to die, your father would never have written to you to come back. . . .

Armand. Marguerite, don't talk like that! I can't bear it! Tell me that you are not going to die! That you don't believe it, that you will not die!

Marguerite. Even if I did not wish it, dear, it would have to be, because it is God's will. Perhaps, if things had been different, if I had really been the good girl you should have loved, I might have grieved more at leaving a world where you are, and a future that was so full of promise. But, as it is, the best and purest of me will be yours for ever. Believe me, God sees more clearly than we do.

Armand [rising]. Don't, Marguerite! Don't!

Marguerite. Must I be the one to give you courage? Come, do as I tell you. Open that drawer. You will find a miniature of me, painted for you, in the days when I was still pretty. Keep it, it will help your memory later. If ever you should love and marry some young and beautiful girl, as I hope you may one day, and if she should find the portrait and ask who it is, tell her that it is a friend who, if God permits, will never cease to pray for you and her. And if she should be jealous of the past, because we women sometimes are, and ask you to give up the picture, do so, dearest. I forgive you, now, already. A woman suffers too deeply

when she feels she is not loved. . . . Are you listening,
Armand, my darling, do you hear me?

Enter NICHETTE, *timidly at first, and then more boldly, as
she sees* MARGUERITE *smiling and* ARMAND *at her foot.*

Nichette. Marguerite, you wrote to me that you were
dying, but I find you up and smiling.

Armand [aside to GUSTAVE]. Oh, Gustave, I am so miserable.

Marguerite. I am dying, but I am happy too, and it is only
my happiness that you can see. . . . And so you are married! . . . What a strange life this first one is, what will the
second be? . . . You will be even happier than you were
before. Speak of me sometimes, won't you? Armand, give
me your hand. Believe me, it is not hard to die.

Enter GASTON.

Here is Gaston come back for me! I am so glad to see you
again, dear Gaston. Happiness is ungrateful. I had forgotten
you. . . . [To GASTON.] He has been so good to me, so
kind. . . . Ah! . . . It is strange.

Armand. What?

Marguerite. I am not suffering any more. I feel better, so
much better than I have ever felt before. . . . I am going
to live. [Appears to sleep.]

Gaston. She is asleep.

Armand [with anxiety at first, then with terror]. Marguerite! Marguerite! Marguerite! [Gives a cry; he is forced
to draw away his hand with an effort.] Ah! Dead! [Runs to
GUSTAVE.] Oh, my God, my God! What shall I do?

Gustave. She loved you dearly, poor girl.

Nichette [on her knees beside her]. Rest in peace, Marguerite. Much will be forgiven you, for you loved much.

OLYMPE'S MARRIAGE

A Play in Three Acts

by

EMILE AUGIER

English Version by

BARRETT H. CLARK

CHARACTERS

(*In order of appearance*)

MARQUIS DE PUYGIRON
BARON DE MONTRICHARD
BAUDEL DE BEAUSÉJOUR
MARQUISE DE PUYGIRON
GENEVIÈVE DE WURZEN
PAULINE, *Countess de Puygiron* ("*Olympe Taverny*")
HENRI, *Count de Puygiron*
IRMA, *Pauline's mother*
ADOLPHE, *a comedian*

PLACE: PILNITZ (*near Dresden, Germany*) *and* VIENNA.
TIME: 1854.

OLYMPE'S MARRIAGE

ACT ONE

The scene is the conversation room at Pilnitz, a watering place. There are three large arched entrances at the back, opening upon a garden; a divan is in the centre; to the right stands a table with numerous newspapers on it; to the left is a small tea table.

As the curtain rises, the MARQUIS DE PUYGIRON *is seated by the table to the left,* MONTRICHARD *on the divan, facing the audience;* BAUDEL DE BEAUSÉJOUR *is likewise on the divan, but only his legs are seen by the audience.*

MONTRICHARD [*Reading his guidebook*]. "Pilnitz, nine kilometers southeast of Dresden, summer residence of the Court. Castle . . . Natural waters . . . Magnificent baths . . . Casino . . ." [*Throwing down the book.*] Palpitation with interest, that little book!

Marquis. Tell me, M. de Montrichard—you are a great authority on modern France—who is Mlle. Olympe Taverny? An actress?

Montrichard. No, M. le Marquis, she is one of the most luxuriously and frequently kept women in Paris. How does it happen that her fame has reached Pilnitz?

Marquis. The *Constitutionnel* announces her death.

Montrichard. Is that possible? A girl of twenty-five! Poor Olympe!

Baudel [*Rising from behind the divan*]. Is Olympe dead?

Montrichard [*After looking for the person who is speaking*]. Did Monsieur know her?

Baudel [*Embarrassed*]. Just as—everyone did—hm—yes, very well.

Montrichard. What was the cause of her death?

Marquis. Here's the item: [*He reads.*] "Our California correspondent writes, 'Yellow fever has just claimed as its victim one of the most charming of our young compatriots,

167

Mlle. Olympe Taverny. A week after her arrival in San
Francisco she met her death.' "

Montrichard. What the devil was she doing in California?
She had an income of ten thousand francs!

Baudel. Which she must have lost in investments.

Montrichard [To the MARQUIS]. It has always seemed to
me the most cruel injustice that these happy young creatures should be exposed to so serious an accident as death,
the same as honest women are.

Marquis. That is the only possible way for them to make
regular their position in society. But what surprises me is
that the papers give her long death notices.

Montrichard [At the right of the table]. You have been
away from France for some time, have you not, M. le
Marquis?

Marquis. Since the Vendée—1832.[1]

Montrichard. There have been great changes in twenty-
two years.

Marquis. So I imagine: *then* things were going from bad
to worse. But—the devil!—then, at least, there was some
sentiment of public modesty.

Montrichard. What can public modesty do in the face
of facts? The existence of this class of women is one of the
facts I refer to. These women have passed out of the lower
strata of society and come into the broad daylight. They
constitute a little world of their own which makes its orbit
in the rest of the universe. They go about, give and attend
dances, have families, and gamble on the Bourse. Men
don't bow to them as yet when they are with mothers or
sisters, but they are none the less taken to the Bois in open
carriages; in the theatre they occupy prominent boxes—
and the men are not considered cynics.

Baudel. Exactly.

Marquis. That's all very curious. In my day the boldest
man would never dream of parading himself in that way!

Montrichard. Well, in your day this new social circle
was still in the swamp; now it's dried up, if not thoroughly
renovated. You used to hunt in high-top boots, buckled up

---

[1] Vendée: Name given the counterrevolutionary insurrection in western
France (including Vendée and Brittany) which took place during the
French Revolution, and which abortively broke out afresh in 1832 in
support of the Bourbons. S.S.S.

to the belt; now we walk about in pumps. Streets have been cut through squares, whole residential sections. Like the city of Paris, society takes in new suburbs every fifty years. This latest is the *Thirteenth Arrondissement*. Do you know, these women have so strong a hold on the public that they have even been made the heroines of plays?

Marquis. In the theatre? Women who—? And the audience accepts that?

Montrichard. Without a murmur—which proves that having made their entrée into comedy, they have done likewise into correct society.

Marquis. You could knock me down with a feather!

Montrichard. Then what have you to say when I tell you that these ladies manage to get married?

Marquis. To captains of industry?

Montrichard. No, indeed—to sons of good families.

Marquis. Idiots of good families!

Montrichard. No, no. The bane of our day is the rehabilitation of the lost woman—fallen woman, we say. Our poets, novelists, dramatists, fill the heads of the young generation with romantic ideas of redemption through love, the virginity of the soul, and other paradoxes of transcendental philosophy. These young women must become ladies, grand ladies!

Marquis. Grand ladies?

Montrichard. Marriage is their final catch; the fish must be worth the trouble, you see.

Marquis [*Rising*]. Good God! And the father-in-law doesn't strangle a woman in a case of the sort?

Montrichard [*Also rising*]. What about the law, M. le Marquis? [BAUDEL *rises and walks slowly downstage to the left.*]

Marquis. Devil take the law then! If your laws permit such shame to fall upon good families, if a common prostitute can tarnish the honor of a whole family by marrying one of its drunkard sons, it is the father's right to take his name from the thief of his honor, even if it were glued to her skin like Nessus' tunic.

Montrichard. That's rather a brutal form of justice for the present age, is it not, M. le Marquis?

Marquis. Possibly, but I am not a man of the present age.

Baudel. But, M. le Marquis, suppose the woman in question does not drag her stolen plumage in the gutter?

Marquis. I cannot admit the hypothesis, Monsieur.

Baudel. Is it not possible that she should like to give up her former life and want to lead a quiet and pure existence——?

Marquis. Put a duck on a lake among swans, and you will observe that the duck misses its mire, and will end by returning there.

Montrichard. Homesickness for the mud!

Baudel. Then you don't believe in repentant Magdalens?

Marquis. I do—in the desert.

The MARQUISE *and* GENEVIÈVE *come in through an archway.*

Marquis. Shh! Messieurs, beware of chaste ears!

Montrichard. And how are Mme. la Marquise and Mlle. Geneviève?

Marquise. Much better, thank you, Monsieur.—Have you seen the papers, dear?

Marquis. Yes, dear, and I am now at your disposal.

Geneviève. No news from Turkey, grandfather?

Marquis. No, my child.

Montrichard. Are you interested in the war, Mademoiselle?

Geneviève. I should so like to be a man and fight!

Marquis. Hush, child.

Geneviève. I'm not so stupid—or if I am, I owe it to you, grandmother.—You shouldn't blame me!

Marquise [*Tapping* GENEVIÈVE *gently on the cheek, then going toward her husband*]. Coming to the spring, Tancrède? It's time.

Marquis. Very well. [*To the others.*] We invalids are here to take the waters.—My arm, Marquise. And you lead the way, granddaughter. [*To his wife.*] Sleep better?

Marquise [*To her husband*]. Almost well; and you?

Marquis. So did I. [*They go out.* MONTRICHARD *escorts them to the door and returns.*]

Baudel [*To* MONTRICHARD]. I am delighted, Monsieur, to have made your acquaintance.

Montrichard. When did I have the honor, Monsieur——?

Baudel. Why—here—just now——

Montrichard. The few words we exchanged together? Good Lord, you are a quick acquaintance-maker!

Baudel. I have known you a long time, by reputation. I have always wanted to be counted among your friends.

Montrichard. That's too good of you! Though my friendship is not a temple of etiquette, people do not as a rule enter it unannounced. [*Aside.*] Who is the fellow?

Baudel [*Bowing*]. Anatole de Beauséjour——

Montrichard. Knight of Malta?

Baudel. I confess it.

Montrichard. Fifteen hundred francs—and what did the title of Beauséjour cost you?

Baudel. Two hundred thousand in land.

Montrichard. Dear enough. You deserve another—a little less expensive.

Baudel. Ha, ha! Good! Baudel, Monsieur, is my patronymic.

Montrichard. Baudel? Just as the Montmorency were called Bouchard. I seem to have heard your name somewhere before, Monsieur. Didn't you apply for membership in the Jockey Club last year?

Baudel. I did.

Montrichard. And you were refused because you were—one moment!—because your father was a milliner?

Baudel. He financed the concern: partner of Mlle. Aglaë.

Montrichard. Partner, yes. Well, Monsieur, if I were your father's son I should call myself merely Baudel. It's no disgrace to be bald; only when one wears a wig does one run the risk of appearing ridiculous, M. de Beauséjour. And so —your very humble—— [*He is about to leave.*]

Baudel [*intercepting him*]. Monsieur, the estate of Beauséjour is situated on the road to Orléans, thirty-three kilometers from Paris. Could you tell me where Montrichard lies?

Montrichard [*Returning to Baudel*]. Three impertinent fellows have asked me the same question. To the first I replied that it was situated in the Bois de Boulogne; to the

second, in the Bois de Vincennes; to the third, in the Forest
of St. Germain.[2] I accompanied each of these three sceptics
to the duelling grounds; they returned convinced—griev-
ously convinced—so convinced that no one has since dared
repeat the question. I trust, Monsieur, that you no longer
desire the information?

Baudel. You refer to pleasure parties on your estates, I
take it? You forget, perhaps, that there are other places for
such? Spa, Homburg, Baden, and—Pilnitz!

Montrichard. Monsieur then insists on a wound?

Baudel. Yes, Monsieur, I need one. I have arranged this
little conversation with that end in view. [*They sit down at
the table.*]

Montrichard. Very well, M. Baudel. But I warn you that
you have already an inch of steel in your arm. Take good
care that the weapon goes no deeper!

Baudel. I am fully aware that Monsieur is the best swordsman in Paris. Your blade stands you in good stead of everything, including a genealogy.

Montrichard. Two inches.

Baudel. Of an ambiguous title, relying entirely upon
chance. You have by your bravado and your cleverness made
an entrée in the world of fashion and high life; you are even
one of the leaders in that world, where you always behave
like a perfect gentleman: spending generously, never bor-
rowing—a good gambler, a good comrade, dead shot, and a
gallant knight.

Montrichard. Three inches.

Baudel. Unfortunately, however, you have recently lost
your luck. You are now without a sou, and are looking for
fifty thousand francs with which to tempt fortune once
again. You cannot find the money.

Montrichard. Five inches!

Baudel. I shall loan you that amount.

Montrichard. Ha!

Baudel. Now how many inches?

Montrichard. That depends on the conditions you make.
You have conditions?

Baudel. Yes.

Montrichard. Speak, M. de Beauséjour.

*Famous places for duelling.

Baudel. It's quite simple: I should like——

Montrichard. What?

Baudel. The devil! It's not so simple as it seemed.

Montrichard. I am very intelligent!

Baudel. Monsieur, I have an income of a hundred and twenty-three thousand francs.

Montrichard. You are fortunate.

Baudel. No, I am not. I have received a gentleman's education and I have aristocratic instincts. My fortune and my breeding call me to the more brilliant realms of society—

Montrichard. And your birth stands in your way.

Baudel. Precisely. Every time I knock at the door, it is closed in my face. In order to enter and to remain, I must fight a dozen duels. Now, I am no more of a coward than the average man, but I have a hundred and twenty-three thousand reasons for wanting to live, while my adversary as a rule would have only thirty or forty thousand. It's not too evenly matched.

Montrichard. I understand: you want to earn your spurs once for all, and you turn to me?

Baudel. That's it.

Montrichard. But, my dear Monsieur, my inserting an inch of steel into your arm will not prove that you're a good swordsman.

Baudel. That is not exactly——

Montrichard. Then what——?

Baudel. It's rather a delicate matter to explain.

Montrichard. Say it out—let us be frank.

Baudel. You are right: I propose a bargain.

Montrichard. For what? You remind me of a bottle of that sort of champagne that takes a quarter of an hour to blow the cork out! Good God, man, ask for a corkscrew!

Baudel. Monsieur, your device is *Cruore dives*, isn't it?

Montrichard. Yes, Monsieur, *Cruore dives; Enriched by his blood.* This was not my own invention: it was given by Louis XIV to my great-grandfather four generations ago; he received eight wounds at the Battle of Senef.

Baudel. What was the estate worth at the time?

Montrichard. One million.

Baudel [*Lowering his eyes*]. Twenty-five thousand francs

a wound. I am not as rich as Louis XIV, Monsieur, but there are wounds and wounds. A scratch on the arm, for instance—doesn't that seem worth fifty thousand francs?

Montrichard [*Severely*]. Do you mean you wish to buy a wound? You're mad!

Baudel. Bear in mind that it is more to my interest than yours to keep the matter a secret. There is nothing reprehensible in the arrangement: the price of blood has always been an honorable thing. Your own device proves that.

Montrichard [*After a moment's hesitation*]. You know, I like you—I couldn't for the life of me say why—but I like you. It will be very amusing to make you a man of the world. I'll take that wound from you, but—gratis, you understand?

Baudel [*To himself*]. That will cost more—but I don't mind!

Montrichard. Send your seconds.

Baudel. But the cause of the quarrel?

Montrichard. Your name is Baudel. I am said to have suggested that you cross the "l." [3]

Baudel. Good! Montrichard, a duel to the bitter end!

Montrichard. And afterward we shall have a housewarming for our new friendship at the Hotel du Grand Scanderburg. I shall await your seconds here, my dear M. Baudel.

Baudel. De Beauséjour.

Montrichard. Yes, yes: de Beauséjour. [BAUDEL *goes out*. There's a queer type! I'll make something of him: first a friend—very attached—with a string to his paw——! This duel is exactly what I needed to set me going once again. Montrichard, the hour of fate has sounded, the hour of marriage! [*He goes to the door, meets* PAULINE *and bows to her.*]

Montrichard. You? You're not dead, then? Why, the papers are full of it!

Pauline. Doubtless a mistake!

Montrichard. Aren't you Olympe Taverny?

Pauline. Ah, I thought so! This is not the first time I have had the honor to be mistaken for that lady. I am the Countess de Puygiron, Monsieur.

[3] Which makes the word "Baudet": ass.

Montrichard. A thousand pardons, Madame! The resemblance is so striking! Even your voice——! You will excuse me for making so natural a mistake? Especially as this is as likely a place to meet Olympe Taverny as the Countess de Puygiron. I beg your pardon once more, Madame.

Pauline [*Going downstage to the right*]. Of course, Monsieur. I was looking for my uncle and aunt here.

Montrichard. They are at the spring. M. le Marquis never told me his nephew was married.

Pauline. For an excellent reason: he didn't know it himself.

Montrichard. Ah!

Pauline. It's a surprise that my husband and I have in store for him. Please be good enough, therefore, not to tell him of our arrival, if you happen to see him before we do. Or—will you please show me the way to the spring?

Montrichard. Do me the honor of taking my arm, Madame. I have the good fortune to be slightly acquainted with your family. [*Bowing.*] Baron de Montrichard—most pleased to—this is nonsense, introducing an old friend!

Pauline. Monsieur!

Montrichard. Are you afraid I'll tell? You know I'm always on the woman's side. You and I can help each other; in my own interest, if for no other reason, I am bound to be discreet on your score.

Pauline. In what way, M. de—de—Montrichard, can I be fortunate enough to serve you?

Montrichard. Ah, you're defiant? Do you want security? I'm only too pleased. I am thinking of marrying: your great-uncle, the Marquis de Puygiron, has a charming grand-daughter. I have just made her acquaintance, but have not as yet been received into the family circle. If you will arrange that for me and further my suit, I shall see to it that whoever has the impertinence to recognise you will have to deal with me. [*He holds out his hand to her.* PAULINE *looks quickly about to see whether anyone else is present.*]

Pauline [*Taking his hand*]. How did you recognize me?

Montrichard. First, your face, then that little pink mark on your beloved ivory neck. The mark I used to adore!

Pauline. Do you still remember it?

Montrichard. You were my only real love.

Pauline. And you mine, dear Edouard.

Montrichard. No, no—Alfred—you're mixing the names. Your "only real love" has had so many names! What the devil put it into your head to marry? You were very happy before?

Pauline. Did you ever happen to notice, when you stepped out into the boulevard, that you had left your cane in the restaurant?

Montrichard. Yes.

Pauline. And you went back for it. There in the private dining room you saw the wreckage of the orgy: candelabra in which the lights were burned out; tablecloth removed; a candle end on the table which was all covered with grease and stained with wine. Instead of lights and laughter and heavy perfumes, that made the place gay not long since, were solitude, silence, and a stale odor. The gilded furniture seemed like strangers to you, to everyone, even to themselves. Not a single article among all this that seemed familiar, not one was reminiscent of the absent master of the house or awaited his return. Complete abandonment!

Montrichard. Exactly.

Pauline. Well, my life is rather like that of the private dining room. I must be gay or utterly lonely—there is no possible compromise. Are you surprised then that the restaurant aspires to the dignity of the home?

Montrichard. Not to mention a certain taste for virtue that you must have acquired?

Pauline. You're joking?

Montrichard. No, virtue is for you a new plaything, I might almost say, forbidden fruit. Let me warn you that it will set your teeth on edge.

Pauline. We shall see.

Montrichard. The career of an honest woman is a fearful undertaking!

Pauline. It can't compare with ours! If you only knew how much energy it required to ruin a man!

Montrichard. No matter, you are now Countess de Puygiron. Now tell me what is the meaning of the news of your death in the *Constitutionnel*?

Pauline. A note my mother sent to all the papers.

Montrichard. How is good old Irma, by the way?

Pauline. Very well and happy. When I married, I gave her all I had—furniture, jewels, income.

Montrichard. That was something of a consolation for losing you.

Pauline. So you see how necessary it was to throw people off the scent? Thanks to this plan, no one will dare recognise Olympe Taverny in the Countess de Puygiron. Now, dear, you know if I had persisted in not being recognised, you would have retired with excuses—that is, if you hadn't given me your security.

Montrichard. Suppose you happen to meet one of your friends who knew of your liaison with the Count?

Pauline. No one knew of it.

Montrichard. Ah!

Pauline. Henri took me seriously from the very first. He was most discreet: Didier and Marion Delorme,[4] you see! You must know that I've played my cards well. I talked of going into a convent; then he asked me to marry him, and I accepted. I pretended I was going to California. Henri met me in Brittany; I married him there a year ago, under my real name, Pauline Morin.

Montrichard. Is he as big a fool as that?

Pauline. You insulting creature! He's a very intelligent and charming young man.

Montrichard. Then how does it happen that——?

Pauline. He never had a mistress—his father was very severe with him. When he became of age, he was as innocent as——

Montrichard. As you—at the age of four! Poor fellow!

Pauline. He's not to be pitied; he's very happy with me.

Montrichard. Do you love him?

Pauline. That is not the question. I strew his path with flowers—artificial, perhaps, but they are prettier and more lasting than real ones.

Montrichard. Truly, do you think the game worth the candle?

Pauline. So far, I don't. We've been spending ten months alone in Brittany—all by ourselves. For the past two months

[4] Main characters in the famous drama *Marion Delorme* (1829), by Victor Hugo. S.S.S.

we've been travelling, alone again. I can't say that we've been hilarious. I live the life of a recluse, going from hotel to hotel; with the maids, servants, and postilions, I am "Madame la Comtesse." All that would be dull enough if I hadn't other dreams for the future—but I have. Now that Olympe Taverny (God rest her soul!) has had time to go to California and die and be mourned for in Paris, I can boldly enter society by the front door, which the Marquis de Puygiron is to open for me.

Montrichard. Is your husband going to introduce you to his uncle?

Pauline. Indeed he is! But he's not expecting the kind of meeting I have planned!

Montrichard. There's a fine fellow caught in a trap!

Pauline. It's all for his own happiness! If he introduces me as an honest woman, he will not be lying: for a year I have been the personification of virtue. I have a new skin.

Montrichard. You have only to shed it, Countess!

Pauline. Impertinent!—Here is my husband! [MONT- RICHARD *walks away and bows ceremoniously to* PAULINE.]

Enter HENRI.

Montrichard. Will you be good enough, Madame, to present me to M. le Comte?

Pauline. My friend, M. le Baron de Montrichard.

Henri [*Bowing*]. Monsieur.

Pauline. We owe our acquaintance to a rather strange accident: M. de Montrichard, when he saw me come in, mistook me for—you know whom I am thought to resemble?

Montrichard. The mistake was all the more inexcusable as the person you speak of recently died in California, and I do not believe in ghosts.

Pauline. Is the poor creature dead? Well, I haven't the courage to mourn her! Let us hope I shan't again be mistaken for her!

Henri. Take care, Madame, perhaps M. de Montrichard feels the loss more keenly than you?

Montrichard. Right, Monsieur, I thought a great deal of the lady. Her heart was much above her station in life.

Henri. Ah? Doubtless Monsieur was in a position to appreciate her better than anyone else?

Montrichard. No, Monsieur, no. My relations with her were always of a very brief and friendly nature.

Henri [*Shaking hands with him cordially*]. I am very glad to have made your acquaintance, Monsieur—we must become friends!

Montrichard. Monsieur! [*To himself.*] I feel sorry for him!

A Servant enters.

Servant. Two gentlemen who wish to see M. de Montrichard.

Montrichard [*To himself*]. Baudel's seconds! [*Aloud.*] Good, I shall be with them in a moment. [*The Servant goes out.*] I hope, M. le Comte, that we shall soon find an opportunity of continuing the conversation?—Madame!

Henri [*To himself, as he sees his uncle*]. My Uncle!

Montrichard [*Meeting the* MARQUIS *at the door*]. M. le Marquis, you find yourself in the bosom of your family.

[*He goes out.*

The MARQUIS *and the* MARQUISE *enter.*

Marquis. It's Henri! My dear boy, what a surprise! [*He opens his arms;* HENRI *kisses him, then kisses the* MARQUISE'S *hand.*] Three years without coming to see us! And not a letter for a whole year! How ungrateful of you!

Marquise. What of it? Family affection doesn't die out like other affection, through absence or silence. Two hundred leagues away, when we were both grieving for the same reason, we were together in our sorrow.

Marquis. We expected you just before your poor father's death. We thought you would feel the need of being with us. [PAULINE *has meantime gone to the archway, without losing sight of the others. She takes off her hat, lays it on a chair, then comes forward.*]

Henri. I was very, very lonely and I thought of you, but important business affairs——

Marquis. I understand—the will and so forth. The most painful part of human bereavements is that we cannot

escape from material worries. Well, here you are at last, and
we are very happy to see you.

Marquise. How did you know we were here?

Henri. The fact is, I didn't. I expected to meet you in
Vienna, at the end of my German tour.

Marquis. Heaven bless the chance that brought you to
us, then! We have you and we mean to keep you.

Henri. I should be only too glad to spend some days with
you, only I was just passing through Pilnitz! I must leave in
an hour——

Marquis. Nonsense!

Henri. It's a matter of great importance——

Marquis. What an idea! There can't be anything to prevent——?

Henri. Excuse me. [*He looks toward* PAULINE, *who stands
near the table. The* MARQUIS *watches him.*]

Marquis. Ah? [*Aside to* HENRI.] You're not travelling
alone? Well, youth is youth! [*Aloud.*] If you have only an
hour to stay here, let us spend the time together at least!
Our hotel is just two steps from here. Give your aunt your
arm. [*The* MARQUIS *takes his hat.* HENRI *offers his arm to
his aunt; they start for the door.*]

Pauline. I shall wait for you here, Henri.

Marquis [*Turning round*]. You lack tact, Mademoiselle!

Henri [*Going to* PAULINE *and taking her hand*]. Uncle, I
have the honor to present to you the Countess de Puygiron.

Marquise. The Countess de Puygiron?

Marquis. Are you married?

Henri. Yes, Uncle.

Marquis [*Severely*]. How does it happen, Monsieur, that
I, the head of the family, knew nothing of this?

Henri. Let me postpone an explanation in which my
self-respect and my duty toward you could not but suffer.
I did not come to Pilnitz to see you, and I have no intention of antagonizing you by my presence here. In leaving
you, I believe that I am paying you all the deference at
present due you.

Marquis. This has nothing to do with deference, Monsieur! In families like ours there exists a solidarity of honor
which is not to be trifled with or put aside by a caprice. Ask
me what I have done with our family name and I shall

answer that I have never spotted it except with my blood. Now I command you to give me your account!

Henri. Command? When I married Pauline, I broke with the family. I therefore have the right to be rid of any duty toward it, as I ask none of its privileges.

Marquise. Henri, my child, can't you be a little more conciliatory?

Marquis. Madame, do not believe for an instant that it is Henri who is speaking! Can't you see that this spirit of revolt has been put into him by someone else?

Henri. You are mistaken, Monsieur: I respect what deserves respect. But the prejudices and absurd conventions, the hypocrisy and tyranny of society—nothing could prevent my despising them as they deserve to be despised!

Marquis. Whom have you married in order to set society at defiance?

Henri. I prefer not to say.

Pauline. Why not, dearest? You must not allow your uncle to believe your marriage worse than a misalliance! That would kill him! Let me reassure him! His sense of honor will surely——? Then we may go.

Henri. Very well. [*He walks away.*]

Pauline. My name is Pauline Morin, M. le Marquis; I am the daughter of an honest farmer.

Marquis. You a farmer's daughter? But your manners, your language——?

Pauline. My dear mother gave me an education far beyond my station.

Marquis. Possibly!—Come, Marquise. [*He offers his arm to the* MARQUISE, *and they turn to go.*]

Pauline. Please stay. I ought to leave if my presence is disagreeable to you!

Marquis. You really cannot expect to be publicly received into a family which you entered in secret? [HENRI *is about to speak.*]

Pauline. And why not in secret? Tell me what you suspect, M. le Marquis? My marriage must seem to you a very treacherous and bold stroke.

Marquis. That would not be at all necessary with a child like Henri!

Henri. But she wanted to go into a convent!

Pauline. It was a comedy, a cruel comedy! Whom could you hope to persuade of my sincerity? Who would admit that a girl of low birth, when she found in you all the intelligence and goodness of heart she had always dreamed, would give up her secret soul to you? You were very simple to believe it—ask your uncle. If I had really loved you, would I not have refused to become your wife? Would I not, M. le Marquis?

Henri. And do you imagine she didn't refuse? She made every possible objection that you yourself would have made.

Pauline. I was defending not only your happiness, but my own. [HENRI *sits down at the table.*] Do you think I had a beautiful dream, M. le Marquis? If you only knew what I am suffering! But I have no right to complain; I anticipated what was going to happen. [*To* HENRI.] I asked God for one year of your love in exchange for the happiness of a lifetime. He has kept His bargain, and given me even a little extra for full measure: for you still love me.

Henri [*His arms extended toward her*]. I *do* love you! I love you as much as I did the first days of our love.

Pauline. Poor dear! You don't realise what is going on within you! Perhaps I'm wrong to tell you—but it's only what you will learn soon enough. Your affection is already waning and you are being worn out by the struggle you are making against the conventions of society. Your family traditions, which you have shattered, and which you call prejudices, are now rising up one after the other——

Marquise [*To her husband*]. That's true enough.

Pauline. You are resisting, I know, and you are already angry that your happiness is not rewarded enough for the sacrifices you are forced to make, but every day these sacrifices grow greater, and the reward less. When you leave here, you will feel the weight of loneliness bearing down on you; you will see with other eyes the woman who ought always to stand you in stead of family, friends, society—and before long the regret of what you have given up for me will change to remorse.

Marquise [*To her husband*]. She doesn't speak like a woman who's trying to deceive us!

Pauline. But never fear, dearest, the day that happens I

shall give you back all you have lost for my sake, and your love for me will be my whole life.

Henri. Who can listen to you and not adore you?

Marquise [*To her husband*]. Poor woman!

Pauline. Good-bye, M. le Marquis, and forgive me for having the honor to bear your name—I am paying dear for it!

Marquise [*To her husband*]. Say something nice to her.

Marquis. Only my rigid principles, which I have always adhered to, separate us—to my regret.

Pauline. Thank you! I go away proud, for I feel that I am at least esteemed by the Great Marquis!

Marquis. Do you know my *nom de guerre?*

Pauline. I am the daughter of a *Vendéen!*

Henri [*To himself*]. What's this?

Marquise. Daughter of a *Vendéen?*

Pauline. Who died with honor on the field of battle.

Marquis. In what battle?

Pauline. Chanay.

Marquis. I wasn't there, but our men fought valiantly that day! What did you say was your father's name?

Pauline. Yvon Morin.

Marquis. I don't recall——

Pauline. I scarcely thought you would: he was only a common soldier—of your cause.

Marquis. We were all equals, made noble by our faith. If there had been distinctions it was death only that made them! [*To* Henri.] Why didn't you tell me you were marrying the daughter of a *Vendéen?* That's not a misalliance! Your father shed his blood with ours, Countess!

Pauline. Oh, M. le Marquis!

Marquis. Your uncle! [*Stretches out his arms toward* Pauline, *who falls into them.*]

Marquise [*As* Pauline *kisses her hand*]. I was sure Henri would not contract a marriage unworthy of him!

Marquis [*To* Henri]. Now you won't leave, will you?

Henri. Uncle——

Marquis. Go if you like, only we shall keep your wife. Come to our hotel, Countess; I should like to introduce you to my granddaughter. This proud nobleman will certainly follow you!

Henri. Yes, we shall join you soon, Uncle.

Marquis. Don't make us wait too long—we shan't sit down to dinner until you come. [*He shakes hands with* PAULINE *and* HENRI *and goes toward the door.*] It's the Lion d'Or.   [*He goes out with the* MARQUISE.

Henri. Swear to me that you didn't know my uncle was here! Swear—on your life!

Pauline. On my life, on my mother! You suspect something too terrible for words, I know!

Henri. Forgive me! You can see how I suffer. I sometimes even doubt you. This story you seemed to invent on the spur of the moment——

Pauline. You think it was prepared?

Henri. I did—and my heart sank.

Pauline. Poor child! You thought I married in order to get into the family, and become a countess?

Henri. Yes.

Pauline. That my sole ambition was to climb? Oh, Henri, how could you have so low an opinion of me?

Henri. Forgive me—I'm not at all well.

Pauline. I know, and for that very reason I wanted you to be with your family once more. My love is not enough in itself—but rather than have you suspect me, I should tell the whole truth to your uncle.

Henri. It would kill him—I know it would kill him! [*He throws himself upon the divan.*]

Pauline [*Sitting beside him*]. Then we'll go tomorrow, if this *lie* is troubling you——

Henri. It is. Your intention was good—thank you for that! But I have no right to fly in the face of my uncle's prejudices with a lie. Every time he shook hands with me, every time you spoke to any member of my family, would be an abuse of confidence for which I should blush.

Pauline [*Embracing him*]. We'll go tonight. Those clouds on your forehead must disappear, you adorable boy! I ask nothing more than to be with you, alone! Come now, let us join those people whose peace of mind gives you so much worry.

Henri. You angel!

Pauline. Ah, *you* have given me wings! [*She gives him*

her arm coquettishly. HENRI *kisses her forehead. To herself.*] Countess, ah!

ACT TWO

The scene is in the MARQUIS' *home in Vienna. The spacious family drawing room is decorated in the style of Louis XIII with recessed walls, wainscoted from top to bottom in carved oak. There are doors at the back and at each side; in the recess of the left wall is a large fireplace above which hangs a full-length portrait of the* MARQUISE. *On each side of the picture is a candelabrum with five candles. In the recess to the right is a deep-set window. Toward the back on the same side is a Venetian mirror.*

As the curtain rises, the MARQUISE *and* GENEVIÈVE *are seated embroidering. The* MARQUIS *stands by the fireplace.* PAULINE *is half-reclining on a small sofa.*

MARQUISE. You must not forget, Tancrède, that we are dining at Mme. de Ransberg's.

Marquis. I shan't forget: you know I adore Mme. de Ransberg!

Marquise. And I believe your affection is returned! If she were thirty years older I might be jealous.

Geneviève. On the contrary, grandmother: rather just because she *is* twenty, it seems to me——

Marquise. That she is no match for you, who are sixty.

Geneviève. Do you think the victor is always the one with the heavy battalions?

Marquise. In matters of friendship, yes.

Marquis. I am very grateful to the dear little Baroness for the way she welcomed our Pauline.

Geneviève. Then you have reason to be grateful to all Vienna, for that matter.

Marquis. I don't deny that. I have been touched and flattered, I admit, by her reception here.

Geneviève. You might almost imagine that we were concealing contraband goods!

Marquis. I'm foolish, like the ass with the burden of relics!

Geneviève [Rising]. Did you hear that, Pauline?

Pauline [Emerging from her reverie]. What?

Geneviève [Going to PAULINE]. So much the worse! See what you've lost! That will teach you to join in the conversation!

Pauline. I'm not feeling well.

Marquise. Not yet?

Geneviève. You're never well, are you?

Pauline. It's nothing. [*To herself.*] What a bore!

Marquis [Sitting by the MARQUISE]. We made you stay up too late last night—you're not used to it!

Pauline. That's so.

Geneviève. But the party was such fun!

Pauline [To herself]. Like a rainy day!

Geneviève. Mme. de Rosenthal is so jolly! She breathes an air of gaiety all about her. Such a brilliant soiree! Even the old people at their whist must have been excited!

Marquise. My partner, the Chevalier de Falkenstein, took my kings every time——

Marquis. His excuse was Pauline's laughter—it distracted his attention.

Geneviève. A deaf man with a sharp ear! Pauline didn't move and she won enormously.

Marquise. Really?

Pauline. Enormously? A hundred francs, at the outside.

Marquis. That's good, at a franc a point. But I have an idea you don't care for gambling?

Pauline. I don't, M. le Marquis, I don't—[*To herself.*] at a franc a point.

Geneviève. Pauline is so serious that I think she's bored by all this frivolous society.

Marquise. Yes, and she seemed, beforehand, to expect a wonderful time!

Pauline. I imagined it was going to be something far different from this!

Marquis. You are too serious for your years, my dear niece.

Pauline. Perhaps.

Marquise. But society is not altogether a matter of frivolity. If you are bored with the young people, why don't you talk with the older ones? You could certainly find something worth while to talk about with them?

Pauline. Madame, I am ashamed to confess that the topics of conversation in society do not appeal to me: I am a barbarian. I've lived too long in our primitive Brittany.

Marquis. We shall civilise you, my dear child. What is the weather like?

Geneviève [*Going to the window*]. Superb!

Marquise. It won't last.

Marquis. Does your wound still pain you?

Pauline. What wound?

Geneviève [*Returning*]. You didn't know that grand-mother was once a soldier?

Marquis. Geneviève!

Geneviève [*Going to the* MARQUIS]. Did that displease you?

Marquise. No, dear.

Marquis. You allow her too great liberty—she's too familiar with you.

Marquise. Familiarity is the small change of tenderness. We are too old to object to that.

Marquis. Very well. That child speaks to you sometimes in a way I shouldn't dare to!

Geneviève. This is between grandmother and me, grand-father. It doesn't concern you.

Marquise. Geneviève, you are forgetting yourself!

Geneviève. You're as severe as grandfather. Did I annoy you, grandfather?

Marquis. No, dear. With me I allow you certain liber-ties——

Geneviève. Then you are as indulgent as grandmother! [*She kisses him.*]

Marquis. That child is twisting us round her little finger, Marquise.

Geneviève [*Taking a hand of each of her grandparents in her own*]. Forgive my little trick: I only wanted to try an experiment. Henri spoke of the respect each of you had for the other——

Marquis. Are you surprised that I respect your grand-mother?

Geneviève. Oh no, but I never dreamed how far it went! Henri called my attention to it: "How beautiful it is," he said, "to see those two lives so bound up in each other! Old age without a blemish! Two hearts that have gone through life inseparable, two beings whom the battles of life have brought closer together. The head and the saint of the family"——

Pauline [*To herself*]. *Philemon and Baucis!* [5]

Geneviève. And tears came into his eyes—tears of admiration and tenderness.

Marquise. Dear Henri!

Marquis. He's right, dear—your grandmother *is* a saint!

Marquise [*Smiling*]. Tancrède, it isn't your place to sanctify me!

Marquis. Would you like to hear about that wound, Pauline? I'll tell you: the Marquise came with me to the Château of Péniscière—you know the details of that terrible siege!—When fire broke out and forced us to leave the Château, we retreated fighting all the way to a little wood where we separated after firing our last volley. The Marquise and I made our way to a farmhouse, where we hid. As the door opened she fainted, and then I noticed that she had been hit by a bullet! [*Taking her hand.*] My dear wife! That wound will be counted among your good deeds, in Heaven!

Marquise. I hope not, dear. You have given me reward enough on earth.

Pauline. Noble! [*To herself.*] Poseurs!

Geneviève. I should like to be your age and have done that!

Marquise. I think you would do the same as I did under the circumstances.

Geneviève. I would! So would Pauline!

Marquise. Of course: she is Bretonne.

Pauline [*To herself*]. They'll soon begin to think that we have done it!

A Servant enters.

Servant. The carriage is ready.   [*He goes out.*

Marquis [*To the* MARQUISE]. Come, my dear—[*To*

---

[5] A poor and aged Phrygian couple who offered hospitality to the disguised Zeus and Hermes, and were rewarded. S.S.S.

Geneviève *and* Pauline.] We'll come back and get you for dinner. Now you may dress, ladies.

Geneviève. We have plenty of time.

Pauline. May I not be excused?

Marquis. Impossible, dear, the dinner is given in your honor.

[*The* Marquis *and* Marquise *go out at the back.*

Pauline [*To herself*]. What a bore! [*To* Geneviève.] Where do they go every day at the same hour?

Geneviève. They say they go out for a drive, but no one ever sees them.

Pauline. A mystery!

Geneviève. I know, but I pretend not to: they visit the poor.

Pauline. But why the mystery?

Geneviève. Shouldn't charity always be secret?

Pauline. Yes, of course. [*To herself.*] Oh dear, what people! I don't know what to do next.

Geneviève. Where is Henri?

Pauline. I have no idea—probably visiting the poor.

Geneviève. He seems rather depressed lately.

Pauline. He's never been over-gay: he's a melancholy boy.

Geneviève. You don't know of any hidden trouble, do you?

Pauline. My dear, melancholy comes from the stomach. Healthy people are never melancholy; M. de Montrichard, for instance. [*She sits down.*]

Geneviève [*Smiling*]. He must have an extraordinary stomach!

Pauline. How clever he is and how gay!

Geneviève. He *is* amusing.

Pauline. And brave! He would make a woman very happy.

Geneviève. You say that as if Henri weren't making you happy?

Pauline. I am very happy, and Henri is charming to me. Only, Mme. de Montrichard would have no occasion to envy me. I should like to see you that woman.

Geneviève. Me?

Pauline. Haven't you noticed what marked attention he pays you?

Geneviève. No. Did he tell you——?

Pauline. What?

Geneviève. That he's paying attention to me?

Pauline. I observed that myself; it's as clear as day. He is in love with you.

Geneviève. Are *you* interested in him?

Pauline. Yes—because I love *you.*

Geneviève. Then be good enough to ask him to stop.

Pauline. Why? Don't you like him?

Geneviève [*Nervously*]. No more than I do anyone else. I'm never going to marry.

Pauline [*Rising*]. I'm surprised. I didn't think your religious devotion went so far as to eliminate marriage?

Geneviève. It isn't a matter of religion—it's only an idea of mine.

Pauline. Then you love someone you cannot marry?

Geneviève. I love no one——

Pauline. You are blushing. [*Drawing* GENEVIÈVE *to her.*] Now, Geneviève, confide in me—am I not your friend?

Geneviève. I tell you, I don't love anyone.

Pauline. Then you *did* love someone?

Geneviève. Let's not talk about it, please. [*Leaving* PAULINE.] I can't. [*She goes to the sofa.*]

Pauline. I understand! [*To herself.*] So much the better for Montrichard! [*To* GENEVIÈVE.] My dear, M. de Montrichard is not a man who cannot forgive a youthful slip. [*She goes to* GENEVIÈVE *again.*]

Geneviève. A youthful slip?

Pauline. He's the ideal husband for you. He'll never inquire into your past life, and if anyone should ever make the slightest allusion to——

Geneviève. To what?

Pauline. What you don't dare tell me— But don't blush, dear! [*She makes* GENEVIÈVE *sit down.*] What young girl hasn't been imprudent once in her life? You meet a handsome young man at a dance; he squeezes your hand; then perhaps you answer a note of his—[GENEVIÈVE *starts to get up again, but* PAULINE *detains her.*] and all in the most innocent possible way. Then you find you're compromised, without ever having done anything actually wrong.

Geneviève. Note? Compromised? I?

Pauline. Then what do you mean by saying you ought not to marry?

Geneviève [*Rising, with dignity*]. I mean, Madame, that there is a man whom I have been brought up to regard as my future husband, and—— But you wouldn't understand! You could suspect——! [*She turns her back to* PAULINE.]

Pauline. I am sorry if I hurt you, dear, but your reticence certainly led me to suppose—and you know I was only trying to be friendly!

Geneviève [*Giving* PAULINE *her hand*]. I was wrong!

Pauline. Now, be brave. There was a man, you say, whom you were brought up to regard as your future husband——?

Geneviève. I gave all I could—respect and submission—to this fiancé. I tried to think and act as he did. I was his companion in my secret thoughts—I—oh, I can't tell you ——! Now I feel like a widow.

Pauline. He's not dead?

Geneviève. Dead to me—he is married.

Pauline. There's no telling what men will do!

Geneviève. He hardly knew me. He met a woman who was worthy of him, and married her—and he was right.

Pauline. Then you should follow his example

Geneviève. With me it's different.

Pauline. Do you still love him?

Geneviève. Even if I once loved him, I should have no right to do so now; his heart belongs to another woman.

Pauline. I don't quite follow your subtle reasoning——

Geneviève. It's simply a matter of keys. [*They rise.*] A husband should be able to open every drawer belonging to his wife, should he not?

Pauline. Of course.

Geneviève. Here is a little gold key which I should have to keep from my husband.

Pauline. What does it open?

Geneviève. An ebony box containing my diary.

Pauline. Your diary?

Geneviève. Yes. My grandmother taught me, ever since the time I was a little child, to write down what I did and thought!

Pauline. How queer!

Geneviève. It's a very good thing to look into one's heart every day. If there are any weeds, it's easy to pluck them out before they take root.

Pauline. Away with dog's-grass, eh? And so you wrote down day by day this romance of yours? Metaphorically speaking, that is the key to your heart?

Geneviève. Exactly.

Pauline. You may as well make up your mind that someday someone will steal it.

Geneviève. In any event, it will not be M. de Montrichard.

Pauline. So much the worse for him—and you!

A Servant enters.

Servant. M. de Beauséjour.   [*He goes out.*

Geneviève. And still less *he!* I can't bear him, the smooth, bragging——! I'm going to dress.   [*She goes out.*

BAUDEL *comes in.*

Baudel. I hope I'm not driving anyone away?

Pauline. My cousin.

Baudel. I should regret it were I able to regret anything in your presence, Countess!

Pauline [*Going to get a small hand mirror which lies on a console table, to the right, and then motioning* BAUDEL *to a chair*]. Very gallant of you, I'm sure!

Baudel [*To himself*]. Alone, strange to say! Let us follow de Montrichard's advice, and may Buckingham preserve me! [*He brings a chair close to* PAULINE.]

Pauline [*Sitting on the sofa*]. Is M. de Montrichard sick, that we see Pylades[6] alone?

Baudel [*Sitting down*]. No, Madame, he is not. He will himself come to present his respects.

Pauline. Do you know, your friendship is worthy the age of chivalry?

Baudel. Cemented in our blood! I owe Montrichard a little revenge, and I shall soon pay my debt!

Pauline. What? Old friends like you?

Baudel. What can I do? He's absurd; he gets on my

---

[6] In Greek mythology, the loyal friend of Orestes. S.S.S.

nerves! Think of it, he persists in noticing your resemblance to——!

Pauline [*Looking at herself in the mirror*]. That poor girl who died in California. Yes. I know. Don't you agree with him?

Baudel. I confess there is something—she resembled you as the goose resembles the swan.

Pauline. She would thank you for that!

Baudel. She lacked that grace, that distinction, that eminently aristocratic air——!

Pauline. Yet Montrichard says we might be taken for sisters.

Baudel. Your homely sister, perhaps! [7] [*He laughs.*]

Pauline. Clever! But you're not at all gallant toward the woman you once loved—you did once love Olympe, didn't you?

Baudel. Not in the least, but she was wild about me!

Pauline. Really?

Baudel. I had the devil of a time making her listen to reason; she swore she was going to asphyxiate herself.

Pauline. Is it possible? Perhaps it was because of you that she went to California?

Baudel [*Rising*]. I am afraid so. Such is life: we love those who do not love us, and do not love those who love us. You are now taking revenge for that poor creature, Mme. la Comtesse.

Pauline. I thought I had forbidden that topic?

Baudel. What then shall I talk about?

Pauline [*Laying the mirror on the sofa*]. Anything else. What did you think of the affair last night?

Baudel. Charming.

Pauline. Take care, I'm laying a trap: I'm going to put your judgment to the test. What did you think of my neighbor?

Baudel. Which?

Pauline. The slim lady to my right, with a head like an ostrich's—whose feet stuck out so from under her dress?

Baudel. That's not kind of you. Well, one would have to be the devil of a naturalist to class her as mammiferous.

---

[7] An untranslatable pun on "soeur de laid": homely sister, and "soeur de lait": foster sister.

Pauline. Not bad. And the mistress of the house, with all her diamonds?

Baudel. I thought the diamonds superb.

Pauline. Like her teeth: half of them false! [*She rises.*]

Baudel [*To himself*]. What a change in her! [*To* PAULINE.] You are a connoisseur, then, Countess?

Pauline. Every woman is an amateur jewel connoisseur.

Baudel. Will you then kindly give me your opinion on this trifle? [*He takes a jewel case from his pocket and opens it.*]

Pauline. Very beautiful. That pearl on the clasp is magnificent. But what are you doing with such a river of jewels? [8]

Baudel. Making it flow—at the feet of—the feet of——

Pauline. Some danseuse, I'll wager.

Baudel. At the feet of—the most deserving.

Pauline. How lucky she is! [*She holds up the necklace so that it sparkles.*]

Baudel [*To himself*]. She does look like Olympe!

Pauline. You're a bad boy.

Baudel. Blame no one but yourself, Madame! [9]

Pauline. You are too clever. This necklace looks a trifle tight.

Baudel. Do you think so?

Pauline. Yes—see! [*She takes it from the box, then gets the mirror.* BAUDEL, *who has taken the box, lays it on the table and returns to* PAULINE, *who hands him the mirror. She then puts on the necklace.*] No, it's plenty large enough. [*To herself, as she looks at herself in the glass.*] How it shows off the complexion!

Baudel [*Aside*]. Montrichard was right; great ladies are as fond of jewels as the others are. What he knows about women——! Now—I—a countess's lover—that will certainly send me up in the world!

Pauline [*Unclasping the necklace*]. Take your diamonds to your danseuse now!

Baudel. After they have touched your neck? It would be the vilest profanation!

[8] "Rivière" means necklace.
[9] Still another pun: Pauline calls Baudel "a bad subject," and he replies that "bad sovereigns make bad subjects."

Pauline. Then what are you going to do with them?

Baudel. I shall keep them as a souvenir.

Pauline. No, no, I wouldn't allow that.

Baudel. Then, Countess, there is but one thing to do: keep them yourself as a souvenir of me, since you object to my having one of you.

Pauline. You're out of your senses! Are such things possible?

Baudel. Why ask? It's very simple. Would you not accept a bouquet of flowers? Diamonds are flowers—which last a long time—that is all.

Pauline. Do you think my husband would look at it in that light?

Baudel [*Laying the box on the table at the right*]. You might tell him that they're paste.

Pauline [*To herself*]. I never tnought of that! What a fool I am; I forget that I have a hundred thousand francs income! [*To* BAUDEL.] Let's not joke about it any longer, Monsieur. Take this back to the jeweller—that will be best. [*She gives him the necklace.*]

HENRI *enters*

Baudel [*To himself*]. Her husband, eh? [*To* HENRI.] How are you, M. le Comte? You're just in time to clear up a mystery of which I am the victim.

Henri. What is the mystery, Monsieur?

Baudel. Madame is trying to persuade me that these diamonds are only paste. [*He hands* HENRI *the necklace.*]

Pauline [*To herself*]. Who would have thought it of him?

Henri. I am no judge. [*To the Countess.*] Did you buy this, Madame?

Pauline. Yes, because of the setting.—It's an old one.— Quite a bargain.

Baudel. I confess my ignorance, Madame, and I promise to keep the secret of the marvellous paste diamonds. It will be to my credit that others are deceived by them. Are you going to wear it tonight at Mme. de Ransberg's?

Henri. Are you dining there, Monsieur?

Baudel. No, M. le Comte, but Montrichard is going to introduce me at the soirée afterward. I hope to make up at that time for not having seen you now, for I must go— [*Bowing.*] Mme. la Comtesse! M. le Comte! [*To himself.*] Things are going beautifully! [*He goes out.*

Henri. You have one great fault, Pauline: duplicity— and you don't scruple to act on every occasion——

Pauline. I don't see——?

Henri. Couldn't you tell me frankly if you wanted diamonds?

Pauline [*To herself*]. Water seeks the river—certainly in this case.[10]

Henri. I never refused you anything reasonable. As you are going into society, I realize you must have jewels, and if I have given you none so far, it was because I had not thought about it. But I repeat, I dislike this underhanded business. [*He gives her the necklace.*]

Pauline [*Taking it*]. I beg your pardon, dear. It was really so small a matter that I was ashamed to speak of it.

Henri. How much do you need for other jewels?

Pauline. Didn't your mother have a jewel-box?

Henri. Yes.

Pauline. Well?

Henri. Her diamonds became sacred objects when she died: they are not jewels, but remembrances. [*He goes to the left.*] Suppose I allow you fifty thousand francs? Is that enough?

Pauline. Thank you. [*A pause.*]

Henri [*Returning*]. Has my aunt gone out yet?

Pauline. Yes, with your uncle. May I ask where *you* have just come from?

Henri. A walk in the country.

Pauline. In those clothes?

Henri. No, I changed them when I came back.

Pauline [*Going to* HENRI]. Why didn't you take me?

Henri. You don't like walking—you prefer driving in the fashionable streets.

Pauline. But the country must be lovely!

Henri. It is.

Pauline. In all the melancholy splendor of autumn!

Henri. What dress are you going to wear tonight? [*He goes to the fireplace.*]

[10] See footnote, p. 194.

Pauline. Henri, you are vexed with me about something? What is it?

Henri. What?

Pauline. I ask you—evidently there is something. I have surely done nothing—have I given you reason to complain?

Henri. Have I given you any cause to be offended?

Pauline. The idea!

Henri. Please, Madame, let us leave these petty family quarrels to the lower classes! You are too dignified to stoop to that.

Pauline. I see: those awful suspicions are troubling you again!

Henri. I have no suspicions.

Pauline. You mean you are sure. Tell me, Henri; my conscience is perfectly clear, and I demand an explanation.

Henri. No use, Madame, you will never have occasion to complain of my attitude.

Pauline. That's complete estrangement, then! Do you think for one moment I'll accept that?

Henri. What difference does it make to you?

Pauline. Now, Henri, for the love of Heaven! Our happiness is at stake, don't you see? Let us both be frank. I'll set you an example: yes, in bringing you to Pilnitz, I knew we should meet your uncle.

Henri. His secretary did tell me of a letter you had written him——

Pauline [*To herself*]. I thought so!

Henri. But I didn't believe that: you promised me you didn't know—you swore on your mother's soul.

Pauline. I would have sworn on the soul of my own child, if I had had one, because you are dearer to me than the whole world, and my first duty is to make you happy! I wanted to bring you back into your proper surroundings again, and allow you to breathe the air that is natural to you—that was my only crime.

Henri. I appreciate what you have done.

Pauline. But the way you say it! Do you for one moment imagine that I was prompted by personal pride—that I wanted to play a part in society, and masquerade as a great society belle? An empty role, dear, and I am only too ready to relinquish it.

Henri. I can believe it!

Pauline. This artificial existence bores me.

Henri [*Sitting down*]. I know.

Pauline. Then what do you accuse me of?

Henri. Nothing. [*He goes to the right of the table and sits down again.*]

Pauline [*Sitting by him on a little table*]. Come, Monsieur, you mustn't scowl! Kiss your wife, who loves only you. [*She offers her forehead;* HENRI *touches it with his lips.*] Do you object to my little trick for getting the necklace? Don't scold me—I don't deserve it. I'm not going to society affairs any more. Then, that matter of your mother's jewels —that was tactless, indelicate of me. I should have realised that a saint's relics should belong only to an angel. Keep them, preserve them religiously, and if Heaven grants us the blessing of a daughter——

Henri [*Violently, as he rises*]. You—a daughter! She might resemble you!

Pauline. Henri! [*She tries to stand up, but he forces her back to her place.*]

Henri. Don't say a word! Let us have no more of this ridiculous farce! I know you only too well! All that virtue you assume so cleverly, your unselfishness, love, repentance —the whole thing has fallen from you like a load, like thick paint—in the warm atmosphere of this family circle! I can see! I am no longer the child you seduced!

Pauline [*Standing up*]. You grow younger, my dear: you had reached years of discretion when you married me.

Henri [*Sadly*]. Twenty-two! I had just lost my father, a man whose severity kept me a child when I should have been a young man. You were my first mistress—I knew nothing of life, except what you taught me. I wasn't hard to deceive; I made an easy rung in the ladder of your ambition.

Pauline. My ambition? Ha, how far has it gone? I'm really surprised at you! You might think I had lived a gay and merry life with you, alone for a year!

Henri. You may well regret all the wasted hours, after what I have just found out. The society our family moves in is not exactly what you had expected, I know, and *your* disappointment has opened my eyes. You feel that this is not quite your place—you feel ill at ease, out of your natural element; you cannot forgive the real society ladies for the superiority of their manners and their breeding——. [PAULINE *is about to speak.*] I can see how bitter you are from every word you speak. You cannot understand the true worth or the essential goodness of this family. You are bored, and as out of place as an unrepentant sinner in church——

Pauline [*Sharply*]. That will do! You don't love me, in other words. There is only one thing to do: separate—on friendly terms.

Henri. Separate? Never.

Pauline. Are you doing me the honor to want my company?

Henri. You bear my name, Madame, and I shall not allow it to be dragged in the gutter. [*A pause ensues.*] Now let us quietly accept the result of our act. We are bound together: let us walk side by side, and try not to hate each other.

Pauline. You will find that difficult.

Henri. Never fear: if I cannot forget how you became Countess de Puygiron, I shall never lose sight of the fact that you are she. Now, I have already shown you too much of what I feel—this explanation is at an end. Let us do our best to keep up appearances.

Pauline. A nice life to look forward to, isn't it?

GENEVIÈVE *enters in evening dress.*

Geneviève. Pauline, aren't you going to dress? They're coming for us soon.

Pauline. I forgot—I was talking with Henri. I'll hurry, though. [*She starts to go.*] Scold your cousin, dear; she wants to be an old maid!

Geneviève. Pauline!

Pauline. Henri is another edition of myself. She wants to remain an old maid in order to be faithful to a childhood husband who deserted her—for three dolls!

Henri [*Troubled*]. Geneviève——?

Geneviève. I don't know what she means?

Pauline [*To herself*]. How troubled they are!

Henri [*To* PAULINE]. You'll never be ready in time!

Pauline [*To herself*]. Ha, is *he* the childhood husband?

I'll soon find out! [*A gesture from* HENRI.] I'm going. You'll talk sense to her, won't you?   [*She goes out.*

Geneviève. Pauline doesn't know what she's talking about. She can't imagine a girl's not wanting to marry without there being some mystery.

Henri. Is it true that you don't intend to marry?

Geneviève. I don't exactly know, but I'm not prejudiced against marriage. I consider it the basis of home life, if not a religion in itself, and I should be too proud to accept a master who would not be a god for me.

Henri. You are right, Geneviève: wait for a man who is worthy of you.

Geneviève. My grandparents have given me so splendid an example of married life that I'd rather a thousand times go into a convent than marry for the sake of convenience, or because it's the thing to do. Rather than accept the first man who happens along——

Henri. The worst misfortune that can befall a human being is an uncongenial marriage.

Geneviève. And I'm so happy here—my people are so good to me! The man who takes me from my home will seem like a stranger—it would be like leaving a temple for an inn.

Henri [*To himself*]. Here was my happiness! So near at hand! [*He turns aside, putting his hand over his eyes.*]

Geneviève. What are you thinking of?

Henri. Nothing; I was looking at that portrait. [*He indicates the* MARQUISE'S *portrait, over the fireplace.*]

Geneviève. It seems to keep watch! How comforting it is! I feel that the whole house is protected by it.

Henri [*To himself, as he looks at the portrait*]. She would have been my mother! [*A servant enters, announces* MADAME MORIN *and goes out.*] Madame Morin?

IRMA *comes in.*

Irma. Where is she? Where is my daughter?—How are you, son-in-law?

Geneviève. How glad Pauline will be!

Irma. Where is she?

Geneviève. Dressing. Don't let her know you are here— we'll give her a surprise.

Irma. You must be her cousin, Mademoiselle? Fine young lady, well set-up! Kiss me, will you, angel?

Geneviève. Delighted, Madame. [*She goes toward* IRMA, *but* HENRI *quickly steps between the two.*]

Henri. To what do I owe the pleasure of seeing you, Madame?

Irma. My maternal affection. [*A carriage is heard outside.*]

Geneviève. Grandfather's coming. I'll tell him you're here.   [*She goes out.*

Henri. What do you want?

Irma. Well—have I a daughter or haven't I?

Henri. You haven't any longer. She is dead to you: you have inherited everything she possessed.

Irma. My dear, that inheritance has taken wings! I've speculated.

Henri. I see. How much will you take to go?

Irma. Heavens! He wants to buy a mother's love!

Henri. I'll give you an income of fifteen hundred francs.

Irma. I must have my daughter.

Henri. Three thousand.

Irma. You poor boy!

Henri. Come, Madame, they'll be here shortly. Tell me how much you'll take.

Irma. Five thousand.

Henri. Very well. But you leave tomorrow morning?

Irma. All right.

Henri. Sh! Here's my uncle.

The MARQUIS *comes in.*

Marquis. I am very glad to see you, Mme. Morin.

Irma. M. le Marquis, the honor is mine.

Marquis. As the mother of a charming daughter! True!

Irma. Excuse my travelling clothes—I should have fixed up a little, but I so wanted to see my girl!

Marquis. Very natural, but your Breton costume would have been dear to the eyes of an old Chouan.[11] It was very wrong of you not to wear it.

Henri [*To* IRMA]. Pretend to understand!

Irma. Oh, one can't travel in such a costume.

---

[11] A member of the band of royalist peasantry who joined the Vendéans in 1793. See footnote, p. 168. S.S.S.

Marquis [*To* Henri]. She looks like a clothes dealer—
but your wife will see to that. [*Aloud.*] Will you see that
Madame's room is made ready?

Irma. A thousand thanks, M. le Marquis, but I'm only
passing through the city. I must leave for Danzig tomorrow
morning.

Marquis. And why must you go to Danzig so soon?

Irma. To collect a debt of a hundred thousand francs. I'll
lose it if I don't go tomorrow. Ask my son-in-law.

Henri. That's so.

Marquis. Then I have nothing further to say. But you
will see us on your return?

Irma. You are too good, M. le Marquis.

Marquis. I should like to know you better. We'll talk
about Brittany—in Breton.

Irma [*To herself*]. Good Lord!

Henri. I think it's time to go to Mme. de Ransberg's,
Uncle. Pauline may stay with her mother: it will be an excellent excuse.

Marquis. Very true.

> *The* Marquise *and* Geneviève *enter.*

Marquise. You are very welcome, Madame.

Marquis. My wife—Madame Morin.

Irma [*Confused*]. Madame—I—this honor—

Marquise. You find your daughter surrounded here only
by friends, Madame.

Irma. Oh, of course—Madame—Madame is too good!

> Pauline *enters in evening dress, wearing the necklace.*

Pauline. Are you ready?

Marquis. You won't have to go, dear.

Pauline. Why? [Geneviève *takes her hand and conducts
her to* Irma.] Mother! [*She steps back, looking nervously at
the* Marquis.]

Irma. Yes, dearie, it's me!

Marquis [*To the* Marquise]. We're in the way here.—
We are now obliged to leave you, Madame; we are dining
out.

Marquise. We should be very sorry, Madame, to be in the
way—you must want to give free rein to your feelings.

Irma. Oh, I—please——

Geneviève [*To* PAULINE]. What lovely diamonds!

Marquis. Well, well, Henri *is* gallant!

Pauline. They're only paste—I just thought it would be amusing to have them!

Marquise. Marvellous imitation—that pearl especially! But, my dear, the Countess de Puygiron should never wear artificial pearls!—Good evening, Madame. [*She takes* HENRI'S *arm,* GENEVIÈVE *takes that of the* MARQUIS, *and they go out. It begins to grow dark.* PAULINE *waits a moment until the others are out of hearing.*]

Pauline. Oh, Mother, how glad I am to see you! [*She kisses her.*] What is going on in Paris? How is Céleste? And Clémence? And Taffétas? Ernest? Jules? Gontran? And how was the ballet at the Opéra? And the Maison d'Or? And the Mont-de-Piété?

Irma. Oh, my!

Pauline. I've been dying to know for a whole year! Let me take off my corsets! God, it's fine to talk with you, Mother, for a minute!

Irma. Pauline's herself again! I knew all this greatness wouldn't change you. You're always the same.

Pauline. More than ever. Did the news of my death make much of a stir in Paris?

Irma. I should say it did! What a lot of people went to your funeral! More than to La Fayette's! I was awfully proud to be your mother—take my word for it!

Pauline. Poor dear! But here I am rattling along—maybe you'd like something to eat?

Irma. Give me some fruit—fresh. It's six o'clock.

Pauline. I forgot—happiness of seeing you! [*She rings.*]

Irma. I'm all excited! [IRMA *takes off her hat and cloak.*]

A Servant enters.

Pauline. Lay places for two. [*To* IRMA.] Shall we eat here?

Irma. Suits me down to the ground.

Pauline [*To the servant, severely*]. You hear? And don't take an hour for it, either!

Servant [*To himself*]. As if I were a dog!   [*He goes out.*

Pauline [*Returning to* IRMA]. What did the girls think of my trick?

Irma. They were all jealous of the gorgeous funeral. Clémence threw herself into my arms and cried: "The idea! Oh, my!"

Pauline. Poor creature! Who's she with now?

Irma. Don't talk about it! She's got better luck than an honest woman! A fine general: fifteen thousand a year!

Pauline. I was a bigger fool than she! [*The Servant brings a table and sets it.*]

Irma. Aren't you happy?

Enter ADOLPHE.

Adolphe. I beg your pardon, Mme. la Comtesse, for the liberty I am taking of——

Pauline. Be seated, Monsieur.

The Servant brings in the dessert.

Adolphe. The day after tomorrow our theatre is to give a performance for my benefit, and I thought that as a compatriot, you would be glad to take a box. Will you be so good as to accept this? [*He gives a ticket to* MONTRICHARD, *who has entered meanwhile, and who hands it to* PAULINE.]

Pauline. Many thanks, Monsieur. I am told that you do impersonations?

Adolphe. Yes, Madame, I owe my success in a foreign country to that.

Pauline. If you are not occupied this evening, we should be delighted to hear you.

Adolphe. Charmed, Madame.

Pauline [*To the servant*]. Bring me another glass, and then go. [*The glass is brought and filled with wine.*] Here, M. Adolphe, drink this.

Adolphe. Thank you, Madame, but champagne does not agree with me.

Irma. It's *Cliquot*, old man; you can't get drunk on that. Here's to you!

Adolphe [*After drinking*]. It's good!

Irma [*Pouring out another glassful for him*]. Say, little one, you squint, don't you?

Adolphe. Yes, Madame, that squint was what induced me to go into comic impersonation.

Montrichard. And is to give us the pleasure of hearing you! [ADOLPHE *drinks.*]

Pauline. Sing us a song, M. Adolphe.

Adolphe. Le Petit cochon de Barbarie? [IRMA *again fills his glass.*]

Pauline. No, a student song!

Adolphe. I don't know any.

Montrichard. But you look as if you'd been a notary's clerk?

Adolphe. I have, Monsieur.

Pauline. You have?

Adolphe. Yes, I come of a good family, Madame; my father was one of the biggest hardware merchants in Paris. He wanted me to go into the law, but an irresistible sense of vocation drove me to the boards. [*He drinks.*]

Montrichard. Your father must have been very angry?

Adolphe. He even refused to allow me to use his name— said I was soiling it by dragging it before the footlights.

Pauline. What *is* his name?

Adolphe. Mathieu.

Montrichard. It would have been downright sacrilege!

Irma. Here's to you, then, son of Mathieu! I like you! You're not handsome and you're something of a fool, but you're nice and simple!

Adolphe [*Displeased*]. Madame!

Irma. Now you mustn't be angry, little one! I was only joking! [*She rises, holding a bottle in one hand and a glass in the other.*] You're good-looking, good-looking—between squints!

Pauline. Come now, let's put our elbows on the table and say foolish things! Why, I can almost imagine myself at the *Provençaux*—I'm born again!

Montrichard [*To himself*]. Homesickness for the mud!

Irma. Can't see decently in here! And I don't like to say foolish things in the dark! [*She hands the bottle to* ADOLPHE.]

Montrichard. Someone'll get wounded!

Pauline [*Taking a candle from the table and putting it in one of the candelabra*]. Let's light all the candles! Help me, Montrichard.

Montrichard. I don't know how many there are—but before long Irma's going to see thirty-six.

Adolphe. Well, I see fifteen. [PAULINE *and* MONT-RICHARD *stand on chairs at either side of the fireplace and light the large candelabra between which hangs the portrait.*]

Irma. A picture? What is it?

Pauline. A barometer.

Irma. That barometer looks to me like an old lady.

Montrichard [*To* PAULINE]. Hm! What if she should come in now?

Pauline. Let them all come! They can send me to the devil with their five hundred thousand francs, if they like!

Adolphe [*Who has taken* MONTRICHARD'S *place*]. I'd like to suggest a toast.

Irma [*Coming downstage on the right*]. Go ahead, but try to be respectable.

Montrichard. Wait for us. [*Near the table.*] We're listening.

Adolphe. To that enchanting sex which is the charm and torment of our existence—in a word: the ladies!

Montrichard. You *are* rather forward, M. Adolphe!

Irma. I call it *risqué!*

Pauline. Comes from a fortunate man, evidently.

Adolphe. Yes, Madame——

Montrichard. You must have all sorts of affairs, a man like you, so exposed in the theatre——

Adolphe [*Fatuously*]. I must admit that opportunities are not lacking.

Montrichard. Then what is, for the love of Heaven?

Adolphe. I'm a respectable man: I'm married.

Pauline. A very grave fault—you must try to redeem yourself.

Irma. And look after your wife! Take my advice!

Adolphe. I beg you, respect the mother of my children!

Montrichard. Oh, Adolphe, hast thou children?

Adolphe. Three: all my living image!

Pauline. I pity the youngest.

Adolphe. Why?

Pauline. He has the longest time during which to resemble you!

Montrichard. All children begin by looking like papa, and end by resembling their father!

Irma. "The voice of blood" is a prejudice.

Pauline [*Raising her glass*]. Down with prejudices! **Down** with the family! Down with marriage! Down with the marquis!

Montrichard. Down with hardware merchants!

Adolphe. Down with hardware merchants!

Irma. Long live us!

Pauline [*Singing*]:

> When you haven't any money
>   And you write to your dad,
> And he answers, "Don't get funny;
>   Don't make love on my cash, lad,
> You can't make love on that,
> And turn night into day———"

[*All join in the refrain, clinking their knives on the glasses.* ADOLPHE *falls from his chair, and* IRMA *gradually dozes.*]

Montrichard [*To himself*]. And to think of all she did in order to become a countess!

Pauline [*Dreamily*]. The dear old songs of my youth! Those lovely old dresses and scarves I used to wear! The dances at the *Chaumière*—dinners at the *Moulin-Rouge*— the old mill I used to throw my hat over! I can see a young girl living in an attic; one day she runs off over the fields to meet her lover for the first time. And the sun! "Open the door, please!"

Irma [*Half-asleep*]. Ah!

Montrichard [*To himself*]. I thought so!

Adolphe [*Rising, quite drunk*]. I tell you—I'm not bad-looking!

Pauline. Then you're a blackguardly imposter! Take off your false nose and your china eyes!

Montrichard. Take off his head, while we're about it!

Adolphe. My wife thinks I'm very distinguished looking.

Pauline. She's unfaithful to you!

Adolphe. Oh, if I thought so———!

Montrichard. You may be sure she isn't, old man! You should never doubt your wife!

Adolphe. Would you swear it on the head of this respectable lady?

Montrichard. Lend me your head, Irma; I should like to oblige this gentleman.

Adolphe [*Sobbing*]. How unhappy I am! She's deceiving me, I know——!

Pauline. How about your good looks, now, you fool?

Irma. There's a fine comedian for you!

Adolphe [*Falling into* IRMA's *arms*]. You, my mother, you understand me!

Irma [*Repulsing him*]. Here now, you fool! Tell us something funny; you came here to make us laugh.

Adolphe. That's right—well—a baptism song! [*He sings*]:

> Little Léon, on his mother's breast
> Was never unhappy——

[*He stops, sobbing again.*] My poor children! They are unhappy.

Pauline. What? Your children?

Adolphe. I bought my wife a cake yesterday, and I haven't paid the baker yet! [*He falls down into his chair.*]

Montrichard [*To himself*]. Poor devil!

Irma. Look, Minette, he's a good-hearted fellow. He's ruining himself for women.

Pauline. Don't cry, baby, we won't send you away empty-handed! Montrichard, give him my purse.

Montrichard [*To* PAULINE]. Charity will be your ruin. [*Giving* ADOLPHE *the purse.*] Here you are, old man.

Adolphe [*Rejecting it*]. No. Monsieur, no—I receive money only from my manager—when he gives it to me. This would be charity. Thank you, I come of a good family!

Pauline. I feel so sorry for him. I don't like to see misery at such close quarters.

Irma. If he's proud, it's his own loss!

Pauline. What *can* I make him accept? [*She quickly takes the pearl from her necklace and gives it to* ADOLPHE.] Here, baby, here's a little trinket for your wife. You can't refuse that.

Adolphe. You are very kind, Mme. la Comtesse. [*He kisses her hand.*]

Pauline. It's late—you must go home now. Take him to

the door, Montrichard. [IRMA *fills* ADOLPHE's *pockets with the remains of the dessert.*]

Montrichard. Take my arm, M. Adolphe. [*To himself.*] Olympe is herself again! God knows where she'll end now!

Adolphe [*To* PAULINE]. You're an angel. [*To* IRMA.] You're both angels.

Montrichard. Don't say that! They won't believe you!

Adolphe [*To* MONTRICHARD]. So are you!

Montrichard. Of course I am. So are you—an impossible angel. Come now, son of Mathieu! [*They go out.*

Irma [*Yawning and stretching herself*]. What an idea! To give him an artificial pearl!

Pauline. Artificial? It's worth at least a thousand francs.

Irma [*Sitting up*]. A thousand francs? Are you crazy?

Pauline. What of it? I didn't have anything else handy. [*Brooding for an instant.*] It will bring me luck! My separation will be a success!

Irma. Got a pack of cards around here?

Pauline [*Taking a candelabrum and going toward the door leading to her room*]. Not here, but I have in my room. Why?

Irma [*Following her*]. I want to try—see how you'll succeed.

Pauline. Do you still believe in card tricks?

Irma. Do I? That's the only thing that's dead certain!

Pauline. Nonsense!

Irma. Stop it! You'll come to some bad end if you don't believe in something.

Pauline. I rely on myself. [*Taking up the candelabrum which she had set down.*]

Irma. You're right; we must help ourselves; then Heaven will help us.

Pauline. Yes, Heaven!

Irma. Figuratively speaking. Now for the cards!

Pauline. My separation!

[*They go out at the left. As* IRMA *passes the* MARQUISE's *portrait, she bows ceremoniously to it.*

ACT THREE

The scene is the same as that of the preceding act. MONT-
RICHARD *and a servant are present.*

SERVANT. Mme. la Comtesse asks M. le Baron to be good
enough to wait a moment for her. Here are the newspapers.
                                                    [*He goes out.*
   Montrichard. Do I arrive in the midst of a crisis? Hardly
tactful, but what's the odds? If I don't succeed in marrying
this lady, I can easily find another. Now I am really quite a
catch. But then why should I marry at all?

                    PAULINE *comes in.*

   Pauline. How are you, M. de Corbeau?[12]
   Montrichard. Do I seem handsome[13] to you?
   Pauline. As everything does which one is on the point of
losing?
   Montrichard. Oh, have I been fortunate enough to cause
you some anxiety, Mme. la Comtesse?
   Pauline. Even sleeplessness—or rather, nightmares. How
inconsiderate of you to stay at Homburg for a week without
writing a line! I dreamed of you as having lost every sou, and
your head was bound up in bloody bandages!
   Montrichard. And you shed a tear for me? Mourned by
Olympe—what an occasion for a beautiful death! I've always missed the exact occasion. Far from blowing out my
brains, I blew up the bank! [14]
   Pauline. Really?
   Montrichard. As really as I have the honor to announce
the news to you.
   Pauline [*Enthusiastically*]. What a man! And what luck!
And you wonder why women love and admire you! If you
were only willing, it wouldn't be that fool Baudel who'd
abduct me——!

[12] Literally, "crow," used in the sense of "vulture."
[13] A pun on "beau": handsome, and "corbeau."
[14] A pun on "sauter la cervelle" and "sauter la banque."

Montrichard. It would be that ass Montrichard—but **you** would be a greater fool than he!

Pauline [*Laughing*]. That's true enough.

Montrichard. What is this joke about the abduction?

Pauline. It's a very serious matter. I have made up my mind to kick over the traces, and I've chosen M. de Beauséjour as my accomplice.

Montrichard. But I was told at his rooms this morning that he went away last night?

Pauline. Yes—to Nice.

Montrichard. But why without you?

Pauline. I remain to negotiate with the honorable family for an amicable separation.

Montrichard. Which you hope to obtain?

Pauline. Which I am sure to obtain. There is an element of chance, because I intend to impose my own conditions; but since yesterday I have found very persuasive arguments, and I assure you everything will be arranged. They thought that when I entered their family I dishonored it! Watch my exit!

Montrichard. But why didn't Baudel wait for you?

Pauline. First, I wanted to get some precious possessions safe out of the way. He took them with him.

Montrichard. Your diamonds?

Pauline. Other things, too. Then he must find a place for me to stay. Do you think I want to stop at a hotel? I'm tired of this life of the past eighteen months. I'm going to make up for lost time, make no mistake about that!

Montrichard. Poor Baudel! Be a good girl, now, Countess, and don't ruin the boy!

Pauline. He will get just what he deserves, he, the prince of fools!

Montrichard. But he's a dear child.

Pauline. Think so? Do you know, he had the audacity to claim that he'd once been Olympe Taverny's lover?

Montrichard. While as a matter of fact he only belonged to the number of those who had not?

Pauline. Now, now——

Montrichard. I beg your pardon, Countess—if I dare still call you by that name?

Pauline. You may dare, old man; I'm not going to drop it.

Montrichard. Maybe the Puygirons will drop it for you?

Pauline. I'd rather give up my money. Their name's a gold mine, dear.

Montrichard. But what if they offered some compensation?

Pauline. They? Poor people! I don't advise them to. I tell you I *have* them!

Montrichard. So tight as that?

Pauline. Yes. I've not lost much time since you've been away: I've been working this last week.

Montrichard. Oh, don't tell me——

Pauline. You're afraid of being dragged in as an accomplice?

Montrichard. I want to be nothing in all this business but a sort of good genius—and then——

Pauline. Then? What do you mean?

Montrichard. That this marriage of mine——well, I'm not so anxious about it now.

Pauline. What!

Montrichard. I'm not ready to make a fool of myself that way until I have nothing left with which to commit more follies. Now I have cash. In the second place, I don't think the young lady is especially attracted to me. If, therefore, she were forced to take me for want of a better, she would have her revenge on me! I should be paying dear! I'd rather she went into a convent than I!

Pauline. I shan't insist, if you look at it in that light. And I must say the child doesn't love you—she loves someone else.

Montrichard. I suspected it.

Pauline. Do you know who that someone is? I give you a hundred guesses.—My husband!

Montrichard. Who said so? She?

Pauline. She has no idea I know.

Montrichard. How did this hopeless love take root?

Pauline. It's not hopeless—that's the nicest part of the business. She's taken it into her head that I'm a consumptive, that I haven't more than six months to live. I don't know where she got that idea!

Montrichard [*To himself*]. I wonder!

Pauline. And she's waiting for my death with angelic serenity. That's the way with these angels! Dealers in morality! Good Lord, *we're* better than they! Don't you think so?

Montrichard. Well, between the person who sets a trap and the one who allows himself to be caught there's hardly a hair's difference. So, I get off scot free, thanks to you——

Pauline. And now that you know how matters stand, be good enough to go away. My dressmaker is waiting for me: I must have a serious talk with her. You don't have to think hard to know I'm not going to show off on the *Promenade des Anglais* those monastic weeds that captured simple Henri's heart!

Montrichard. Shall I see you again, then?

Pauline. In this family, no, but I have a notion you'll walk into Nice some day and want to be set on your feet again.

Montrichard. That reminds me! [*Taking out his pocketbook.*] Will you do me a favor? Take this check on the Bank of France to Baudel. I intended to give it to him this morning as soon as he was up——

Pauline. For fifty thousand francs? What is this?

Montrichard. A loan.

Pauline. Do you still continue to pay your debts, you overgrown child?

Montrichard. None of us is perfect!

Pauline. If I were you, Baron, I should keep that little check—for a rainy day.

Montrichard. No, no, it might rain on me before it does on him, and I should be forced to use it. Let us keep our honor intact!

Pauline. Take this back. I don't like to carry scraps of paper worth so much.

Montrichard. Very well. I'll send it through the banker. Good-bye, Contesina. [*He kisses her hand.*]

Pauline. Good-bye, Baronino. [*He goes out.*] What a queer mixture! I thought he had more backbone! Really, I think there *is* no perfect man!

Geneviève comes in, looking for something.

Pauline. Good morning, Geneviève.

Geneviève. I beg your pardon, I didn't see you! How are you this morning?

Pauline. Very well, as usual.

Geneviève. As usual!

Pauline. Were you looking for something?

Geneviève. A little gold key I lost yesterday.

Pauline. The key to the famous box? The key to your heart?

Geneviève. That's the one.

Pauline. I told you someone would steal it.

Geneviève. Oh, I'll find it.

Pauline [*Putting on her hat*]. You can find everything except lost time——

Geneviève. Are you going out?

Pauline. To the dressmaker's.

Geneviève. Can you think of dresses——?

Pauline. This is a happy day for me.

Geneviève. You're better, then?

Pauline. Little Miss Obstinate, I'm as healthy as possible.

Geneviève. You said something very different the other day.

Pauline. No matter what happens, don't forget that you've sworn never to repeat a single word of what I told you.

Geneviève. It's not fair to make me promise that—please don't keep me to it.

Pauline. I must. If you talk too much to your grandparents about me, they're likely to want to look after my welfare a little too carefully. I couldn't remain here! Now, let's say nothing more about it.

Geneviève. But I shall at least have done all I could?

Pauline. Yes, your conscience may be clear! See you later, angel.   [*She goes out.*

Geneviève. I have an idea—but how can I open the subject with grandfather and grandmother? [*She sits down, her head resting on her hand. She is plunged in thought.*] Oh, Henri! My dear Henri!

The Marquis *and the* Marquise *come in.*

Marquis [*Pointing to* Geneviève]. What is she thinking about? Statue of meditation!

Marquise. She looks very sad.

Marquis. Very.—What's the trouble, dear?

Geneviève [*Startled*]. I didn't know you were there!

Marquise. Didn't you hear us come in? What awful thought was absorbing you so?

Marquis. Has someone troubled you?

Geneviève. Oh, no.

Marquise. Do you want anything?

Geneviève. No. [*Interrupting herself.*] That is——

Marquis. That is—yes. Come now, don't sulk—what is it?

Geneviève. I want to see Italy!

Marquis. What? Italy—right off, at once?

Geneviève. It's the spleen—I don't like Vienna. I'll be sick if I stay here any longer.

Marquise. How long have you felt this way?

Geneviève. For a long time. I didn't intend to say any-thing about it— I hoped I should get over the feeling. But it only gets worse. Please—take me to Rome!

Marquis. This isn't reasonable!

Marquise. Silly idea of a spoiled child!

Geneviève. No, I declare it isn't. I must make that trip. I don't usually take advantage of your kindness, do I? You don't know what it's costing me now to ask you to break in on your quiet life, your regular habits——

Marquis. Oh, our habits! The main consideration is that you should be happy, and it seems that you are not that here. What do you say, Madame?

Marquise. We are at home wherever Geneviève is happy.

Geneviève. Well, if you take me to Rome, I promise to sing like a songbird from morning to night; you'll have me with you all day; there won't be any dances to deprive you of your granddaughter. We'll have such a good time together!

Marquis. All together!

Geneviève. You can teach Pauline and me whist.

Marquis. Is Pauline to come?

Geneviève. Of course—it's to be a family party! Every evening you'll have your little game just as you do here, only it'll be nicer. I'll be your partner and you may scold me every time I make you lose a king. Here you don't dare scold grandmother!

Marquis. Well, I don't say no to that. If the Marquise consents, we'll talk it over later.

Geneviève. Talk it over?

Marquis. We must have some time to become accustomed to the idea.

Geneviève. And you will show me Rome yourself, grandfather. All young women go there with their husbands, who explain the sights to them. But I'd rather go with you.

Marquise. She's right, dear; we should take advantage of the time she is still with us.

Marquis. If someone had told me an hour ago that we should spend the winter in Rome I should certainly have been surprised!

Geneviève. Then you will? Oh, thank you!

Marquise. She's looking better already.

Geneviève. When do we leave?

Marquis [*Laughing*]. Give me my cane and hat.

Marquise. How much time will you give us to get ready?

Geneviève. I'll get ready for you—you have only to step into the carriage.

Marquis. Give us a week.

Geneviève. Too long. You'd have time to change your mind!

Marquise. Four days?

Geneviève. Three.

Marquis. You'll sing, you say, from morning to night?

Geneviève. And I'll play whist with you.—I'll read your paper.—I'll do anything you like! I do love you so! [*She throws herself into his arms.*]

Marquise. Really, I like the idea of this trip. Shall we leave tomorrow?

Geneviève. I gave you three days—I'm reasonable! We must have time to persuade Pauline and Henri.

Marquise. I hardly think they'll object.

Geneviève. If they do—well, you're the head of the family, grandfather; use your authority.

Marquis. It seems to me that you are the head of the family!

Geneviève. I warn you now that if Pauline doesn't come with us, I shan't go. If you're anxious for the trip you must induce her to come, too.

Marquis. Very well, Mademoiselle, I shall make use of my authority. [*To the* MARQUISE.] When we have great-grandchildren, they'll make us walk about on all fours!

A Servant enters.

Servant. This gentleman [*showing card*] would like to see M. le Marquis.

Marquis [*Taking the card*]. Mathieu—Adolphe. I don't know him. What does the gentleman look like?

Servant. He is an actor I once saw at a little theatre—I believe he is the same one.

Marquis. What can he want with me? An artist, a Frenchman? Ask him to come in.   [*The Servant goes out.*

Marquis [*To* GENEVIÈVE]. Go to your room.

[GENEVIÈVE *goes out.*

ADOLPHE *comes in.*

Adolphe. Forgive me for disturbing you, Monsieur and Madame. I wished to see Mme. la Comtesse, but she is out, and I took the liberty of——

Marquis. Very glad to see you, my dear Monsieur—I have always had a liking for artists.

Adolphe. I beg your pardon, Monsieur, but it is not as an artist that I come to see you, but as a man. You see before you a prodigal son who was drawn to the footlights by an irresistible sense of vocation, but who in leaving the stage has found again the position and manners befitting his status.

Marquis [*Dryly*]. That is different.—What can I do for you?

Adolphe. Let us go back a little, if you please. I lately had the honor of sitting at your table.

Marquis. My table? Are you dreaming, Monsieur?

Adolphe. Not in the least. The scene—there is no other word for it—took place in this very room. There is the picture which we illuminated. [*Looking at the* MARQUISE.] An

excellent likeness, Madame, very noble! My compliments!
Good portraits are so rare nowadays! I wanted to have one
of Mme. Mathieu——

Marquis. Indeed, Monsieur?

Marquise. When was this?

Adolphe. Last Saturday.

Marquise [To her husband]. The day Mme. Morin came.
We were dining out.

Adolphe. Yes, you were not at home. There were four of
us; your charming niece, an elderly lady—very distinguished
looking—a gay gentleman, and your humble servant, who
had the good fortune to happen in at the time.

Marquis. What brought you?

Adolphe. I came to offer a box for my benefit performance.

Marquis. Then why not come to the point at once, Monsieur? I don't go to the theatre any longer, but, as a compatriot, I am ready to subscribe.

Adolphe. Very kind of you, but the performance took
place yesterday.

Marquis. Was it successful?

Adolphe. We didn't cover expenses.

Marquise. I see. What is the price of my box?

Adolphe. I was not asking for charity, Monsieur. My
father was a gentleman, one of the largest hardware merchants in Paris.

Marquis [Smiling]. Noblesse oblige! I had no intention
of offending you, Monsieur.

Marquise. We are ready to offer any excuses.

Adolphe. I ask for none, Madame.

Marquis [Offering him a chair]. Sit down. [*Taking his
snuffbox from his pocket and handing it to* ADOLPHE.] Will
you have some snuff?

Adolphe. Just a pinch.

Marquis. How do you like it?

Adolphe. It's delicious! So—where was I?

Marquis. At the table——

Adolphe. Oh, yes. After dinner, I was asked to sing.
Naturally, I couldn't think of receiving money for my serv-
ices, because I acted in my capacity of man of the world.
Then Mme. la Comtesse induced me to accept this pearl—

as a present to my wife. [*He takes the pearl from his pocket.*]

Marquise [*Quickly*]. Let me see it, Monsieur. [*She takes it.*] Didn't this belong to a diamond necklace?

Adolphe. Yes, Madame.

Marquis [*To himself*]. Very bad taste on her part!

Adolphe. I wanted to keep it as a souvenir, but you see I was counting on that blessed benefit yesterday to pay off some debts——

Marquis. Are you in debt?

Adolphe. Gambling debts. [*To himself.*] At the bakery! [*To the others.*] They fall due in twenty-four hours, you understand, so that I had to take this to the jeweller's.

Marquis. And he told you what it was worth?

Adolphe. Yes, Monsieur. Now, I can hardly believe that Mme. la Comtesse intended to make me so valuable a present.

Marquis. So valuable!

Adolphe. The jeweller offered me a thousand florins.

Marquise. Then it's real. [*She knocks the pearl against the table.*] Yes, it is!

Marquis. What does this mean?

Adolphe. What do you think? That I came here to ask for money? Nothing of the kind——!

Marquis. You bring it! Shake hands, Monsieur, you are a true gentleman. As for that pearl, my niece *did* know what she was doing when she gave it to you—it is yours. But please allow me to buy it from you. I should like to return it to her. [*He takes some banknotes from his pocketbook.*]

Adolphe. Ah, M. le Marquis!

Marquise [*To the* MARQUIS]. Poor fellow, he's so embarrassed!

Marquis. Since you seem to like my snuff, allow me to present the box to you—as a souvenir. [*He takes out his snuffbox.*]

Adolphe. M. le Marquis, I promise you I shall always keep it.

Marquis. Au revoir, my friend.

Adolphe. Then you will allow me to come and see you occasionally?

Marquis. Honest people like yourself are always welcome in the homes of honest people like ourselves.

Adolphe. M. le Marquis, you have given me a signal honor!

Marquis [*Laughing*]. The Order of the Snuffbox. [ADOLPHE *goes out.*] A fine fellow—and he carries away with him one of my old-fashioned prejudices.

HENRI *enters.*

Here, nephew, give this pearl to your wife, and ask her not to play any more tricks on us. In other words, ask her not to try to deceive us with any more paste imitations!

Henri [*Going to the* MARQUISE]. What's this?

Marquise. This pearl is real; so are the diamonds, in all probability.

Henri. Then why did she lie to us?

Marquise. Probably she was afraid you would scold her for her extravagance.

Henri. I gave her fifty thousand francs with which to buy jewels. She should have told me she'd spent some of the money in advance.

Marquise. False pride, perhaps.

Henri. Possibly.

Marquis. Here she is. I shall take particular pleasure in making it embarrassing for her!

Enter PAULINE, *wearing her hat.* HENRI *goes to the left and watches her intently.*

You're just in time, niece. We were speaking of your paste imitations and marvelling at the immense progress in chemistry.

Pauline [*Taking off her hat and shawl*]. Diamonds are so cleverly imitated that it is almost impossible to distinguish the artificial ones from the real.

Marquis. Will you show me your necklace?

Pauline. I haven't it any longer—I sent it back to the jeweller's.

Marquis. Why?

Pauline. Madame told me that the Countess de Puygiron should not wear artificial jewels.

Marquise. Take care, child.

Henri. Aunt!

Marquise. No, I don't want to see her any more involved in her lie. We know that the stones are real.

Pauline. Well—I confess——

Marquis. That you haven't returned them to the jeweller's?

Pauline. I did return them! Yes! I was afraid the trick would be discovered—so I put an end to all that nonsense!

Henri. How much did you lose on the exchange?

Pauline. Nothing.

Henri. Nothing at all?

Pauline. Of course not.

Henri. Not even the price of this pearl? [*He shows her the pearl.*]

Pauline [*To herself*]. The devil! [*To the others.*] I didn't want you to know—I was going to pay for it out of my savings.

Henri. Where does the jeweller live?

Pauline. Never mind, I'll see to it.

Henri. Where does he live?

Pauline. Monsieur, the way you insist——!

Henri. Answer me and don't lie!

Pauline. Do you suspect something?

Henri [*Violently*]. Yes, I suspect that these diamonds were given you by M. de Beauséjour!

Pauline. Oh, Henri!

Marquise. Remember, she's your wife!

Henri. If I am mistaken, let her give me the address of the jeweller, and I'll make sure at once.

Pauline. No, Monsieur, I refuse to stoop in order to justify myself. Your suspicion is too vile. Believe what you like.

Henri. You forget that you have no right to be so haughty about it.

Pauline. And why, if you please? I defy you to say!

Henri. You defy me?

Marquis. You don't know what you are saying, my boy. It is very wrong, of course, for your wife to be so obstinate, but what the devil! think of it; you're accusing her of an infamy!

Marquise [*To* PAULINE]. Pauline, take pity on him! He doesn't know what he is saying. Prove that he's wrong.

Pauline. No, Madame, I shan't say another word.

Henri. She's vile! She sold herself!

Marquis. Henri, your conduct is not that of a gentleman! Ask your wife's pardon.

Henri. I beg *your* pardon—all of you! That woman is Olympe Taverny! [*The* MARQUIS *is thunderstruck. The* MARQUISE *stands at his side.* PAULINE *is at the right,* HENRI *at the left.* HENRI *goes to his uncle, and falls to his knees.*] Forgive me, father, for having dishonored the name you bear, for having allowed that woman to impose on me, for having polluted this pure house by her presence!

Marquis. I disown you!

Marquise. But he loved her then, and thought her worthy of us, because he believed her worthy of himself. This marriage was the fault of his youth, not a crime against his honor as a man. Don't disown him, dear—he is very unhappy! [*After a pause, the* MARQUIS *offers his hand to* HENRI *and helps him rise, without looking at him.* HENRI *kisses his aunt's hands profusely.*]

Henri. A duel to the end with M. de Beauséjour now—pistols—ten paces!

Marquis. Good! I'll be your second! [HENRI *goes out. The* MARQUIS *opens a drawer and takes out a case of pistols, which he places on the table in silence.*]

Pauline. Don't trouble to get those ready, M. le Marquis. Your nephew is not going to challenge M. de Beauséjour, for the excellent reason that M. de Beauséjour left Vienna last night. I have just now allowed Henri to leave, because his presence here would have interfered with an explanation which we are going to have.

Marquis. An explanation between us, Mademoiselle? Your explanation will be made in court.

Pauline. I can easily imagine that you would like to drag me into court—that is what I should like to discuss. There is one point which you know nothing of: I shall enlighten you.

Marquis. The lawyer will see to that. Leave us.

Pauline. Very well. [*To the* MARQUISE.] Will you be kind enough to give Mlle. Geneviève this gold key? She has been looking for it since yesterday.

Marquise. The key to the box?

Pauline. Which contains the record of her heart's history.

Marquise. How do you happen to have it?

Pauline. I simply took it. Indelicate of me, was it not? You see, I have not been well brought up. I thought I should find in that box just the weapons I might need some day.— I was not mistaken. Will Mme. la Marquise be pleased to hear some extracts? [*She gives the* MARQUISE *a slip of paper.*]

Marquis. Another blackguardly trick!

Pauline. A rather brutal way of putting it! But I am not one to defend your granddaughter!

Marquise [*Unfolding the paper*]. This isn't her handwriting!

Pauline. You don't think I'm foolish enough to let you have the original? That is in safekeeping, in Paris.—Read.

Marquise [*Reading*]. "April 17.—What is happening to me? Henri doesn't love Pauline any more. He loves me——"

Marquis [*To his wife*]. Would Henri be so——!

Pauline. Undignified as to make love to his cousin? Looks like it, doesn't it? But you needn't worry: I told her.

Marquis. You, Madame?

Pauline. And I told no more than the truth.

Marquis [*To his wife*]. Does Henri love his cousin?

Marquise [*Reading*]. "I love him. Oh, now I am sure I have never felt otherwise toward him——" Poor dear!— "God have pity on me! That love is a crime! Grant me the power to tear it from my heart! I considered him dead! Why has he come back again?"

Marquis [*To* PAULINE]. Yes, why?

Pauline. Continue, you will hear!

Marquise [*Reading*]. "April 20.—My heart is deeply troubled: what can I do with this love—which, after all, might become legitimate? He will always feel remorse. He is dishonored by the fearful hope which he feels—in spite of me. But is it my fault if Pauline cannot recover from the illness that is killing her?"

Marquis. You again? [PAULINE *bows.*]

Marquise. That is why she wanted to have us all to go to Italy!

Marquis [*To* PAULINE]. If a *man* were capable of such

infamy, I'd shoot him like a dog! But a woman, it seems, may do anything!

Pauline [*To the* MARQUIS, *smiling*]. It is most fortunate that we have the privileges accorded us by reason of our weakness, you must admit. But to return to your grand-daughter: I think the reading of her little romance will attract more admirers than husbands. Don't worry, though, I shan't publish this precious document unless you force me to—and you won't do that, I'm sure.

Marquis. Make your conditions, Madame.

Pauline. At last, thank God, you are reasonable. I shall follow suit. All I ask is an amicable separation, and that I keep the money agreed on in my contract.

Marquis. You will not use our name?

Pauline. Oh, M. le Marquis, I realize its value!

Marquis. We shall pay you!

Pauline. You are not rich enough. And what would you think of me for selling the title? No, I have it and I intend to keep it. An amicable separation cannot take from me what a legal one cannot—you must at least be just.

Marquise [*To her husband*]. She has us bound, hand and foot!

Marquis. Very well!

Pauline. Now we are agreed. You must arrange it all with Henri. I'll rid you of my company at once. [*She turns to go.*]

Marquis. One moment—first we must have Geneviève's diary.

Pauline. I told you it was in Paris.

Marquis. Write to the receiver of stolen goods to return it at once.

Pauline. Nothing is simpler. But, really, if I give up my only weapon, what guarantee shall I have——?

Marquis. My word as a gentleman.

Pauline. Good; between people of honor a given word is enough. Well, I give you my word that I shall not misuse my precious treasure. What would be the good for me?

Marquis. The pleasure of revenge. You must hate us, for you realise how we despise you.

Pauline. Is that the way you hope to persuade me?

Marquise. The Marquis uses strong expressions—it's very

wrong of him. Be kind, Madame! Please, for our dear grand-
child's sake, take pity on our gray hairs! I shall pray for you!

Pauline [*Smiling*]. Good for evil, Madame!

Marquis. That will do, Marquise! [*He passes in front of*
PAULINE, *without looking at her. To the* MARQUISE.] Leave
me alone with her.

Marquise. But, my dear——

Marquis [*Conducting the* MARQUISE *to the door*]. Leave
us! [*The* MARQUISE *goes out. The* MARQUIS *sends her a long
kiss with his two hands, and comes downstage again.*]

Pauline. You're pale, M. le Marquis.

Marquis [*His arms crossed as he stands immovable*]. You
would be paler than I if you knew what I was thinking!

Pauline. Ah, threats?

Marquis [*Slowly*]. We have begged, but there was no use.
My dear saint of a wife has prostrated herself before you.

Pauline. Well?

Marquis [*About to seize her*]. Well, you damned——!
[*He stops.*] Our salvation lies in our own hands now,
understand?

Pauline. I'm not afraid; I've gagged bigger men than you.

Marquis [*Staccato*]. Write as I dictate.

Pauline [*Shrugging her shoulders*]. You're dawdling,
Marquis.

Marquis. Write this instant, do you hear me? Tomorrow
will be too late!

Pauline. Because?

Marquis. Because if once my granddaughter's secret is
known, the only possible reparation will be her marriage
with your husband, and, by God, if that happens, she *shall*
marry him!

Pauline [*Smiling*]. You mean that you'll—suppress me?
My dear Monsieur, do you take me for a child? [*She tries
to go.*]

Marquis [*Laying his hand on the pistols*]. Take care!

Pauline. Why? Don't mind about those pistols—they're
not loaded. Now let's stop trifling—you're bound to lose
in the end.

Marquis [*Composing himself*]. Write as I tell you, and
I will give you half a million francs.

Pauline. You offer to buy my artillery on the day of

battle? Your humble servant. Adieu, dear Uncle—— [*She goes toward the door at the left.*]

Marquis [*Taking up a pistol*]. If you try to pass that door, I will kill you.

Pauline [*On the threshold, as she hums an air from "Les Etudiants"*]:

> When you make love to a little girl
> And compromise her——

Marquis [*Fires.* PAULINE *screams and falls, outside the door. The* MARQUIS *takes another pistol and loads it*]. God is my judge!

A SCRAP OF PAPER

A Comedy in Three Acts

by

VICTORIEN SARDOU

English Version by

LÉONIE GILMOUR

CHARACTERS

(*In order of appearance*)

CLAUDINE ⎫
HENRI ⎬ *servants*
BAPTISTE ⎭
SOLANGE, *housekeeper*
PAUL, *in love with Marthe*
MARTHE, *Clarisse's sister*
THIRION, *Paul's tutor*
COLOMBA (*Mme. Thirion*)
PROSPER BLOCK, *a traveller and collector of curios*
BUSONIER, *Custom house inspector*
VANHOVE, *a country gentleman*
CLARISSE (*Mme. Vanhove*)
SUZANNE, *Prosper's adversary—later his wife*

PLACE: *Near* CHINON, FRANCE.
TIME: *Mid-nineteenth century.*

A SCRAP OF PAPER

ACT ONE

A *salon in the chateau of* M. *and* MME. VANHOVE. *The style is that of* LOUIS XVI.

Enter BAPTISTE, HENRI, *and* CLAUDINE.

CLAUDINE [*contemptuously whirling around an armchair that she is dusting*]. Just look at that, will you! Is that old-fashioned enough for you—that ridiculous piece of furniture!

Henri [*nailing the carpet down*]. You must come to the suburbs of Chinon[1] to see such rubbish.

Baptiste. Yes, that's another of monsieur's fine ideas—to come out here to the country to hunt. . . . [*Stretching himself on a settee.*] And I had thought to take him to some watering place—for my sciatica.

Henri [*stopping and sitting cross-legged on the carpet*]. I'm beginning to have enough of this! Here we've been swallowing dust ever since five o'clock this morning!

Baptiste. Yes, and for people who've been trundled over a railroad for a whole day.

Claudine. Second-class, too—and that's anything but comfortable.

Enter MADAME SOLANGE.

Solange. Well! I declare! You won't wear your shoes out in a hurry at that pace, you three.

Claudine. Hello! To whom have we the honor of speaking?

Solange. You have the honor of speaking to Madame Solange, housekeeper of the château, my dear, and nurse to madame.

Baptiste. My compliments to your nursing, Madame Solange; but as to your housekeeping—

Solange. Well! What about it?

[1] Chinon: the site of the ruins of a famous twelfth-century castle.

Baptiste. It won't kill you. It must be two years since you've handled a broom in this room, hey?

Solange. No! Three!

Baptiste, Henri, Claudine [*laughing*]. Three!

Solange. Yes, three years! . . . Since the departure of my old mistress, Madame de Crussolles (the mother of madame; ah, you didn't know her). . . . Since her departure for Paris, with Mademoiselle Clarisse, who was going there to marry M. Vanhove! . . . Stay! It all comes back to me! It was at daybreak; they had gone for the post horses to harness them to the old barouche; and madame said to me, in a low voice, from the coach door: "Solange, shut up everything tight, my girl, for fear of burglars!" (That was her mania, poor woman, to be afraid of burglars!) "And you are not to open the salon again until my return, do you hear?" "Yes, madame." "Whip up, driver." Then I did as I was told—I shut everything under bolt and bar, awaiting the return of madame. Alas! She didn't return, poor lady. A year after the wedding she was no longer of this world; and so the apartment has never been touched until yesterday evening, when Mademoiselle Clarisse, now Madame Vanhove, arrives at midnight with her husband, without a word of warning, and says, as she jumps from the carriage: "Hurry, nurse, open the salon and have it cleaned early in the morning; I have company tomorrow, to lunch, to dinner!" So I opened the room, and that good and early; for, say what you please, I always obey orders.

Henri. And so that's why the salon was all upside down, as if the folks had just left yesterday!

Solange. Yes, that's the reason; only, instead of standing there chattering, you'd better finish your work.

Henri. Bah! two touches of the feather duster and it's done! [*He starts to dust a statuette of Flora.*]

Solange. Wretch! Don't touch Flora!

Henri. But she's covered with dust, your Flora!

Solange [*stopping him*]. Never mind! Don't touch it! It's forbidden! Since the accident to Zephyr——

All. Zephyr!

Solange. Yes, it was the companion piece to the Flora. See! [*She points to the other pedestal.*]

Claudine. Well, where is it?

Solange. Ah, poor thing! broken to a thousand bits. And madame cherished it as the apple of her eye! A real old Sèvres! And so nobody was to touch it! And when madame became paralyzed in both arms, it was always Mademoiselle Clarisse who dusted it. No one else! [*To* HENRI, *taking the duster.*] Here, give me that, I'll finish this job.

Claudine. So! There's nothing more to do here; I'm going to take my cup of chocolate.

Henri. And I my bath.

Baptiste. And I to get my letters ready!

Henri [*with a mock courtesy to* SOLANGE]. Adieu, Lady Solange.

Baptiste [*bowing*]. Housekeeper of the château.

Claudine [*bowing*]. And nurse!

[*Exeunt* CLAUDINE, BAPTISTE, *and* HENRI, *laughing.*

Solange [*alone*]. A fine lot! So devoted to their masters! A pity about his "chocolate"!

Enter PAUL, *tiptoeing.*

Paul [*in a low voice*]. Solange!

Solange. Monsieur Paul! Here, in the house of M. Vanhove!

Paul. She sleeps?

Solange. Who? Madame Vanhove?

Paul [*timidly*]. No, Mademoiselle Marthe.

Solange. What! You know Mademoiselle Marthe, then?

Paul. Oh, yes.

Solange. There's no need of blushing about it.

Paul. But I'm not blushing. [*Aside.*] What a tiresome woman! [*Aloud.*] It was the suddenness of your question——

Solange. Yes. . . . And pray where did you make the acquaintance of Mademoiselle Marthe, who hasn't been at the château since she was eight years old?

Paul. Why, at Paris, two months ago, when I went there with my tutor, M. Thirion.

Solange. Ah! It was our neighbor, M. Thirion, who introduced you to Madame Vanhove?

Paul. And to Mademoiselle Marthe.

Solange [*laughing*]. Ah! that's it!

Paul [*embarrassed*]. Yes, that's it!

Solange. What a boy! There's no need of asking him what's up. It's plain enough.

Paul [quickly]. Plain! what is plain? I didn't say anything.

Solange. No, but you've told everything.

Enter MARTHE, *in riding habit.*

Marthe. Good morning, Monsieur Paul.

Paul. Mademoiselle Marthe!

Solange. He thought you still asleep.

Marthe. Asleep! I've already made the tour of the village twice on horseback, all alone, English fashion. Here, nurse! [*She gives her her hat and whip.*]

Solange [aside]. With a young man like that—I can leave them alone, with an easy conscience.   [*Exit.*

Paul [eagerly]. Ah! Mademoiselle!

Marthe [mimicking]. Ah, Monsieur Paul!

Paul. How have you been since last I had the happiness of seeing you?

Marthe [still mimicking]. Oh, pretty well, I thank you. And you?

Paul. There you are making fun of me again, just as you did at Paris.

Marthe. Oh, no! Not at all! What good have you been doing these two months?

Paul. Good? Oh, nothing.

Marthe. What else?

Paul. Writing poetry.

Marthe. Verses! You must let me see them.

Paul. Oh, no!

Marthe. Why not?

Paul. Because there are things in them that I shouldn't like to say.

Marthe. Well, you needn't say them. I'll read them.

Paul. Never! No, mademoiselle, let me take my hat and go. I feel as though I were sliding down a precipice. You can say anything without fearing to vex me, while I—no! Decidedly, mademoiselle, another time, later—[*He takes his hat.*]

Marthe. Then you've finished? I may go? [*Pretends to go.*]

Paul. So soon?

Marthe. But, gracious, if you've nothing more to say to me——

Paul. Ah! If I dared——a thousand things.

Marthe. That's too many. You are embarrassed. Do you know what you ought to do, Monsieur Paul?

Paul. What, mademoiselle?

Marthe. You should go walk in the park for an hour or two, to calm yourself. And above all, don't make verses. No! you must reason with yourself in simple prose, and then you'll say something like this: "It must be admitted that I am a great bungler."

Paul. Very true.

Marthe. "Here I've been waiting for someone, a friend, with a certain degree of impatience."

Paul. Yes, indeed, counting every second.

Marthe. "Counting every second. And when she arrives, I dare not tell her what is in my heart."

Paul. Most true.

Marthe. "As if all that were not perfectly proper and polite"—

Paul. Oh, perfectly.

Marthe. "As if Mademoiselle Marthe could be vexed by that."

Paul. Ah, mademoiselle, that is——

Marthe. That is what you are going to say to yourself under the trees—then you'll come back—you'll speak—I'll listen!——

Paul. Ah, permit me!

Marthe. And we shall see whether I am vexed. Good morning, Monsieur Paul.   [*Exit.*

Paul. Well, truly—it's over.—I've said it—that is—no; it was she who made me say it. But it comes to the same thing. Ah, I should never have believed that I could have gotten through it so well. But that's what it is to be plucky.

Colomba [*from without*]. Paul!

Paul. My guardian, and his wife! Let me escape with my happiness! They'd spoil it for me.

[*Exit precipitately towards the park.*

Enter THIRION, COLOMBA.

Colomba. Paul! Paul! Where can he be?

Thirion [*holding up a net with a butterfly in it*]. The butterfly? Here he is.

Colomba. Who's thinking of your butterfly? I'm speaking of Paul. I saw him in this salon.

Thirion. Paul, always Paul! You've nothing but Paul in your head.

Colomba. And you—you'd better be looking after him than be forever chasing flies and butterflies.

Thirion [*sitting down by the table*]. Entomology is a passion which hurts no one. [*Sticks the butterfly onto his hat with a pin.*]

Colomba. I tell you you're not living up to your duty as guardian to that child.

Thirion. "That child" is twenty years old.

Colomba. His wits have gone woolgathering since you took him to Paris on that ridiculous journey—against my wishes, mind you.

Thirion. It was to make the acquaintance of his lawyer, my dear. He's got to know his lawyer sometime. My guardianship will come to an end; and when the time comes for him to marry——

Colomba. To marry! What, he's going to be married, then?

Thirion [*astonished*]. What's the matter? If——

Colomba. I forbid you to put such ideas into his head.

Thirion. Pshaw!

Colomba. The mere fact of having seen those frivolous décolleté Parisian women at the ball, at the theatre—

Thirion. Oh, as to the décolleté—the fact is—but indeed he's only seen very respectable women—Madame Vanhove, for instance.

Colomba. Ah, truly! a coquette—who got herself talked about nicely at Chinon—before her marriage. And I suspect that odd friend of yours, M. Prosper, knows something about that, too. Just arrived from India the other day to pay you a visit and hasn't even come to say good morning to me today.

Thirion. What does Prosper know? A mere bit of girlish folly. Really, to hear you talk——

Colomba. I don't care who hears me! It's just trouble wasted trying to bring up this young man to a sense of decorum and modesty, if he's to be spoiled by those Parisian women.

Thirion. Oh, as to that! You don't imagine that boy will remain forever—Confound it—— You make me forget myself. But in fact, even I, who speak to you, I, Madame Thirion—— Hang it. But at his age—I, too——

Colomba [*aside*]. You too!

Thirion. And what if this young man should have an intrigue——

Colomba. An intrigue with a woman! Speak!

Thirion [*aside, biting his lips*]. Ah, blockhead! and Colomba such a prude! What an idiot I am!

Colomba. But continue—go on—speak!

Thirion. No, no, my dear, I was jesting.

Colomba. Monsieur Thirion! You are hiding something from me.

Thirion. No, no, I tell you.

Colomba. But I shall force you to tell me. I will know it, whatever comes of it.

Enter PROSPER, *at the back.*

Thirion. Come, come, Colomba.

Colomba. I will know everything. Speak!

Thirion. But——

Colomba. But speak, I tell you.

Prosper [*clad in white, with a Chinese parasol*]. No, don't speak, Thirion.

Thirion. Prosper!

Prosper. Don't speak! After trying violence, Madame Thirion will be forced to have recourse to persuasiveness. Turn and turn about. Let yourself be persuaded, my friend, and don't speak.

Thirion [*to* PROSPER]. Would you believe it?

Colomba. Enough! [*To* PROSPER.] Have you been going around the village in that garb?

Prosper. Just as I went around the world, madame, and always with the greatest success. Just now, for instance, I met a lady on horseback who didn't attempt to hide her extreme delight at the sight of me. A most charming creature

Colomba. To be frank—for a man—that fan, that parasol
—it's very bad form.

Prosper. What do you mean by *form*, my dear lady?

Colomba. Why, the fashion.

Prosper. Talk of fashion to a man who has just traversed
two hemispheres, running across men and women of every
color. It's not good form at Chinon; but it's good form at
Peking—and that's all there is to it.

Thirion. Ugh! the Chinese!

Prosper [*imitating him*]. Ugh! the Chinese. That's my
good European, who thinks all is said when he disdainfully
exclaims *the Chinese!* But to them, you are the Chinese,
you Chinonese! With your side whiskers and your stovepipe
hat in broad daylight!

Thirion. I!

Prosper. Yes, you, and madame, and all like you. Just so
many Chinese, in another China, and with as many ridiculous Chinese customs. Thirion's Chinese. He doesn't eat
larks' nests but he devours pickled oysters, and snails à la
provençal. And madame's Chinese; she doesn't imprison
her little feet in thimbles, but she mutilates her figure with
a tight corset. And Prosper Block, here, is Chinese. He
doesn't smoke opium, but he smokes twenty cigars a day,
ruins himself, makes an offensive brute of himself. Chinese!
Bah!

Enter BUSONIER.

Busonier. And Busonier, too! Here's one you haven't
mentioned.

Thirion. Busonier! you here!

Busonier [*shaking hands*]. Here I am! I heard of Madame
Vanhove's arrival and started for the country the first thing
in the morning, so as to be the first to announce to her the
great news.

Thirion. The great news? What news?

Busonier. What! You don't know? [*Bursts out laughing.*]
Bah! you really don't know?

Thirion. What is it?

Busonier [*laughing*]. You're certainly the only ones——
Such a thing to happen to me—custom house inspector—
why, my friend, it's the only topic in the cafés, in the

theatres, in the papers, everywhere. Why, man, I'm famous, thanks to Madame Busonier.

Thirion. Your wife! I understand.

Busonier. You catch on? And you, Prosper?

Prosper [*grasping his hand*]. I'm with you.

Thirion [*enthusiastically*]. I'm delighted!

Busonier. Eh?

Thirion. You deserved it long ago. I always said to Madame Thirion: "That's all he lacks. But it will come to that finally."

Busonier [*to* MADAME THIRION]. He told you that—

Thirion. A woman like Madame Busonier, so intelligent, so clever! Ah, I was sure——

Busonier. Hold on! Allow me! What is it you think has happened?

Thirion. Why, an increase in the family!

Busonier. An increase in the family? Well, yes. But not as you understand it!

Colomba. Ah! I understand. Madame Busonier——

Busonier. Heavens! She's had herself abducted.

Colomba. Horrors!

Thirion. My dear fellow, before Colomba!

Busonier. Faith! Madame Thirion can't take it tragically no more than I; and seeing that I turn the thing into a jest——

Thirion. A jest!

Busonier. What! Do you think I'm going to be such a fool as to tear my hair, to draw more ridicule upon myself! Hardly! Busonier is not such a fool as to give his friends the satisfaction of pitying him! At the first news, another man would have hidden himself! But I—took my cane, put on my hat, and went straight to my club. As I enter, someone holds out his hand to me with an air of condolence. I burst out laughing. The crowd retorts. But I was the first to laugh, and my laugh killed theirs. Let a hunchback forget his hump, and nobody thinks of it!

Colomba. You take it philosophically!

Busonier. Do you want me to take it like a hoodwinked husband? Am I so joined to the frivolities of Madame Busonier that my thirty years of well-known probity should become bankrupt owing to the loss of her virtue? Thank

God, my honor is my own—as her dishonor is hers. I was
an honest husband! I remain an honest man! She loses both.
—So much the worse for her!

Prosper. There's a man without prejudices for you!

Busonier. To be sure; and that is also the opinion of a
sensible and intelligent woman to whom I related the affair
this morning.

Thirion. Who's that?

Busonier. Mademoiselle Suzanne.

Thirion. She here!

Busonier. At Chinon, where I left her in the midst of her
trunks. She has come to spend the autumn at the château.

Colomba. Who is this Mademoiselle Suzanne?

Busonier. Ah, true! Madame doesn't know her. Mademoiselle Suzanne is a Parisian, a little cousin of Madame Vanhove's and godmother to her younger sister, who, coming
into a snug little fortune on the death of her parents, has
steadily refused the best matches, out of sheer love of in-
dependence.

Colomba. An old maid!

Busonier. A charming woman, just verging on thirty, and
who, consequently, has the right to know in theory many
things which young girls are supposed not to know. Spirit-
uelle, with a frankness of manner that would perhaps be
offensive in another—but which she renders amiable; moving among the best people in Paris; and more virtuous in
her liberty than many another in chains—as Madame
Busonier can testify.

Prosper. Bah! don't talk of Madame Busonier; it's laugh-
able.

Thirion. Oh, she! Gad! She'd shrug her shoulders at such
trifles.

Prosper. That she would.

Thirion. Yes, in China it's tolerated indulgently.

Prosper. And in the Marquesas Islands it's quite an honor.

Thirion [*trying to hush him*]. Softly, my friend. Colomba!

Prosper. An honor! Intrigued for! Solicited! Implored!

Thirion. My friend, Colomba! Colomb——

Prosper [*continuing and rising*]. Bah! Madame will soon

understand all that. It's a matter of latitude. What is honor, in such a case? A mere shadow! Now all travellers will tell you that the nearer you come to the equator, the shorter the shadows, on account of the perpendicularity of the rays of the sun. At Java, for instance, a deer, an elk, or Busonier, might walk with impunity in broad daylight without blushing at their shadows. But let them go northward, and presto! —there is the shadow——which lengthens, lengthens—— and the fear of ridicule grows with the length of the shadow.

Thirion. Then that is why Vanhove is so jealous.

Prosper. He is from the North?

Thirion. A Hollander.

Prosper. He is afraid of his shadow.

Enter VANHOVE *crossing through the park at the back.*

Colomba. Good morning, Monsieur Vanhove. Did you have a good night?

Vanhove. Thanks. Yes.

Busonier. Is Madame Vanhove down yet?

Vanhove. I believe so.

Thirion. Then we'll go say good morning to her with Monsieur. M. Prosper Block—the friend of whom I spoke last night. He would like to have an interview with you.

Vanhove. Very well.

Prosper [*aside*]. What ice!

Thirion. We'll see you later.

[*Exeunt* COLOMBA, THIRION.

Vanhove. You've come to join us in the chase, sir?

Prosper. The chase? No. That is, yes, but another sort of chase.

Vanhove [*coldly*]. Indeed.

Prosper. Let me come to the point at once. I am a bachelor, and, you'll be surprised to hear, have just come from India for the purpose of getting married. But I will say at the outset that my hand is forced.

Vanhove. Indeed.

Prosper. I'll tell you how: I am only heir to a very rich uncle, who's even more pigheaded than he is rich. And as for my patrimony—swallowed up, shipwrecked, in the course of long voyages.

Vanhove. Indeed.

Prosper. You'll perhaps want to know why I undertook such long and expensive journeys?

Vanhove. No.

Prosper. No! Then perhaps you wouldn't like to hear about woman's treachery and the cruel mishap that forced me to seek oblivion on the foamy brine?

Vanhove. No.

Prosper. No! But still you must be impatient to learn the causes that make marriage a necessity to me?

Vanhove. No.

Prosper. Excuse me—But it's absolutely indispensable that you should be impatient to learn about them. Otherwise I should have no reason for telling you about them.

Vanhove [*coolly*]. As you will. I'm all impatience.

Prosper. Then I will yield to your desire, and begin; but don't be alarmed, I'll make a short story of it. A month ago, after three years of wandering over land and sea, I turn up, with my whole cargo of stuffed crocodiles and parrots, at the house of the uncle of whom I spoke to you, who lives alone in a kind of a dovecot, about a mile from here. He opens his door, and, instead of embracing me: "Ah vagabond," he cries, "is it you?" "It's myself, uncle!" "At least you're married?" I rack my brains to recall whether in Oceania or elsewhere—"No, uncle, no, I'm not married." "What, you heartless knave——here I've condemned myself to celibacy, all on your account, in the hope that your house would be mine, that your wife would cook my gruel— and instead of that, you leave me alone in my pigeon house, with Athénaïs." Athénaïs is his housekeeper. "Do me the favor to go and get yourself a wife, at once." "But where shall I find her?" "Why, anywhere, vagabond! There are adorable girls everywhere." "But, uncle!"—— "I give you six weeks, and if by that time you don't bring me your betrothed, I'll publish the bans for my marriage with Athénaïs—— Be off!" With that he slams the door in my face, leaving me in the street, with all my traps. Now what do you say to that?

Vanhove. Nothing.

Prosper. Nothing! Then don't let's talk of it any more. So then I made up my mind to take up my quarters with your neighbor, my friend Thirion, who has kept my room ready for me these ten years. "I have it!" says he—— "Just the thing for you! M. Vanhove has just arrived with his wife and his little sister-in-law. She's a pearl. Go find him, make your request, and it's done." I come to you, make my request for the hand of your sister-in-law—is it done?

Vanhove. Well, I don't say no.

Prosper. Then it is yes?

Vanhove. Oh, no.

Prosper. Then what is it, my good sir?

Vanhove. Go see my wife—her sister. It concerns her more than me. [*Rings.*]

Prosper. You are right. And I am the more pleased, because three years ago, when I was on a visit to my friend, Thirion, I had the honor of making the acquaintance of Madame de Crussolles; and if I've never seen Mademoiselle Marthe, who was then at the convent, I am well-known to Madame Vanhove.

Vanhove. Ah, indeed! [*Rings.*]

Enter CLAUDINE.

Vanhove [*to* CLAUDINE]. Tell madame someone wishes to see her.

Prosper. Wait! Give her this card!   [*Exit* CLAUDINE.

Vanhove. You'll stay to lunch and to dinner?

Prosper. You are too kind.

Vanhove [*looking at his watch*]. Nine o'clock! I am going to see whether my dogs are here. I'll be back directly.

Prosper [*alone*]. Don't hurry! Well, now I'm sure of the husband, and I have no doubt about his wife. His wife! What memories! And how many changes in three years! But the salon at least hasn't changed; there is the little table, the lamp, the Flora. Even the bit of embroidery—God bless me—is the same. And this book—the very book. Oh, we were just going to look up "Genevieve." [*Reading.*] "Genev—" What a strange sensation. [*Coldly.*] Very surprising—— Surely it's the castle of the Sleeping Beauty. Everything has been asleep.

Enter CLARISSE.

Clarisse. And you come to awaken us!

Prosper. Clarisse! Madame!

Clarisse. I couldn't believe the card. Is it indeed yourself?

Prosper. Come, like the prince in the fairy tale, through a thousand brambles and briars, to see what has survived the grand trumpet blast.

Clarisse. Oh, nothing.

Prosper. Nothing! In your heart, perhaps; but mine will never forget three months of the most budding, tenderest, purest love—born among flowers and sunshine!

Clarisse. It is dead!

Prosper. Dead?

Clarisse. Sit down and tell me where in the world you come from, so early in the morning—to talk of all that again.

Prosper. I come from the other world, madame, and to speak of other things!

Clarisse. Indeed. Of what?

Prosper. Of my marriage, madame.

Clarisse. With whom?

Prosper. With your sister Marthe, if you will permit it.

Clarisse. Marthe. What folly! A mere child!

Prosper. Oh, there are no more children. Only little women.

Clarisse. She hasn't even met you.

Prosper. A tremendous advantage. The unforeseen!

Clarisse. But how do you know she doesn't love another?

Prosper. O, I am counting on that.

Clarisse. What, you count upon her loving—

Prosper. To be sure. Will you permit an Oriental simile to a man just come from Calcutta? How did you use to make tea every evening, in this same salon? First you poured a few drops of boiling water on the leaves to soften them and take out the bitterness; and after throwing away this first water, the next infusion was the more savory! So it is with the first love of a young girl. It's thrown off and all the fragrance remains for the first cup.

Clarisse. You always were a crackbrained fellow!

Prosper. Besides, are you happy?

Clarisse. Perfectly.

Prosper. You perhaps repent of having married M. Van-hove?

Clarisse. Not in the least! I love him, and I have only one regret—to have believed for an instant that I ever loved another.

Prosper. You've found the true recipe for happiness—to throw overboard the man you love in order to marry the one you don't love! Then why not give me Mademoiselle Marthe? She'll follow in your footsteps and become the happiest woman in the world.

Clarisse. You want to know the truth?

Prosper. The real truth?

Clarisse. The real truth! Here it is. I should be most unhappy if this marriage should take place;—I won't deceive you—it will not take place.

Prosper. Why not?

Clarisse. Why not? How can you ask? You've known me as a light, frivolous woman—a flirt, if you will. And, however little cause I have to blush for that schoolgirl love of which you spoke just now, still it cannot give me pleasure to recall it. Can you not understand that I should be most reluctant to see in my husband's house, the man whom I permitted to say to me, before he did—

Prosper. Ah—what you replied to me: "I love you."

Clarisse [*hastily rising*]. You see you give me reason for my prejudice. Come, be chivalrous, I ask no sacrifice of you. You don't love my sister; you haven't met her. Withdraw your request. Let us say good-bye and you will carry away with you not only the consciousness of having done a good deed but also the assurance that you have in me a true friend.

Prosper. Ah, but that is what I can't believe.

Clarisse. You can't believe——?

Prosper. In your friendship. No more than I advise you to believe in mine—for under the ashes of love I have kept a smoldering brand—what a glowing brand!—an inextinguishable hatred—which I've carefully kept alive these three years, all by myself. I'm not sorry to draw some sparks of it from your eyes; for really a woman can't trifle with a man as you trifled with me—in the space of five hours!

Clarisse. I!

Prosper. Listen. We are here in this room again; all the surroundings are the same. It's only you who prevent these three years from seeming like one night and that last night we saw each other——yesterday. Ah, yesterday. You were there and I here. And I was reading aloud from this book— see, it's still here. And you were embroidering this bit of tapestry—(there's witchcraft in it; everything is the same) —and in this armchair sat your mother, apparently asleep, but her watchful eye followed us everywhere, and reduced our love-making to the mute interchange of glances and little scraps of notes. Ah, those little notes! You remember them—faintly scented, charming—I burned them as I received them—as I had sworn to do—in my divine candor. And the letter box, so well chosen—for none touched it but you and I—our Flora is there still, as it was yesterday. Yesterday, Mademoiselle Clarisse, I left you saying: "Until tomorrow"—"Tomorrow," you answered. And this morning you are Madame Vanhove. That's what I call rather abrupt.

Clarisse. Who willed it so? You!

Prosper. I?

Clarisse. Were you beside me to prevent it? Where were you?

Prosper. Where was I? That's just what I am going to explain to you. When I left you, madame, last night, or three years ago, as you will, instead of going straight to Thirion's, I take a turn under the trees. I light a cigar, and after the fashion of platonic lovers, lean against a tree and gaze at the light in your window, giving vent to a thousand sighs. Suddenly——

Clarisse. Suddenly?

Prosper. Two steps away, I see shining under the trees a little glowing light—not a glowworm—a cigar!

Clarisse. A cigar!

Prosper. With, of course, a man at the end of it: one of my good friends and your admirers—M. de Rivière. Mutual astonishment and stupefaction at the discovery of a new light in the mass of rhododendrons. Third cigar, M. Tonnerieux, secretary to the prefect.

Clarisse. Ah!

Prosper. Three hearts on fire, burning their incense under your windows. I drag these gentlemen off to my room. Stormy explanations ensue. Each claims that he has the right to give you this little serenade. Sarcasm and retort discourteous. Two duels on my hands!

Clarisse. Good Heavens!

Prosper. We take down our swords, make for the duelling ground, and there in the moonlight I wound Tonnerieux— a mere scratch; de Rivière stabs me through the arm; I fall, am carried away,—and that's where I was: in bed, with fever and delirium.

Clarisse. But I never knew——

Prosper. Naturally. Except for Thirion everyone thought it was a hemorrhage of the lungs; and, moreover, to add to the dramatic situation, at the very moment when I fell a post chaise was carrying Madame de Crussolles and her daughter to Paris, where M. Vanhove awaited them. Your marriage was the first news to greet my convalescence: result —a relapse, followed by my first voyage to the Marquesas Isles.

Clarisse. But—my letter?

Prosper. Your letter!

Clarisse. The letter I wrote—at the very moment when you were waiting under my window. The letter in which I told you everything—M. Vanhove's proposal—the implacable will of my mother—our departure at night for Paris! That letter which told you to join us in Paris at any price— that I was ready!—oh, a thousand foolish things that I should blush to repeat and which you know very well.

Prosper. It's the first time I ever heard of it.

Clarisse. Ah, do not say that! I slipped down here in the night to put the letter in the usual place, sure of your finding it in the morning, as you had the others.

Prosper. But in the morning—I was in bed with a fever, madame.

Clarisse [*rising, frightened*]. But then, the letter! If you haven't it, where is it?

Prosper. Why, where you put it—under the Flora—unless someone—

Clarisse. My writing. Oh, if my husband! Fortunately this salon has not been opened.

Prosper. Then it must be there.

Clarisse. Oh, you've frightened me so! I dare not look!

Prosper. I will look.

Clarisse. No, no—let me.

Prosper [*stopping short*]. Someone——

Clarisse. My husband!

Enter VANHOVE, BUSONIER, THIRION, MADAME THIRION, COLOMBA, *finally* PAUL *and* MARTHE.

Prosper. Well, sir, are your hounds ready?

Vanhove. Yes. [*To* CLARISSE.] What's the matter?

Clarisse. Nothing—the excitement—what monsieur was telling me——

Vanhove. This marriage?

Prosper. Precisely. My marriage.

Vanhove [*to* CLARISSE]. Well?

Prosper [*to* CLARISSE]. Well, as I understand it, the matter is settled, is it not?

Clarisse. Entirely! Monsieur understands my reasons. He withdraws his request. [*Movement of surprise on the part of* PROSPER.]

Vanhove. Indeed!

Prosper. But pardon me, madame. I cannot so easily renounce the honor of an alliance with your family. I should like first—I should be glad——

Marthe [*embracing* CLARISSE]. Good morning, sister.

Prosper [*aside*]. Ha! my enchantress—the lady on horseback— [*Aloud.*] But no, no, no. I don't withdraw. Not at all!

Clarisse [*uneasy*]. Ah!

Prosper. And I implore madame to permit me to offer my suit before judging it unacceptable.

Vanhove. Naturally. [*Moves to one side.*]

Clarisse [*aside to* PROSPER]. Your conduct is neither charitable nor courteous—and it is utterly useless.

Colomba [*aside to* PAUL]. I forbid you to speak to Mademoiselle Marthe.

Prosper [*looking after* CLARISSE]. What great thinker was it who said: "When a woman ceases to love us she hates us." I'd like to have lived before that gentleman so as to have said it first; for it is an incontrovertible truth.

Thirion. What is that you are saying?

Prosper. I say that it's confoundedly rough on a fellow to make the tour of the world all for the sake of a coquette who treats you like a lackey when you return—under the pretext that in the interval she has become as virtuous as Cornelia, mother of the Gracchi![2]

Thirion. A refusal?

Prosper. Worse—a dismissal! And as a result I am now madly enamored of the charming creature, who was an object of utter indifference to me this morning. Plague take it! Shall I go back like this, with my parasol?

Thirion. Gad! A husband who is both jealous and brutal; a woman who hates you. Better give it up!

Prosper [*looking at* CLARISSE *who softly moves up toward the mantelpiece*]. No, by Heavens! I hold her under my thumb. I shall stay, and I shall do my courting in spite of her.

Thirion. What's that?

Prosper. What's that? did you ever see two hunters after one partridge?

Thirion. Well?

Prosper. Well! Just watch Madame Vanhove prowling around the Flora. The partridge is there.—She is watching it—I too. And I'm thinking it will be a strange kind of a game.

Thirion. A partridge?

Prosper [*turning and seeing* CLARISSE *on the point of lifting the Flora and taking the letter*]. Confound it! Too late! She's taking aim!

Enter SUZANNE.

Suzanne [*gayly*]. It is I! [*All turn abruptly and* CLARISSE *withdraws her hand without having taken the letter.*]

Busonier. Mademoiselle Suzanne!

Marthe [*running up to* SUZANNE]. My godmother!

Prosper [*seeing* CLARISSE *go to embrace* SUZANNE]. Saved! My turn now! [*He starts towards the Flora, but* COLOMBA *stops him midway.*]

---

[2] Gracchi: Two Roman statesmen of the second century, B.C. Cornelia was the epitome of virtuous motherhood in ancient Rome.

Suzanne. Good morning, dear friend! Good morning, pet!

Marthe. I'm going to get your room ready.   [*Exit.*

Suzanne [*embracing everyone*]. Good morning, cousin Vanhove. You're a bear. But I'll permit you to embrace me. I don't make my arrival every day. And M. Thirion, too. And M. Busonier—Oh, not you—I've seen you before, this morning. Who else?

Thirion [*presenting* PAUL]. My pupil whom you saw in Paris!

Colomba [*stopping* PAUL]. I forbid you to kiss——

Suzanne [*drawing* PAUL *to her*]. Ah, M. Paul! He will blush! [*Kisses him.*] He did blush! [*Bowing to* COLOMBA.] Madame!

Colomba [*dryly*]. Mademoiselle! [*Talks apart with* PAUL.]

Suzanne [*turning and seeing* PROSPER, *who is about to lift the Flora and take out the letter unperceived*]. Who is this gentleman in white?

Prosper. Missed! Try again.

Clarisse [*hastening to introduce him so as to force him to come forward*]. M. Prosper Block! A friend! [*Moving past him.*]

Suzanne [*looking at them*]. Ah, indeed! [*Aside.*] There's something in the wind.

Prosper. I have long coveted the honor of being introduced to madame!

Suzanne. You are interested in curiosities?

Thirion. Oh, tremendously! He has just returned from Asia, the Pacific islands, the ends of the earth.

Suzanne. How fortunate to be a man! But to run about the world in skirts!

Busonier. They didn't embarrass Madame Busonier.

Suzanne. Tell me, sir traveller, what is the most curious thing you have seen in the world?

Prosper. The most curious? Woman.

Suzanne. Ah, you are a student of the species?

Prosper. Exclusively! As Thirion studies insects, and others mushrooms.

Suzanne. You wish to imply that there are some venomous kinds?

Prosper [*watching* CLARISSE *as she hovers about the*

Flora]. Some, and they are generally the most beautiful. [*Aside*.] Ah! We begin to beat about the bush again.

Suzanne. And like a true naturalist, you stick little labels on us as they do with the stuffed birds in the *Jardin des Plantes*.

Prosper. Just what I was saying to Madame Vanhove. Excuse me. [*Everyone turns towards* CLARISSE *who comes forward without the letter;* PROSPER *offers her a seat which she is obliged to accept.*] Woman is a bird with a very slender beak, long claws, plumage of a greater or less degree of brilliancy, which she is constantly occupied in keeping bright.

Suzanne. And wings?

Prosper. The wings are wanting. She has nothing in common with the angels. [*Everybody protests.*]

Suzanne. Oh, sir, think of your mother, who perhaps hadn't so much wit as you, but who had heart enough to rock your cradle all night long—and your sister, a bit of a coquette perhaps, but who pawns her jewels to pay your gambling debts—and your wife?—

Prosper [*interrupting*]. Now there's where you spoil the simile.

Suzanne. No, there's where you spoil us! For it's you who make our faults; but you don't make our virtues. And someday, when poverty and disease cast you upon a hospital cot—then it is you find your natural history at fault. For there beside you is neither wife, nor beak, nor claws; only a sister of charity—with wings.

Prosper. The exception proves the rule. And in the case of woman, it is a general rule—

Suzanne. General rule! There are only exceptions.

Prosper. Well, madame, twice I thought I had met with exceptions—in Java and in Borneo; and do you know what happened? I was poisoned twice! And even in our own country, where poisons change their nature and are transformed into every sort of treachery and backbiting, I've sworn never to take a step without an antidote.

Thirion. An antidote? Of what sort?

Prosper. Oh, any little object that might scare the enemy and hold him off—— Such as, for instance, a letter.

Clarisse [*aside*]. He wants the letter.

Suzanne [*aside*]. There's a letter in the case!

Busonier. Fie! Such a weapon—and against a woman.

Prosper. Pardon me. I spoke of defense, not of attack. The shield is legitimate where it would be infamous to use a sword. Among all peoples——

Thirion. He's going to cite the Chinese. Just see if he doesn't!

Prosper [*quickly*]. Our masters in many things—even the manufacture of porcelain. Show me any object in this salon comparable to their masterpieces. Take this little Sèvres, for instance. [*To* CLARISSE.] A Flora, is it not? [*Taking the Flora.*]

Clarisse [*trying to stop him*]. Sir!

Prosper. Oh, don't be alarmed—I know its value.

Clarisse [*frightened*]. Give it to me. It's covered with dust.

Prosper. Don't give yourself the trouble. [*Aside.*] I feel the letter.

Clarisse [*taking a handkerchief, as if to dust it herself*]. Let me——

Prosper. A thousand thanks! By just blowing— [*Turns aside, under the pretext of blowing off the dust.*]

Suzanne [*staying* CLARISSE'S *hand*]. Vanhove is watching.

Clarisse. Oh, if you knew! [*The letter falls.*] Ah! [PROS-PER *quickly puts his foot on the letter.*]

Suzanne [*aside*]. A letter! I was sure of it.

Prosper [*handing the Flora to* CLARISSE]. It is evident you are alarmed for this little work of art.

Clarisse [*in a low voice*]. Oh, this is infamous!

Prosper [*softly*]. A shield, madame! All is fair in love and war. [*The bell rings for luncheon.*]

Enter MARTHE.

Marthe. Luncheon is ready!

Thirion [*rising*]. Well, I'm not sorry for that!

Busonier. Nor I!

Paul. Nor I!

Colomba [*aside to* PAUL]. You are not to sit beside Mademoiselle Marthe!

Paul. But—

Colomba. I forbid you.

Marthe. Give me your arm, Monsieur Paul!

Colomba. I forbid you. [*Turns and finds herself facing* Busonier.]

Busonier. Madame! [Colomba *takes his arm,* Clarisse Thirion's.]

Suzanne [*to* Prosper, *who stands with his foot on the letter*]. Aren't you going to offer me your arm?

Prosper. Beg pardon! I just dropped——

Suzanne. What?

Prosper [*letting his handkerchief fall*]. My handkerchief.

Suzanne [*in a low tone*]. Come, give it up with a good grace—

Prosper. Give what up?

Suzanne. The letter.

Prosper. My antidote! Never.

Suzanne. I shall force you to give it up.

Prosper. I'll wager you don't.

Suzanne. I'll wager I do.

Prosper. A declaration of war?

Suzanne. To the death!

Prosper. And we are to begin hostilities?—

Suzanne. After luncheon. But give me your arm—her husband is watching us.

Prosper [*offering his arm*]. Madame, may I?

Suzanne [*aloud*]. And so you like the Chinese; and do you eat with little sticks too?   [*Exeunt.*

ACT TWO

Prosper's *room at* Thirion's. *Curios everywhere: a mummy case, stuffed animals, a case of shells, strange weapons, etc. Among other objects are a box of cigars, matches, a lamp, and a tobacco jar.*

Prosper [*seated before an open fire, wrapped in a fur dressing gown*]. A nice climate, upon my word! In the morning it's hot as Senegal—at two o'clock cold as Lapland. [*Throws a log into the fire.*] Disgusting! [*Another stick. Shooting heard in the distance.*] Ah, shooting! The gentlemen are hunting. Much joy to them!

Enter a Servant.

What do you want? I didn't ring.

Servant. A letter for you, sir. They're waiting for an answer.

Prosper. Ah, from my uncle. Good! I know his letter by heart. Every morning he writes the same thing: "Vagabond, have you found a wife?" [*Reading.*] "Vagabond, have you found"—— Just so. Fifteenth edition. [*Throws it in the fire.*] Say I'll take the answer myself, within an hour, and have my horse ready at three.

Servant. Very well, sir.   [*Exit.*

Prosper. A quarter of an hour to go, another to return. I'd rather make the run and see that savage uncle myself. I'll tell him I've found my wife—[*Looks for a cigar.*]—that she is a charming blonde, and adores me! [*Rolling a cigarette.*] As for Mademoiselle Suzanne, I don't know whether she is as virtuous as her friend; but one thing there's no doubt about, and that's her challenge—"I will have the letter by force!" Did you ever hear the like! So you're going to outwit me—bless your little heart!—and filch my letter—American fashion. Clever Suzanne! But far more clever Prosper! We'll see who wins—— Once in possession of the letter, there were several ways of defending it—First, to keep it on my person, day and night. At night I hardly think the young lady—No! But day and night there are a thousand ambushes to be feared. To hide it in the lining of my hat! I tried that at Surinam with the love letter of a pretty little Dutch woman—but of course I managed to leave the hat at the house of her husband, who serenely took possession of it and has worn it ever since. I didn't dare claim it. So the hat won't do. Now from the moment I gave up the plan of carrying the letter about with me, I had no other resource but my room with its furniture—or a friend —or the hollow trunk of a tree. But as to the tree trunk— out of the question; for first you must find your tree, and then, having found it, you mustn't use it, for fear of rats. Then for the friend.—There is only Thirion, married, consequently allied to the fair sex, and not to be trusted. Third, there's my bedroom.—Nothing in it mine, nothing to be trusted—neither servants nor locks. Supposing I should put it in this casket with the secret lock. The casket can't be opened. But the windows are only six feet from the ground, and a casket of this shape has wings. Just see how an apparently simple problem may become complicated! All for a wicked little scrap of paper, no bigger than that. In short, another man than Prosper Block would have been at his wits' end. And so it is with almost delirious enthusiasm that I proclaim myself a genius in hiding it in the only place that will never be suspected, in—— [*A knock at the door.*] Someone knocks—Come in!

Enter PAUL.

Prosper. Ah, it's you, my young friend. Then you didn't go shooting with the rest?

Paul [*embarrassed, and trying to be dignified*]. No, sir.

Prosper. I understand. Madame Thirion is afraid. Good. Sit down and have a cigar. [*Offering cigars.*]

Paul. Thank you. I don't smoke.

Prosper. Ah, indeed. Madame Thirion objects to the odor?

Paul. Sir, I didn't come here to smoke, but to talk seriously with you. .

Prosper. Indeed!

Paul. This morning I learned, from a chance word dropped by M. Thirion, that you had asked M. Vanhove for the hand of Mademoiselle Marthe in marriage.

Prosper. Well?

Paul. Well, sir, I will not conceal from you that I love Mademoiselle Marthe, and that my greatest desire is to obtain her hand in marriage.

Prosper. Provided Madame Thirion consents.

Paul [*gently*]. Sir, there is no question of Madame Thirion here. It's between you and me. Kindly tell me whether you persist in your suit, yes or no?

Prosper [*aside*]. The boy is amusing. [*Aloud.*] Well, yes, I persist.

Paul. Then, sir, since one of us must necessarily yield his place to the other, and since I am not disposed to do that, it is indispensable that we fight.

Prosper. Indispensable?

Paul. I leave you to judge of that.

Prosper. Well, granted. Only you know, my dear young man, there are many modes of fighting: which do you prefer?

Paul. It is for you to choose, sir.

Prosper. I confess to a weakness for the custom of Japan.

Paul. I agree to the custom of Japan. I shall have the honor to send you my seconds, and——

Prosper. Oh, that's quite unnecessary. The matter can be decided between ourselves, with closed doors, and immediately, if you wish it. [*He goes to his wardrobe.*]

Paul [*laying aside his hat and gloves*]. It's contrary to all rules, but I'm your man.

Prosper [*presenting two Malayan daggers*]. Here are two daggers. Be so kind as to choose.

Paul. What are those?

Prosper. The weapons. [PAUL *takes one.*] And now [*sitting down*] be good enough to begin.

Paul [*turns quickly, weapon in hand, but stops short on seeing* PROSPER *seated*]. To begin!

Prosper. Certainly. You provoke the quarrel; it's for you to begin.

Paul. All alone? How shall I begin?

Prosper. Why, by ripping open your stomach.

Paul. My stomach?

Prosper. The custom of Japan—Invariable rule: the aggressor is to rip open his stomach before his adversary, and the latter is bound to do likewise at the very same instant. You are the aggressor. Begin! I'll follow suit.

Paul. You are making sport of me, sir! We are not in Japan, but in France, and your custom is utterly absurd.

Prosper. A question of appreciation. I find your custom detestable.

Paul. Detestable for one who has neither courage nor honor.

Prosper [*gayly*]. Oh, as for courage, young man, I've fought with tigers—quite as dangerous as you;—and as for honor, you see everyone hasn't the same opinion about that, since in Japan it's different from what it is here. And mark, the Japanese reason far better than you; for supposing we were to fight in the French fashion: I should inevitably kill you.

Paul. Oh!

Prosper. Oh, I'll answer for that! And afterwards I should be only the more sure to marry: there you are away off from your object! On the other hand, suppose we fight like the Japanese. You rip yourself open—I rip myself open.—You won't get married, that's sure; but neither will I! And you can rest in peace.

Paul. You treat me like a child, sir.

Prosper [*rising and holding out his hand*]. Rather, like a friend, young man. For, to make an end of the matter, the two methods are equally unreasonable; and the man who has washed his honor in blood can say with Diogenes on coming from a bath of questionable purity, "Where can I wash myself clean after this?" But what is welcome in all places and at all times, what suits every age and stature, is the fair and courteous competition—with the head and heart for weapons—that I offer you. You love Mademoiselle Marthe. She, perhaps, loves you. So much the better for you—for I swear I will not marry her against her will. But since you have found means to please her, permit me to believe that I shall not be less skillful, and allow me to go through my term of probation.

Paul. In what manner?

Prosper. Ah! I haven't asked you your methods. The young lady will choose, the vanquished will retire from the field—and intact.—Consolation ready at hand!

Paul. And how long do you require for this trial, sir?

Prosper. My dear friend, don't haggle over the time. You are not of age, you haven't the consent of your guardian, and I am certain you never will get it.

Paul. Never? Why not?

Prosper. Why not?

Colomba [*from without, knocking*]. M. Prosper!

Prosper. Listen—That's why! I am not presentable; let me get out of the way.

Colomba and Marthe [*from without*]. May we come in?

Prosper. Yes, you're quite welcome, ladies.

[*He enters his dressing room.*

Enter COLOMBA *and* MARTHE.

Colomba [*looking around for* PROSPER]. Well?

Marthe. Where's M. Prosper?

Prosper [from within]. Excuse me. I am a bear. I should have frightened you.

Colomba. We beg your pardon. We thought we should find Mademoiselle Suzanne and the gentlemen here. They wish to visit your museum.

Prosper. Visit it, ladies, by all means.

Marthe. Oh, what pretty things! [*Frightened.*] Oh! a mummy!

Colomba [aside to PAUL]. You know I don't wish you to associate with M. Prosper. He is a very undesirable acquaintance for you.

Paul. But really, if I listened to you, I shouldn's speak to anybody. Now it's M. Prosper, now Mademoiselle Suzanne, then Mademoiselle Marthe——

Colomba. Especially the latter. And I must say you pay great attention to my wishes. You never fail to sit beside her at table and to chatter with her in an undertone in a most improper manner—in spite of my disapproving looks——

Paul. But madame——

Colomba. But I give you warning, that if you don't mend your ways, I'll have you sent back to Chinon this very evening, to study for your degree.

Paul. But, madame!

Marthe. Monsieur Paul!

Colomba. And as a beginning, I here formally command you to give your whole attention to me.

Marthe. Monsieur Paul!

Colomba [to PAUL]. You hear? [*Sitting down by a table.*]

Marthe. Must I come for you, then? [*She sits down on a divan.*] Ah! I understand. Madame Thirion has been making eyes at you ever since this morning, and now she has forbidden you to speak to me.

Paul. Oh! madame——

Colomba. Paul, bring me a footstool, please.

Paul. Yes, madame.

Marthe [aside to PAUL]. I forbid you to give it to her.

Paul [footstool in hand]. But——

Marthe [pointing to her feet]. And put it there at once.

Colomba. Paul, don't you hear me? A footstool.

Paul. Pardon! but I—don't know——

Colomba. Why, you've got it in your hand!

Paul [*looking at* MARTHE, *who points to her feet*]. Yes, but Mademoiselle Marthe asked me——

Marthe. What's that? If madame wishes it, give it to her, by all means.

Colomba. You are too kind!

Marthe. Don't mention it, madame. It is a deference that my age owes to yours.

Colomba [*pushing away the footstool which* PAUL *presents*]. The difference is too slight for me to accept it.

Marthe. Then take it as a delicate attention of Monsieur Paul—which I yield to you.

Colomba [*aside, rising*]. Which she yields! What insolence!

Marthe [*aside, rising*]. Checkmated!

Colomba [*to* PAUL]. You shall go this very evening.

Paul. But——

Marthe [*aside to* PAUL]. If you answer her, I'll never speak to you again.

Paul. Then—I— [*Sits down on the footstool.*] Ah!

Enter THIRION, BUSONIER, SUZANNE, *and several hunters, with their rifles.*

Thirion [*at the door*]. May we come in?

Prosper [*coming from his room, dressed*]. Come in! Come in!

Suzanne. Beat the drums! Blow the trumpets! [*To* PROSPER.] I hope to make a good fight. Was it rash to come upon you in your stronghold with an armed force?

Prosper [*bowing*]. I can only answer in Oriental phrase:— "A ray of sunshine has the right to enter everywhere!"

Marthe. And when one isn't a ray of sunshine?

Prosper. Perfume of roses has the same privilege.

Marthe [*to* PAUL]. He is more gallant than you.

Prosper [*to* THIRION *and* BUSONIER]. I thought you had both gone hunting?

Busonier. Yes, yes. But this is between the acts.

Prosper. And what have you killed since noon?

Thirion. Between the two of us, we've killed one dog.

Prosper. And Vanhove?

Busonier. Oh, Vanhove! He's a mighty hunter before the Lord, as a rule. But today I don't know what's the matter with him. He is moody and absent-minded. Misses every shot.

Colomba. Madame Vanhove didn't come with you?

Busonier. No, she is not feeling well.

Thirion [*coming upon* PAUL]. Hello! What's he doing here?

Colomba. It is imperative that this young man should go to Chinon.

Thirion. How's that? Why?

Colomba. To prepare for his examinations.

Thirion. Pshaw! I don't see the necessity of it.

Paul. Nor do I.

Colomba. But I do.

Thirion. Why?

Colomba. I have good reason to.

Thirion. That's another matter. He shall go. [COLOMBA *moves away.*] [*Aside.*] Some pranks, I'll wager. What a simpleton it is! Can't manage his affairs without Colomba's knowledge. [*To* PAUL.] Oh, you are a simpleton!

Paul. Sir?

Thirion. Go pack your trunk.

Paul [*sighing*]. Ah! When a woman takes a grudge against you! But I'm not at Chinon yet.

Thirion. What's that?   [*Exit* PAUL.

Suzanne. A truly remarkable collection this—and collector.

Prosper. All bric-a-brac. It's the fashion, you know. Our furniture, our books, our ideas and customs—bric-a-brac—mere bric-a-brac. We only care for what is foreign.

Suzanne. Show me a man seated in an American rocking chair, like this one, before a Flemish table covered with an Algerian cloth, drinking Chinese drinks out of Saxon porcelain, smoking Turkish tobacco, after a Russian dinner, where he talked sport to his wife in English, while she answered with Italian music—I'll tell you at once—This is a Frenchman!

Marthe. Just look at these little shells!

Prosper. Souvenir of a Honolulu lady.

Colomba. A bracelet!

Prosper [*in an undertone to* SUZANNE *and* COLOMBA]. A dress, rather.

Colomba [*rising*]. Oh, monsieur!

Suzanne [*aside*]. Too much virtue to be virtuous.

Marthe. Monsieur Paul! What, is he gone?

Suzanne [*aside*]. Oh! Monsieur Paul again!

Marthe [*to* PROSPER]. A thousand thanks for your kindness. Are you coming, godmother?

Suzanne. Run along. I'm coming.

Thirion [*seeing* MARTHE *go towards the little door at the right*]. You're not going out that way?

Marthe. Yes, it's the shortest road to the château. [*Aside.*] And he went out by this door. [*Aloud.*] Good day, gentlemen.   [*Exit.*

Thirion [*to* BUSONIER]. Supposing we resume our shooting.

Busonier. And kill another dog?

Colomba [*about to go out by the door at the rear*]. Aren't you coming, mademoiselle?

Suzanne. No, madame. I shall go with Marthe.

Thirion and Busonier. Good-bye.

               [*Exeunt* THIRION, BUSONIER, COLOMBA.

Suzanne. Good sport, gentlemen! [*To* PROSPER.] Monsieur, I have the honor—[PROSPER *bows and shuts the door after* BUSONIER *and* THIRION. SUZANNE *quickly closes the little door at the right, returns, and takes a seat.*]—to salute you.

Prosper. Indeed! I thought you were beating a retreat.

Suzanne. Before the battle? It's clear you don't know me. But are you still holding on to the letter?

Prosper. Yes, I'm holding on to it!

Suzanne. Well then, before coming to open hostilities, suppose we exchange a few diplomatic notes.

Prosper [*sitting down by the table*]. By all means.

Suzanne. First note: We appeal to the honor of our adversary and ask him whether simple probity authorizes him to keep a letter which he has—how shall I express myself——

Prosper. Stolen!

Suzanne. Let us be parliamentary and say—intercepted! What have you to answer?

Prosper. I answer that the letter, being addressed to me, taken by me, is in possession of its rightful owner.

Suzanne. You didn't receive it, therefore it belongs to us.

Prosper. You sent it to me, therefore it belongs to me.

Suzanne. There was no emissary.

Prosper. Pardon me. A point of good faith. The Flora represents in this case the letter box, and the point in dispute is this: Does a letter dropped into a letter box belong to the sender or to the person to whom it is addressed?

Suzanne. To the sender.

Prosper. To the person addressed.

Suzanne. Let us say to both.

Prosper. Then it's mine.

Suzanne. But it's also ours.

Prosper. Where rights are equal, possession gives the title. Let us go on to the next point.

Suzanne. We ask what you purpose to do with our handwriting?

Prosper. I have already replied categorically on that point. Observe strict neutrality, and on the day when I give up all hopes of Mademoiselle Marthe, I will bid an eternal farewell to Madame Vanhove, and burn the letter before her eyes.

Suzanne. You will do that?

Prosper. On my word of honor—and I swear I should have done it this morning, without telling you, of course, if your challenge hadn't provoked me to combat.

Suzanne. Well, then, I withdraw my challenge. Burn it before me. See, here's a pretty fire. Clarisse will know nothing about it, and the effect will be the same for you. Come, a good deed!

Prosper [*smiling*]. I'd lose too much.

Suzanne. But what?

Prosper. The immense satisfaction that I promise to my artistic instincts in seeing you find the letter where I have hidden it.

Suzanne. Surely wit spoils the heart.

Prosper. Not always, mademoiselle. You are a proof to the contrary.

Suzanne. And that is your last word?

Prosper. The last.—Negotiations broken off!

Suzanne. At least I hope I have observed all the forms, and given you three summonses.

Prosper. Yes.

Suzanne. Then let the trumpets sound for battle. Since it is I who prevented your destroying this scrap of paper, I shall be forced to repair the injury I've done you, and to make you destroy it before my eyes.

Prosper. As you please. The letter is here.

Suzanne. Here?

Prosper. Here! Find it, and I'll authorize you to burn it yourself.

Suzanne. Oh, I'm something of an artist, too. And I shall not be satisfied unless you burn it with your own hands—in that fire.

Prosper. Madame, I swear that if you succeed I will renounce Mademoiselle Marthe—and I will start this evening, madame, this very evening, to find a wife in the Marquesas Islands.

Suzanne. You swear?

Prosper. I swear it.

Suzanne. A coward he who retracts! I warn you I am obstinate.

Prosper. I too!

Suzanne. That the fear of gossip will never deter me.

Prosper. Nor me!

Suzanne. Especially when there's a good deed to be done.

Prosper. Oh, for my part, in the matter of good deeds—don't mention it!

Suzanne. And I'm going to begin by a regular siege. I shall attach myself to you, bore you to death with my presence. I shall be tiresome, unendurable, altogether odious. I will never leave you until you say—"What a nuisance of a woman! I'd rather burn the letter than have her around."

Prosper. Was ever anyone threatened with so delightful a punishment! My soul is intoxicated with joy to think of the many pleasant hours we shall spend together. Do me the honor to sit in this armchair and make yourself at home. Here is a fire, books, and some sketches to which I venture to call your attention. The cases are open—here are my

shells; there, Thirion's insects. All the keys are in their locks.
Let me see, are they? [*Looks.*] Yes—excepting this little
casket, which contains papers on matters of no interest to
you. Open and rummage through everything—turn everything topsy-turvy—I shall be only too delighted if they
charm your leisure during a little visit that I am obliged to
make to my uncle; and if you're still here when I return I
hope to continue our most entertaining conversation.
Would it were never to end!

Suzanne. But——

Prosper. Good day, madame.   [*Exit.*

Suzanne [*alone*]. What? Gone? He's decidedly interesting. Did you ever hear such insolence! "Search, madame,
search!—Everything is open—excepting this casket." How
particular he was to emphasize the casket—with his important papers. Poor man! I can be sure at least his letter
isn't in the casket. But it is in this room—Where can he
have hidden it? [*Someone knocks at the little door to the
right.*] Already! No. It is the little door leading to the park.
[*Louder knocking.*] Who's there?—I'm compromised!—
Come to my aid! [*She opens the door.*]

Enter CLARISSE.

Clarisse. You are alone?

Suzanne. Clarisse!

Clarisse [*shutting the door*]. I saw him pass my windows
on horseback, and as you didn't return—why, I couldn't
keep still. I threw this shawl over my shoulders and came
over.

Suzanne. Rash woman! What if your husband had seen
you!—Or Madame Colomba, that embodiment of charity!

Clarisse [*throwing her shawl on the sofa*]. Pshaw! Since
we are alone, tell me. Have you got it?

Suzanne. The letter? No, he refuses to surrender it.

Clarisse. Oh, Suzanne, he's left it somewhere around here.
Find it, I implore you. I no longer dare look M. Vanhove
in the face. He acts as if he had guessed everything—as if he
knew all.

Suzanne. My poor friend! What a lesson to young girls, if
they could only hear you.

Clarisse. Oh, they'd never do any more writing, I assure you.

Suzanne. Avoid all double-dealing, there's a simple rule of conduct for you.

Clarisse. Oh, don't lose any time!—Let us search.

Suzanne. But I am searching!

Clarisse. Like that?

Suzanne. With my head. It does better work than my hands could.

Clarisse. But we must rummage over everything—examine everything.

Suzanne. Do so—I have permission. But that's not my way of doing it.

Clarisse. What!—you're just going to sit still?

Suzanne. My dear child—Nature, in making us women did us such an ill turn that she tried to recompense us by giving us a sixth sense—like the butterflies. Have you ever examined a butterfly?

Clarisse. Oh, I don't know. What a question!

Suzanne. Well, just look in that case there. Let's see! [CLARISSE *quickly picks up the case and takes it to her.*] That is Thirion's collection. Just examine their heads. How pretty they are! They have two long slender horns to feel and to touch things at a distance.

Clarisse. Well?

Suzanne. Well, my dear, it's the same way with us women. We, too, have little horns all around our heads—so fine that no one perceives them, so delicate that they find out everything. Some are like tendrils, to twine around the men, others are sharp-pointed, to blind them.

Clarisse [*pettishly, putting back the case*]. And that's how you're going to find my letter?

Suzanne. Search!—I'll show you how to make use of your horns.

Clarisse. I'd rather trust my two hands. [*Begins to open all the drawers.*]

Suzanne. That's right—Go ahead! Upset everything. Don't forget to search the mouth of the lizard, and the hollow of the guitar. What a child!

Clarisse. Could he have hidden it in the bookcase, perhaps?

Suzanne. Three hundred volumes to examine—Look at the edges of the shelves!

Clarisse. Why?

Suzanne. Are they dusty?

Clarisse [*climbing on a chair to see*]. Yes.

Suzanne. All along?

Clarisse. All along.

Suzanne. Then it isn't there. In pulling out a book he would have disturbed the dust.

Clarisse. That's so.

Suzanne. Now look there—at that little bit of paper folded under one foot of the table.

Clarisse. This?

Suzanne. Yes—no, it's not worth the trouble.

Clarisse. Why not?

Suzanne. Because the edge of the paper is worn and discolored.

Clarisse. And besides, that wouldn't have been clever—right in plain sight. [*She continues to hunt about.*]

Suzanne. For that very reason it would have been extremely clever. It's clear you don't know how to use your little horns, my dear. You confound the hiding places of simpletons with those of clever people. A clever man will take so little pains to conceal an object that you'd never think of hunting for it where it is. And I'll wager that if we don't find this wretched letter it's because it's staring us in the face.

Clarisse [*after hunting awhile*]. Nothing! But there's still another room.

Suzanne [*smiling*]. Go ahead! I am privileged to look everywhere.

Clarisse. But if he should come back—Well, I don't care—I can defend myself. [*Enters the bedroom.*]

Suzanne. Now where can it be? He's clever enough to have simply put it—under his paperweight—[*She lifts the paperweight.*] Nothing there! Or here, in the tobacco jar—[*Looks into the jar.*] Cards, a stick of sealing wax—paper for cigarettes—tobacco—some torn and crumpled letters. [*Reading.*] "To Monsieur Prosper Block—To monsieur, monsieur"—[*Going over the letters.*] And here's an odd-looking one, all covered with stamps. It must have done considerable travelling. [*Starts to put it into the other hand, with the rest, but changes her mind.*] "To Monsieur Prosper Block, care of the Reverend Sir Edward, Honolulu, Island of Oahu"—[*Reflecting.*] Honolulu! But that can't be of recent date. Why is it here? Very odd! [*Weighs the letter.*] Who could have sent a little billet-doux, weighing no more than that, to Monsieur Prosper Block, at Honolulu? Make a man pay five francs postage just to bid him good morning! It's certainly very odd. [*Holds the letter up to the light.*] It's a little square piece of paper. [*Calling.*] Clarisse!

Clarisse [*from the other room*]. I can find nothing.

Suzanne. Tell me, my dear—Was your letter very big?

Clarisse. No—a half sheet, folded once.

Suzanne [*feeling the letter. Aside*]. A half sheet, folded once!—yes. [*Aloud.*] White paper?

Clarisse. No, blue. I saw it this morning.

Suzanne [*peeping into the envelope*]. It is blue!

Clarisse [*from the other room*]. Oh, Suzanne!—A box full of papers!

Suzanne. All right. So much the better. [*Smelling the envelope.*] Perfume—but very faint. [*Looking more closely through the envelope.*] Let's see the handwriting. [*Makes a movement to take out the letter. Stops short.*] Softly! This is a matter of honor. Have I the right to read it? Why not? He gave me permission to look at everything that was open —everything. This envelope is open—It's not quite the thing—and it's not my custom, although a woman. [*Fingering the envelope.*] But if it should be the letter! My fingers twitch!

Clarisse [*coming out from the bedroom, in despair*]. Ah, my dear friend—It's no use—I give it up. We shall never find it—never!

Suzanne. I can't see her cry like that! [*Snatches the paper from the envelope and presents it to* CLARISSE.] Clarisse! Was your letter anything like that?

Clarisse [*unfolding the letter*]. It's my letter!

Suzanne [*laughing*]. Ah, my dear—My little horns! What did I tell you?

Clarisse. Oh, yes, it's the very letter. [*Reading.*] "I leave tonight; but far or near, my love—" my love! If Monsieur Vanhove—— [*Violent knocking at the little door.*]

Suzanne. Someone knocks!

Clarisse. Someone knocks?

Vanhove [*from without, knocking louder*]. Open the door!

Suzanne. Vanhove! Give it here! [*Takes the letter.*]

Clarisse. Oh, where shall I hide?

Suzanne [*sotto-voce, going to open the door*]. Always the same! Don't hide—Stay.

Clarisse [*losing her wits*]. No, no. He would see my agitation—He would guess. [*Looks around.*] Ah, in this room! [VANHOVE *knocks again.*]

Suzanne [*her hand on the doorknob*]. Stay here!

Clarisse. No! [*Enters the bedroom and closes the door.*]

Suzanne. Ah, foolish woman! [*Opens the door.*]

Enter VANHOVE *in shooting dress, with his gun.*

Vanhove. You?

Suzanne [*calm and smiling*]. Yes, I. What an uproar you've been making, cousin.

Vanhove. You here?

Suzanne. As you see—Looking at the collection.

Vanhove [*looking around him*]. Alone?

Suzanne. As you see. [*She sits down before the cases of shells.*] There's a wonderful collection of shells!—Just look!

Vanhove [*putting down his gun*]. I thought I heard talking in here.

Suzanne. Yes—I was trying to decipher these labels aloud. These scientific men give such outlandish names to things. Here, just look at that. Isn't it pretty?

Vanhove. Suzanne, you weren't alone—Clarisse was here!

Suzanne. Clarisse! What should she be doing here?

Vanhove. No good, evidently, since she has fled.

Suzanne [*laughing and still looking at the shells*]. Indeed! Are you often taken that way, cousin?

Vanhove. I tell you she was here.

Suzanne. Then, why shouldn't she be here still? Come, my friend, do you think she has hidden herself under the table?

Vanhove. Then why didn't you open at once?

Suzanne. Because I thought the knocking was at the other door, and opened that door first.

Vanhove. You opened it to let Clarisse make her escape. That's the way she went!

Suzanne. How tiresome you are! If she went out that way, go and satisfy yourself, and leave me in peace with my shells.

Vanhove. Suzanne, I noticed that my wife was very much agitated this morning, after talking with this man—who knew her in the past. They spoke to each other in an undertone before lunch. What did they have to say to each other during that affair of the statuette?

Suzanne. They probably were saying that M. Vanhove was a funny kind of a man with his jealousies.

Vanhove. He asked for the hand of Marthe without even having seen her. How transparent! A mere pretext for introducing himself into this house in order to see her again. This marriage is merely a blind to divert my suspicions. [*Seizing* SUZANNE'S *hand.*] Look me in the face, and tell me that it isn't.

Suzanne. Of course it isn't.—But let go my hand, Vanhove,—you hurt me. And see what a mess you've made of my shells. [*Opens her hand and shows a shell in powder.*] This isn't nice of you.

Vanhove. Do you want to know what I have done? I left off shooting abruptly, to return to the château. I asked for madame. She had gone out. I had with me my dog Myrrha, who is as much attached to her mistress as to me. I said: "Search, Myrrha, search for her."

Suzanne. Oh—if it is possible.

Vanhove. Oh! [*Mocking her.*] And Myrrha darted into the park and came straight to Thirion's house, stopping at the door at the foot of this stairway. I tell you my wife is here, Suzanne. Where is she?—Where is she?

Suzanne. How do I know? Call Myrrha, my dear friend. If you're going to hunt your wife with dogs——

Vanhove [*falling into a chair*]. Ah, Suzanne! You are right. What a miserable wretch I am! This jealousy is a frightful passion—It blinds and maddens me. My head is on fire—I am no longer a man, but a wild beast, without understanding or reason. [*Weeping.*] Oh, let me weep. It will relieve me. Oh, my God, what torture!

Suzanne. Why, Vanhove!—My friend! Now I'm going to

scold you—you great baby! Spoiling your happiness in that
fashion, when you have the most charming, the most
lovable wife—who thinks of no one but you, who lives only
for you.

Vanhove. I know it!—I know it! I am reasonable again,
Suzanne. I am calm. But the first occasion—if I should
ever believe—[*Sees* CLARISSE's *shawl and leaps upon it.*] Ah,
you see she's been here—That's her shawl!

Suzanne. Her shawl!

Vanhove. Don't deny it. Who put it there?

Suzanne. I did—I took the first that came to hand.

Vanhove. I don't believe you. The shawl is here—She
hasn't gone. She is hidden somewhere. But I swear that I'll
find her

Suzanne. Vanhove!—Stop!

Vanhove [*searching, in spite of her*]. Leave me!

Suzanne [*trying to stop him*]. Think of what you are
doing!

Vanhove [*finding the door to the other room*]. A door!—
She's there! [SUZANNE *throws herself between him and the
door.*] She's hidden in that man's room! Let me pass, I say!
And on my life—[*picks up his gun*] I'll kill lover and
mistress together.

Suzanne. Ah, wretch! Then kill me! For I am his mistress.

Vanhove. You!

Suzanne. You drive me to say it, madman! since by your
uproar you are turning it into a public scandal. What! You
didn't understand at once, from my confusion, my agitation
—Do you think a woman comes to visit a man alone, to
look at his butterflies and shells? I didn't open the door at
once, it's true—because I was afraid of being found here.
Your dog stopped at the door—because it had tracked
Clarisse's shawl. Clarisse refused to give Marthe to Prosper
—because she knows of our liaison. Prosper wants to marry
—because he thinks I've deceived him and wants to be
revenged on me. Clarisse spoke low to him—to try to move
him and prevent this marriage—which will never take place.
For I, too, am jealous, Vanhove—jealous as you. And I
can tell you that when once I am aroused! Well!

Vanhove. Is it possible! You, Suzanne! So virtuous!

Suzanne [*sighing*]. Ah, my poor friend. There are days and moments——

Vanhove. Yes, yes. He spoke this morning of having fallen in love with a woman three years ago.

Suzanne [*sighing*]. It was I.

Vanhove. He spoke of treachery!

Suzanne [*sighing*]. My treachery!

Vanhove. But why did you not tell me that at once?

Suzanne. You are so good! And do you think a woman makes such a confession voluntarily? But you were in such a rage—and your outcry! You can't imagine it! Then the terrible fright, and then—but it's all told now, isn't it? And my reputation, my position—you understand, Vanhove? [*Aside.*] And ta ra ta ta ta! I'm in such a muddle I don't know what I'm saying.

Vanhove. Calm yourself, Suzanne—No one shall know what you have confided to me. And from this wrong great good may result.

Suzanne. How?

Vanhove. For now it is no longer Marthe whom Monsieur Prosper shall marry—it is you.

Suzanne. Me? [*Aside.*] I never thought of that!

Vanhove. Trust me. I'll take it upon myself.

Suzanne. But, my friend——

Vanhove. No, no. I will see him myself. I will speak to him—and that at once. Where is the gentleman to be found?

Suzanne. Oh, my dear friend. Not before I—at least you'll grant me the joy of luring him back. Come now! [*Insisting.*] Ah, Vanhove!

Vanhove. Well, as you will. But I swear that if he hasn't made up his mind before dinner, I'll take him by the collar—

Suzanne. Oh, Heavens.

Vanhove. And make him marry you—I'll answer for it! Dead or alive! A woman like you to be suspected, accused! It's like Clarisse! My good, pure Clarisse! Whom I— [*Laughing.*] What a fool I am! But he shall marry you! I am so happy I want everybody else to be happy. He shall marry you!—And we'll dance at your wedding! By Saint Hubert!

—Suzanne, you shall be happy! I am entirely satisfied. Now, to my shooting! [*Taking his gun.*] Come, Myrrha, we're going ahunting, my girl.

Suzanne [*aside*]. And they say this man can't talk.

Vanhove. But not a word to Clarisse, Suzanne.

Suzanne. Be at ease, my friend. She shall know no more about it than she knows at this minute.

Vanhove. To the hunt, Myrrha! Ah! What a joyful day!

Suzanne. Ah, what a joyful day! [*Exit* VANHOVE.] Oh!

Clarisse [*coming from the bedroom*]. Gone?

Suzanne. Hush! [CLARISSE *draws back.*]

Vanhove [*from without*]. To the hunt, Myrrha! Come, my girl!

Suzanne. He's gone.

Clarisse. Oh, Suzanne!—My friend, my sister! Blessings on you! You've saved me twice.

Suzanne. Nonsense! We must stand by each other against the common enemy. Only, I am lost.

Clarisse. Lost?

Suzanne. If I've got to marry this man I'll kill him first. I'll kill him on the wedding night.

Clarisse. Good Heavens! If my husband persists in seeing him, in speaking to him, everything will be found out. We must get him out of the way.

Suzanne. He shall go. But be off, quickly! Vanhove may go to the house again.

Clarisse. Burn the letter. I'd like to stop to see it burn, at least.

Suzanne. Hurry, I tell you. You must be there before him.

Clarisse. Someone may see me.

Suzanne [*opens the little door*]. Go this way. The road is clear.

Clarisse. I will escape this way.

Suzanne [*snatching her shawl from her*]. Leave the shawl!

Clarisse. That's so! Oh, I'll go quickly—I'm lighter than when I came.   [*Exit.*

Suzanne [*draws the letter from her pocket*]. Easy enough to burn the letter—But how to make him go? That's another matter. He'll want his revenge. [*Looks at the clock.*] Half-past four. He would still have time to pack up and take the nine o'clock train this evening. [*Crumples the letter to throw it in the fire.*] Wouldn't that be fine! [*Stops and looks at the letter.*] But there's the envelope—Give unto Cæsar what is Cæsar's. [*Takes the paper from the envelope.*] I'll just slip in the first scrap of paper that comes to hand. [*Picks up a scrap of paper from the table and puts it in the envelope.*] There!—right in the midst of the to-bacco—"To M. Prosper Block, Honolulu." [*Places it among the other letters in the tobacco jar.*] That's done! Now for the billet-doux. [*Approaches the fireplace.*] It's not just what I had counted on; it would have been such a joy—[*Holds it over the fire.*] to make him burn it himself. [*The paper catches fire. She pulls it back and blows it out.*] Himself! Stay! What was it he swore?—"If you make me burn it with my own hands, in this fire, I give you my word of honor that I'll leave this evening to go look for a wife in the Marquesas Islands." That would just suit us! Has he a word of honor, a man like that? He must have. Poor head and weak brain—but I'll trust to his word of honor. Let's see—Would it be very difficult to make him burn that?— [*Looks around the fireplace.*] If I put it there, near the fire! [*Twists the paper and puts it near the fireplace.*] Looks as if it had already been used to light a cigar. [*Goes off, and looks at it from every side.*] This whets my appetite—I do love these little contests of skill. Here's a paper to be burned! Now, for a change, he shall amuse me; for he has bored me enough ever since morning. [*Listens.*] Someone coming up stairs. It is he. Oh, I forgot the matches! [*Throws them all into the fire.*] There! [*Sits down in an armchair.*] Let me appear worn out, utterly worn out. [*Pretends to be dozing. PROSPER knocks softly.*] Ah! All right!—go on knocking.

Enter PROSPER, *softly opening the little door at the right.*

Prosper. Asleep! Fatigue! Exhaustion! Despair! [*Looks around him.*] Well, she's managed to turn everything topsy-turvy. [*Looks into bedroom and laughs.*] And the letter?— Have we found it? [SUZANNE *watches him from the corners of her eyes, while he looks into the tobacco jar and perceives the envelope.*] It's there. Ha! ha! The cunning sex is beaten! [*Looking closely at* SUZANNE.] Beat— [*Breaking off.*] But asleep, like that—she's pretty—remarkably—[*looks closer*] pretty. Exquisite! [*Turns around her.*] As for her eyes!——

Suzanne [*opens her eyes wide, and looks at him*]. What did you say?

Prosper [*drawing back*]. Oh! dazzling!

Suzanne [*pretending to awake*]. I beg your pardon. I must have fallen asleep.

Prosper. Pray consider yourself at home, madame.

Suzanne. What time is it?

Prosper. Five o'clock.

Suzanne. So late!

Prosper. Tell me, joking aside, have you found it?

Suzanne. No, but I haven't given up. You see I am at my post—and I shall stay here.

Prosper. All the evening?

Suzanne. All the evening.

Prosper. And the night?

Suzanne. And—bah! I'll have it before then.

Prosper [*laughing*]. On my soul, madame, that's very fine and chivalrous of you. The most heroic obstinacy I've ever seen in my life.

Suzanne. Obstinacy? You call it obstinacy.

Prosper. Call it pride!

Suzanne. Neither the one nor the other.

Prosper. Don't defend yourself. You have a reputation for cleverness to save. This contest, that you've so rashly entered upon, may tarnish its lustre by a defeat. You make a desperate appeal to all your forces, you swear to die in the breach. That is fine! It's great! sublime! If the chances of war hadn't made me your enemy, I'd like to fight under your standard and help you recover this wretched letter. [SU-ZANNE *shivers.*] You are cold—pardon me! [*Throws a stick into the fire.*]

Suzanne. Seriously, do you imagine my only motive is the silly vanity of outwitting you?

Prosper. Don't call it vanity—call it pride, madame! And legitimate pride! You're pitted against a man who has fought with red Indians. Here's a tomahawk that I captured from a great chief—"The sachem who weeps over his posterity." I too am a great chief—a great chief of the pale-faces, keen of scent, cunning on the trail. It would be no small glory for you to take my scalp. [*It grows dark.*]

Suzanne. Well then, to follow out your simile:—In spite

of the pleasure I should have in scalping you, oh great chief! a better motive than that has sent me on the warpath. Only be good enough to light your lamp, for really it's getting quite dark.

Prosper [*rising to take the lamp from the mantel*]. Yes, madame. But, in default of pride, what motive can drive you to this desperate contest?

Suzanne. You won't admit that more serious motives may exist?

Prosper. I confess that—[*The lamp sputters.*] So! That fool of a servant hasn't put any oil in. [*Rings.*]

Suzanne. Light a candle—that will be quicker.

Prosper. That's so. [*Looks for the matches.*] As I was saying, madame, if it is not the desire—very natural in a woman—especially—Ah! no matches now.

Suzanne. A bit of paper!

Prosper [*bending down and seeing the twisted scrap of paper*]. This will do. [*Picks it up.*] The very natural desire of a woman not to let herself be outwitted by a man— [*Holds the paper over the fire. It burns.*]

Enter Servant, with lighted lamp.

Servant. You rang, sir?

Prosper [*extinguishing the lighted paper and keeping it in his hand*]. Yes—Good! Thanks! That's what I wanted.

Suzanne [*aside*]. How vexatious. It was almost done.

　　　　　　　　　　　　　　　　　　[*Exit Servant.*

Prosper. By a man—(I'll perhaps manage to finish my sentence.) I don't really see what can set you against me.

Suzanne. How about the desire to save my friend? You don't take that motive into account?

Prosper [*still holding the scrap of paper*]. A friend! A friend! Pardon the question, madame. But is it possible for a woman to be so much the friend of another woman as to pull her out of a scrape? [*Aside.*] She's ravishing by lamplight.

Suzanne. I might be offended by the question. I prefer to laugh at it.

Prosper [*picking at the paper*]. Ravishing! [*Aloud.*] Note that I haven't any better opinion of my own sex than of yours. I don't believe in the goodness of either. [Suzanne *mechanically takes up the envelope and fictitious letter, from the tobacco jar, and plays with it.* PROSPER *starts.*]

Suzanne. You judge others by yourself.

Prosper [*laughing to see the letter in her hand*]. If you mean that I am selfish—[*Aside, delightedly.*] Oh! the letter! [*Aloud.*] I confess that I try my best to be so; others only do evil to me, and I don't see what I should gain by doing good to them.

Suzanne [*throwing the letter back into the jar*]. The pleasure of doing good. If you knew how a kind act brightens the sky, seasons one's food, and softens one's pillow— Ah, Sir Egoist!—you'd be good for your own sake! Of all that you have spent during your life, think what is left to you. The little that you have given——

Prosper. Perhaps, yes! [*Aside.*] What a smile—and what a soul!

Suzanne [*aside*]. If I were to put out the lamp, he'd be forced to light it again. [*Starts to turn the wick up and down.*]

Prosper [*springing forward*]. Allow me, madame! Is it smoking?

Suzanne. Yes, a little. [*Puts out the lamp.*] Oh, there now! [*Takes off the chimney and fixes lamp for lighting it again.*]

Prosper [*aside*]. So much the better! [*Aloud.*] Ah! madame, if you believe all you say, if you are really prompted only by goodness of heart—Ah, no, it's not enthusiasm that you inspire in me, it's veneration, idolatry, religion! You're not merely a woman of adorable beauty, charm, wit—but a being come I know not whence, I know not how, to be adored by me without my knowing why—I only know that I must adore you whether I will or no, or be insensate. For of all women you are the only woman that is worth marrying.

Suzanne. Talk about a proposal! That's certainly one! But it would be less obscure if you'd light your lamp.

Prosper [*approaching her*]. No, madame, no. There's nothing so beautiful as the light of an open fire on an autumn evening—or so fitting for what I have to say to you.

Suzanne. Light the lamp, or I shall go.

Prosper. Command me, I am your slave—But I have no matches!—And I swear to you——

Suzanne. Light the lamp!

Prosper. Yes, I swear it. I swear that since my return you have hypnotized me—bewitched me——

Suzanne [*pointing to the lamp*]. Yes, but——

Prosper. I'm mad! Or is it reason returning with love?

Suzanne. Ah, I'm going.

Prosper. You shall not go. No, no! You shall not leave your work unfinished. You've made me believe for an instant that supreme virtue and perfect goodness could exist on this earth. I wish to believe it all my life, and to prove to you that I am worthy of it. See!—here is the letter, madame, the letter—precious talisman—that has drawn you down from heaven to me. I will destroy it—and burn with it, before your eyes—[*Takes letter from jar.*]—my past, and all its errors—which I here abjure. [*Throws envelope in fire.*]

Suzanne [*aside*]. I could embrace him for that.

Prosper [*holding up the envelope with the tongs*]. Look, madame. It burns! It burns!

Suzanne [*aside*]. I shall never have the courage to send him away, now. Bah! I'll take him in my confidence, and he'll stay.

Prosper. Do you want the ashes at your feet?

Suzanne [*laughing*]. Are you quite sure it's the letter?

Prosper. Do you doubt——

Suzanne. Your good faith! No, indeed! But give me the little scrap of paper you had just now.

Prosper [*searching on the floor*]. The scrap of paper! I don't understand!

Suzanne [*laughing*]. There it is. [PROSPER *picks it up with astonishment.*]

Prosper. Well, what then?

Suzanne [*listening*]. Hush! What's that?

Prosper. The barking of dogs. [*Goes to the window.*] Thirion, Busonier, and Vanhove are coming back this way.

Suzanne. They may come up. Quick! Give it to me!

Prosper. Ah, I understand! You're afraid of being surprised with me in the dark. Don't be alarmed. [*He lights the paper again.*]

Vanhove [*outside, under the window*]. Here, Myrrha, here!

Suzanne [*watching the paper burn*]. It is fated that he shall burn it. [PROSPER *lights the lamp and throws the burning paper out of the window.*] Ah!

Vanhove [*without*]. That's the way to set fire to a house, Monsieur Prosper!

Suzanne. Good Heavens!

Prosper [*turning from the window*]. Fear nothing. It went out as it fell—and I see someone is picking it up.

Suzanne [*terrified*]. Vanhove! All is lost!

Prosper. What?

Suzanne. The letter! It was the letter!

Prosper. The letter? What!—that scrap of paper!

Suzanne. Yes, yes—that scrap of paper! Quick!—Run! Run, I tell you!

Prosper [*rushing to the window*]. But which way?

Suzanne [*pointing to the door in the rear*]. There!

Prosper [*going to the other door*]. I run!

Suzanne. No—this way!

Prosper. This way! [*Upsets chairs and reaches door.*]

Suzanne. Meet me at the greenhouse.

Prosper. Dead or alive, I'll have it!   [*Exit at rear.*

Suzanne. That's what comes of being too clever!   [*Exit.*

ACT THREE

A greenhouse, attached to the château, with dining room adjoining. Exotic plants; terrace furniture.

Enter SOLANGE, BAPTISTE, *and* HENRI.

SOLANGE [*takes some fruit from a basket, puts it on a plate and hands it to* HENRI, *to prepare for dessert*]. Here!

Baptiste. Hurry, hurry! The gentlemen will come upon us hungry as wolves after their hunting and the table isn't even set yet.

Solange. This newfangled craze for having the dessert on the table, together with the soup, instead of keeping it for a little surprise, as in my day! [*Noisy shouts and laughter from without.*]

Henri. There they are!

Enter THIRION, BUSONIER, *and three other hunters,
laughing.*

Thirion. I tell you I could have killed him if I had wanted
to. [*Redoubled laughter.*]

Busonier. A partridge scotched! A growl from Thirion!

All [*laughing*]. Long live Thirion!

Thirion. Long live Thirion! What sorry jesters you are!
Everyone to his taste, I say. Here's Monsieur d'Espars,
who only cares for one kind of hunting, and that's deer-
stalking. Busonier prefers to hunt hares. Mr. Tax-collector
laughing in his corner over there—snipe. Vanhove—Oh,
he'd hunt elephants if he had his way. But I have more
modest tastes—I hunt butterflies and young ladies.

Busonier. With a gun?

Thirion. Let me tell you how I came to miss that accursed
partridge. I had him at the end of my gun, didn't I! Well!—
and I was about to kill him—when, looking down, I spied a
tiger trotting along to his nocturnal lair—a tiger——

All. A tiger!

Thirion. A tiger!—A tiger-beetle!—A gold-winged tiger!
—I am carried away by my naturalist instincts. I keep one
eye on him—like that. I draw on the partridge while eyeing
the beetle. I miss the partridge, but I leap upon the other—
and you see I'm not such a bad hunter, since there he is, in
this horn. [*Shows a horn of blue paper stuck in the barrel
of his gun.*]

Busonier. If that were all we had brought back for
dinner!

Thirion. Dinner! That reminds me—I, for one, could
dine——

All. Yes, yes!

Henri [*aside to* BAPTISTE]. And the table isn't set.

Baptiste. Would the gentlemen perhaps like to brush the
dust off first?

Busonier. That's so!— We shouldn't be the worse for an
ablution.

Baptiste. The gentlemen's rooms are this way.

[*Exeunt the hunters.*

Busonier. Where's Vanhove?

Thirion. Can't say! He left us abruptly as we passed my house. [*To* SOLANGE.] Hasn't my wife come yet?

Solange [*entering with a pile of dishes*]. No, sir.

Thirion [*looking at his watch*]. Making her toilet! [*Aside.*] Colomba is always so particular. No décolleté in dress or in language! To think that she's never even called me by my first name.   [*Exeunt* THIRION *and* BUSONIER.

Enter CLAUDINE.

Claudine. His wife, good man! Isn't she that thin blond who's always running after Monsieur Paul? [*She and* HENRI *exchange glances.*]

Solange. Hold your tongue, gossip!

Henri. Say, Madame Solange, do they take their coffee here?

Solange. Yes.   [*Exit* HENRI *to dining room.*

Claudine. Then I'll leave you to get the cups ready. I'm going to change my tie—this one's so unbecoming—makes me look like a nursemaid.   [*Exit.*

Solange. Oh, indeed. Can't stitch a hem, but she can play on the piano. What are we coming to!   [*Exit.*

Enter PROSPER *and* SUZANNE.

Prosper. In the conservatory, she said. Here at last!—Thank Heaven!

Suzanne. Thank Heaven! Well?

Prosper. Well?

Suzanne. You have it?

Prosper. You haven't it?

Suzanne. Not I.

Prosper. Nor I.

Both. Ah!

Suzanne. Then what did you mean by saying—"Thank Heaven"?

Prosper. I meant: I haven't it, but she must have it—thank Heaven!

Suzanne. But I came in after you!

Prosper. Just so! I rush downstairs, four steps at a time.—I reach the bottom.—No one there—no paper. I say to myself: One of two things must have happened: either Van-hove stamped on the paper to put it out, or picked it up to see that it was extinguished. The paper isn't here, therefore the second hypothesis is the correct one. He has picked it up, then thrown it away. Dogs have a mania for chasing everything. His dog, seeing the paper, must have seized it, then dropped it a few steps farther on. Follow the trail, and I'll find it. I followed the trail——

Suzanne. And you found nothing?

Prosper. But my reasoning was good!

Suzanne. It was the wind that chased it.

Prosper. There is no wind.

Suzanne. Then the first hypothesis was the correct one.

Prosper. Just what I said to myself: Vanhove trod on the paper. I didn't look carefully! But fortunately Mademoiselle Suzanne is more clever than I—She has found it.

Suzanne. But I didn't look for it. I came down—you weren't there—so I said to myself: He's got it—run! And so— I ran!

Prosper. By a thousand crocodiles! Then I've got to begin over again tomorrow, at daybreak?

Suzanne. Tomorrow?—right away!

Prosper. Without an overcoat!

Suzanne. What's an overcoat got to do with it?

Prosper. But mademoiselle, consider!

Suzanne. Would you have the first passer-by pick it up?

Prosper. No.

Suzanne. And take it to Vanhove?

Prosper. I'd blow out what brains I have left.

Suzanne. Well, march then!

Prosper [*buttoning his coat and shivering*]. Yes, mademoiselle!—Br-r-r.

Suzanne [*throwing* CLARISSE's *shawl over him*]. You're cold. There, take my shawl.

Prosper. No, no, mademoiselle.

Suzanne. Yes, yes!

Prosper [*letting himself be wrapped in the shawl*]. She dazzles me, fascinates me, intoxicates me! I am disarmed, subdued—[*The shawl stops his mouth.*] muzzled.

Suzanne. Quick—march!

Prosper. Yes, mademoiselle! Muzzled!   [*Exit.*

Suzanne. Here I've been running about like a squirrel in its cage, ever since morning, all for a wicked little scrap of paper—and on account of that—Poor boy! He's taking trouble enough to undo the mischief he's done—I won't speak ill of him. But cursed be all scribbling, scribblings and scribblers! Anything goes in conversation. "I love you," is a pretty phrase to speak, but to write it! It freezes on the way. I might send a world of kisses by letter to—well, this man, for instance! A lot of satisfaction he'd get! He wouldn't even blush. [*Rising.*] Strange!—It's I who am blushing. How absurd! Surely I wouldn't play such a trick on myself as to hide any afterthought on his account? Come, come! Let's see!—what does this mean? Ah, Mademoiselle Suzanne, I'm going to keep my eye on you.

Enter MARTHE.

Marthe. Ah! It's godmother! Have you seen Monsieur Paul?

Suzanne [*aside*]. Here's one who doesn't mince matters. [*Aloud.*] No, I haven't seen him; but have you seen Monsieur Vanhove?

Marthe. No. He's walking up and down in his room.

Suzanne. Walking up and down! We're lost!

Enter BUSONIER.

Busonier. Who's this walking up and down at half-past six o'clock? Don't people dine here?

Marthe. I'll go and find out.   [*Exit.*

Suzanne. Busonier, my good friend, answer me quickly!

Busonier. What is it?

Suzanne. You were with Vanhove when Monsieur Prosper threw that burning paper from the window?

Busonier. What? You know——

Suzanne. Who picked it up?

Busonier. The paper?

Suzanne. Was it Vanhove?

Busonier. Vanhove?

Suzanne. Answer me! You kill me with suspense!

Busonier. But give me time, my dear friend. What strange interest!—

Suzanne [*impatiently*]. Well?

Busonier. Ah! I recollect. It was I who picked it up.

Suzanne. You?

Busonier. I'm sure of it.

Suzanne. And then?

Busonier. Then?

Suzanne. What did you do with it?

Busonier. What did I—? What strange interest!

Suzanne. Oh, what a man!

Busonier. Heavens, I believe I threw it—no, no, I didn't throw it away.

Suzanne [*eagerly*]. You have it?

Busonier. No, I gave it to Thirion.

Suzanne. To Thirion? [PAUL *appears at the rear and disappears quickly.*]

Busonier. Or rather he took it out of my hands. I'm sure of it. That was it!

Suzanne. Thirion!—a fool!—Unlucky chance! Tell me at lcast where he is—I want to speak to him.

Busonier. He was here with me just now. [*Calls.*] Thirion!

Suzanne [*stopping him*]. No, no! Don't call him!

Busonier. I must not call him?

Suzanne. Let us look for him—find him.—Come!

Busonier. But—What strange int——

Suzanne [*dragging him*]. Come, come!   [*Exeunt.*

Enter PAUL, *in travelling dress.*

Paul. Nobody! I'll venture. [*Coming down.*]

Enter SOLANGE.

Solange. Monsieur Paul! you here?

Paul. Hush!

Solange [*lowers her voice*]. And Madame Thirion told me to take away your plate!

Paul. I believe you, Solange. She drives me away! She sends me to Chinon to study for my degree!

Solange. But at least you'll take dinner before you start?

Paul. Oh, I started some time ago. Under the pretext that my place had been engaged in advance, she made me take the five o'clock stagecoach, in front of the door, putting me under the driver's special care. I've been en route an hour already.

Solange. How's that?

Paul. You see: I was alone in the coach. We had reached

the outskirts of the village, near the little hill—I opened
the door softly, jumped to the ground without being seen—
and came across the fields.

Solange. What for?

Paul. What for, Solange? Why, to see her—you know
whom I mean—to tell her that I love her—that I love her
much more than this morning—a thousand times more—
and that I don't wish to leave her—and that I want to marry
her—and that I needn't be a Bachelor of Arts for that!

Solange. If Mademoiselle Marthe should hear you! What
a lecture!

Paul. Marthe! Not she!

Solange. My stars! He has lost his senses!

Paul. She'd be only too glad to see me!

Solange. To see you! You count on seeing her?

Paul. I should think so—during dinner.

Solange. And where, if you please?

Paul. Here! The conservatory will be awfully convenient.
—Very comfortable here.—I can hide here all winter. And
I shall see her—and I'll talk to her all day—and I'll be free,
like the savage in his native forests, without guardian or
preceptress! No more Colomba! Down with Colomba!

Solange. What a daredevil!

Paul. And to begin, I'll write a little note to Mademoiselle
Marthe. [*Hunts through his pockets.*] Well, my notebook
will do! Ah! I must have dropped it when I jumped from
the coach! Here's a piece of a pencil, at any rate. Give me
some paper, quickly. Paper!

Solange. I? Oh, I dare say.

Paul. You refuse?

Solange. You'll want me to deliver your letter, too, very
likely.

Paul. Of course.

Solange. Well, just wait a minute. Did you ever hear the
like? [*Aside.*] I must go, or he'll end by coaxing me.

Paul. Solange, my dear Solange.

Solange. None of that! Go away, you saucy boy.   [*Exit.*

Paul. And I counted on her. What shall I do? [*Feels in
his pockets.*] There's the pencil all right—but the paper?
Ah! [*Falls upon a bench and finds himself facing* THIRION's
horn of paper.] Oh, Providence! This horn! [*Takes it up*

and shakes it.] What's that?—a little bell? [*Opens and looks in.*] A beetle!—Some of my guardian's game. Bah! One more or less in his collection! He'll think he lost it on the way. [*Shakes out the beetle.*] That animal should offer up a candle to love—he's saved from the camphor bottle. [*He tears off the burnt edge.*] So! That looks better! It's written on, but there's one side blank. What luck! [*Writes.*] "I have returned. They want to make me study for my bachelor's degree, but I don't want to be a bachelor, I want to be your husband. I am hidden in the conservatory. Yours for life"—

Thirion [*outside*]. The paper?

Paul [*rising*]. Somebody—my guardian!

[*Disappears among the plants.*

Enter SUZANNE, BUSONIER, *and* THIRION.

Thirion. But what paper?—But which paper? I don't understand a word of what you're saying.

Suzanne. Don't scream so loud.

Thirion [*lowering his voice*]. What paper?

Suzanne. That Prosper—

Thirion. Lighted!

Suzanne. Threw from the window—

Thirion. That I picked up!—

Suzanne. That you took from his hands.

Thirion. Ah! The bit of burnt paper. Speak!—Was that it?

Suzanne. At last!

Thirion [*without heeding her*]. Now, just put yourself in my place. You say, "The paper." What paper? There are so many pa—

Suzanne [*impatiently to* BUSONIER]. Oh! He's even more provoking than you.

Thirion. If you had said at once the scrap of paper—

Suzanne. Well then, the scrap of paper. So! The scrap of paper. Where is—the scrap of paper?

Thirion. Strange! You want that paltry fragment——

Suzanne. Yes!

Thirion. But you know it was burnt.

Suzanne and Busonier [*exasperated, accenting every syllable*]. What—did—you—do—with—it?

Thirion. Why, I made a little horn of it.

Suzanne. A little horn?

Thirion. Yes, to hold my coleoptera, which was tickling the palm of my hand most abominably!

Suzanne. Where is this horn?

Thirion. Why, there! In the barrel of my gun.

Busonier. At last!

Thirion [*grumblingly*]. At last!

Suzanne. At last I have it!

Thirion [*looking into his gun*]. Gone!

Suzanne. Lost!

Thirion. Oh, that rascal of a beetle. He must have worked about until he tumbled to the ground—cage and all.

Suzanne. Then he can't be far. Let us look for him. [*All hunt on the floor.*]

Thirion [*searching among the plants*]. Remarkable!—The intelligence of these animals! What an interesting paper I can write about it for the entomological society of Chinon. [*Uttering a cry.*] Ah! [SUZANNE *and* BUSONIER *run up, thinking he has found the horn.*] I will call it—"A Prisoner's Escape"—or, "A Coleoptera in the Bastille"—or——

Suzanne. Nothing!

Thirion and Busonier. Nothing!

Suzanne. Oh, there's no use saying: "We must find it." Look for it—Look! [*Perceiving* VANHOVE.] No!—Don't look!

Busonier and Thirion [*stupefied*]. Ah!

Enter VANHOVE, CLARISSE, MARTHE, COLOMBA, *the hunters,* BAPTISTE, *and* HENRI.

Vanhove. Well, aren't we going to dine today?

Marthe. Yes—dinner is ready.

Baptiste. Dinner is on the table, madame.

All. Ah!

Busonier. Welcome news!

Clarisse [*aside to* SUZANNE]. He's gone?

Suzanne [*still searching with her eyes*]. The beetle? Yes, he's gone.

Clarisse. The beetle?

Suzanne. Oh no! Him!—Prosper! Yes, yes, my friend. [*Aside.*] Poor boy, searching out there.

Clarisse. He's gone!—and the letter burned! Ah, Suzanne, at last I breathe again.

Suzanne [*aside*].I——suffocate.

Vanhove [*aside*]. She is worried. She cannot have succeeded with that man. Now I must take the affair upon myself. [*Offers his arm to* SUZANNE]. Suzanne!

Suzanne [*with a last look on the ground, takes his arm mechanically*]. Thanks, my friend.

Marthe. Have you lost anything?

Suzanne. Yes, a little brooch.

Vanhove. There?

Suzanne. Oh, don't stop to look for it. It's not worth the trouble. [*To* MARTHE.] Tell Solange to come here a minute.

Marthe. All right. [*Aside.*] To think that Paul hasn't come! [*Exeunt to dining room.*

Enter PAUL.

Paul [*coming out from the foliage, on all fours, letter in hand*]. At last! There I've been listening to the buzzing of words for a quarter of an hour. [*Rubbing his hands and legs.*] Anything but comfortable in there!—with plants pricking my arms, plants pricking my legs—I say, who's going to carry my letter?

Enter CLAUDINE.

Claudine [*admiring lace collar she is wearing*]. There! Now I look like somebody! [*Seeing* PAUL.] Hello! The little dark-eyed fellow! The tall blonde's young man.

Paul [*turning away in alarm*]. Oh!

Claudine. The gentleman is perhaps looking for the dining room?

Paul. Oh, Mademoiselle—Don't tell anybody you saw me. Not a word!

Claudine. Make your mind easy. It's my business to be discreet.

Paul [*aside*]. Discreet! In fact—my letter! I've read of such things in novels. If I were to try! [*Aloud.*] Mademoiselle!

Claudine. Sir?

Paul [*embarrassed*]. You are very pretty.

Claudine. So I've been told, sir.

Paul [*looking down*]. And with good reason. Only—there's one thing lacking——

Claudine [*looking at him*]. What's that? Eyes?

Paul. Oh, no. They're all right. [*Timidly.*] I meant, a pair of pretty earrings.

Claudine [*aside*]. Oho! Bribery and corruption.

Paul [*aside*]. I hope she won't be offended. [*Aloud.*] If I dared. [*Slips his purse into her hand.*]

Claudine. Anything you please, sir.

Paul [*delighted*]. May I? Then take this little note, will you?

Claudine. I needn't ask who it's for.

Paul. You'll give it—

Claudine. While I'm changing the plates.

Paul. Ah! Marton or Lisette! Wait! I must kiss you!

Claudine. That one's for me. I'll keep it.

[*Exit to dining room.*

Paul. I'm coming on! A runaway! Clandestine billet-doux! Conquest of a soubrette!—Again somebody! The devil take him. [*Hides.*]

Enter PROSPER, *wrapped in his shawl.*

Prosper. Nothing, nothing, nothing!—Nothing but a beastly cold and the appetite of a wolf. They're dining without me. This is the last straw. I enter panting and blowing, in an absurd costume, with the appetite of a drover—absolutely ridiculous! Ah, Prosper!—After three years of voyaging, to be wrecked by a woman's breath—blush at thine own disgrace!—And if there's any pride left in thee, behold thyself in this shawl. What grotesque monster dost thou resemble? Hercules in the shirt of Nessus. It devours thee, it eats into thy flesh, it burns thy bones, and thou hast not the wit to take it off. Thou wearest it for the sake of its owner, whom thou lovest. Speak out, miserable wretch! Thou lovest her—thou lovest her so that with the appetite of a wolf thou'lt stand reciting thy monologue, instead of going to dinner. Go eat, buffoon!—go eat!

Enter SOLANGE.

Solange. Monsieur!

Prosper. Don't stop me—I'm hungry. [SOLANGE *tries to hold him by his shawl.*] Don't touch my shawl!

Solange. But are you not Monsieur Prosper?

Prosper. Yes—Prosper Block, who's half famished! But don't touch my shawl.

Solange. But Mademoiselle Suzanne——

Prosper [*turning quickly*]. Mademoiselle Suzanne?

Solange. She said I was to watch for monsieur on his return——

Prosper. Speak!

Solange. And to say to monsieur that she'd lost a little horn——

Prosper. A horn?

Solange. Of paper, with a little bug in it.

Prosper. A little beast? A horn of paper with a little bug? Well, what's that to me?

Solange. She said to beg you to look for it immediately.

Prosper. Look for it? Immediately? And my dinner?

Solange. She didn't say anything about dinner.—Only she said I was to ask you for her shawl.

Prosper [*gives up the shawl*]. Her shawl! The last straw! [*Falls upon a bench.*] I am dead.

Solange. Sir!

Prosper. Go! Go!—[*Exit* SOLANGE.]—If I search, I don't dine. If I don't search, but enter, I don't dine; for her threatening eyes will destroy my appetite. I am her slave, her Negro slave. [*Rises.*] She wants her horn—immediately! —and her little bug. Some ridiculous whim—Absurd! No matter, I enter upon my duties. Bridled, muzzled! I would have it so. Come, search, Bowwow.—Search for thy mistress' horn, and the little bug. Search! [*Begins to hunt about, and disappears in the shrubbery for a moment.*]

Paul [*coming out*]. I hear nothing. He must be at dinner. [*Looking towards the dining room.*] Ah, the door is open— I see them all. They're going to change the plates. [PROSPER *comes down, hunting to right and left.*] There's Claudine making a sign to me. Yes, yes! Now she's taking a plate.— Now she's going—where is she going then? Oh, the stupid, it is not—She's given the letter to Colomba. [*Cries out.*] Oh!

Prosper. What's that?

Paul. Somebody!—I'm lost. [*Vanishes in the shrubbery.*]

Prosper. I heard a cry. I must have stepped on the beast. [*Looks around and picks up the fragment of burnt paper.*] It can't be that! [*He opens it.*] A fragment of burnt paper! Blue paper! [*Reads.*] The ends of words—"My mother— hove—hove—" Vanhove! It's the letter. Here! Torn! How?——

Enter VANHOVE.

[*Turns and sees* VANHOVE.] Ah, good. That's how!

Vanhove. I thought I heard a cry.

Prosper [*aside*]. We're to cut each other's throats here, it seems! Very good! But after dinner!

Vanhove [*perceiving him*]. Ah, it's you.

Prosper. I beg your pardon, sir, I'm afraid I've kept you waiting. [*Starts to enter the dining room.*]

Vanhove. Two words, sir, if you please.

Prosper [*aside*]. It's decreed I shall fight on an empty stomach.

Vanhove. Do you still persist in the request you made me this morning, sir? [*Clatter of plates.*]

Prosper [*with a regretful glance at the dining room*]. Yes —and no. [*Aside.*] Confound it, I'd forgotten all about that. [*Aloud.*] Yes, on principle—but, in reality, no, no!

Vanhove. Explain yourself!

Prosper. I will explain.—Madame Vanhove showed such a great repugnance to this union——

Vanhove. For good reasons.

Prosper. Reasons! [*Aside.*] I'm spoiling everything. A little assurance. [*Aloud.*] What reasons, sir? For what reasons?

Vanhove [*quietly*]. Possibly your forgetfulness of an old love which it would pain her to see sacrificed to a new one.

Prosper. Indeed! [*Aside.*] He's come to the point at once. So much the better. [*Aloud.*] I see you know all, sir.

Vanhove. All!

Prosper [*rising*]. Then perhaps you'll be willing to defer our conversation until after dinner.

Vanhove. No, sir! The matter is too serious to admit of any delay.

Prosper. Oh, not so serious as you imagine. I loved the lady—whom, you know; we exchanged a few confidences, a few letters, it's true. But permit me to say that I confined myself to the most respectful homage—the purest kind of love—and that her virtue——

Vanhove. No, sir!

Prosper. No, sir? What do you mean?

Vanhove. No, sir! No!

Prosper. Thunder and lightning, this is a most un-fortunate misapprehension, and I give you my word of honor——

Vanhove. Don't swear. She is guilty. She has confessed it to me.

Prosper. She has confessed?

Vanhove. All.

Prosper. But what? All what? There wasn't the half, nor the quarter——

Vanhove. All.

Prosper. She can't have accused herself of what didn't exist. Woman's slander doesn't go that far.

Vanhove. All, I tell you. Your desertion, for an imagined betrayal; your voyages; your return, and the light way in which you treat the love which she still feels for you.

Prosper [*aside*]. The love—Well! Her choice of a con-fidant is what tickles me. [*Aloud.*] Then she told you? Quite simply, like that?

Vanhove. No matter how—she told me.

Prosper. Charming! And you have come?

Vanhove. Yes.

Prosper. To offer me?

Vanhove. Yes.

Prosper. A duel?

Vanhove. No—a reconciliation with her.

Prosper. What? Beg pardon?

Vanhove. I said—a reconciliation with her.

Prosper. You! To reconcile me!

Vanhove. The honor of my house demands it.

Prosper. Oh, it's your honor. [*Aside.*] He understands it as they do in the Marquesas Islands.

Vanhove [*offering his hand*]. And so, sir, I offer you my hand as a friend.

Prosper. Ah, you are very kind! Very kind, indeed! [*Aside.*] Too kind!

Vanhove. Make her happy——

Prosper. Yes, sir. Yes, sir.

Vanhove. And me too.

Prosper [*aside*]. And him too! He says that with an air of dignity!—[*Aloud.*] Thunder and lightning, sir, have you thought over what you are proposing to me? If I should refuse, sir?

Vanhove. If you should refuse! Ah! I would kill you.

Prosper. Ah!

Vanhove. Without fail! For it shall not be said that a gentle and good woman trusted to your love and that you refused her the satisfaction which she has a right to expect.

Prosper. The satisfaction—I refuse her—

Vanhove. That's what I said.

Prosper [*aside*]. Satisfaction! What high-sounding words!

Vanhove. Your choice, sir?

Prosper. It's all up. I prefer to fight. But, thunder and lightning, surely this will be the first time that ever a husband fought in order that his wife might——

Vanhove. Sir, I beg you not to mix my wife's name up in this.

Prosper. Sir, it's necessary.

Vanhove. No, sir, it's not necessary. Your weapons?

Prosper. Are those you choose.

Enter SUZANNE *and* CLARISSE.

Suzanne [*aside*]. Just what I feared!

Clarisse [*aside*]. A challenge?

Suzanne [*throwing herself between them*]. Ah, Prosper! Have Vanhove's arguments been of no more avail than my tears?

Prosper [*surprised*]. Hey?

Suzanne. Must I then throw myself at your feet while I appeal to your honor?

Vanhove [*restraining her*]. Isn't that what you want?

Prosper. What under the sun does all this mean?

Suzanne. No, my friend! No! Your Suzanne has never

been guilty. [*Softly to* PROSPER.] Bear me out in all I say. [*Aloud.*] No, I have never betrayed my vows. You know it well. [*Softly.*] Talk as I do.

Prosper. But!——

Suzanne. But never was truer love repaid with such ingratitude.

Prosper. Me?

Suzanne. Stupid! [*Aloud.*] And if you refuse to retrieve my honor——

Prosper [*softly*]. I—

Suzanne. I will kill myself. Yes!—And it's you—you who will have dealt the fatal blow. Speak, sir, speak! Speak!

Prosper. Ah! I must then—[*Aside.*] I don't understand a word, but I have her now. [*To* VANHOVE.] Ah, I must then——

Vanhove. Yes!

Prosper. Very well, very well! I understand, I understand.

Vanhove. What is your answer?

Prosper. Well, my answer, my answer—[*Resolutely.*] Is all that quite true, madame?

Suzanne [*effusively*]. Ah! [*Apart to him.*] Bravo! Well done!

Prosper [*aside*]. Bravo! Well done! Oh, just wait a bit. [*Aloud.*] You swear that you have been faithful to me?

Suzanne. Ah! Do you ask that?

Vanhove. Do you ask that?

Prosper. No, sir, no! I no longer ask it.

Suzanne [*aside to* PROSPER]. Good! Courage!

Prosper. You love me?

Suzanne [*with ardor*]. Ah! [*Aside to* PROSPER.] Make-believe.

Prosper [*aside*]. Ah! Of course! Make-believe. [*Aloud.*] And I too, madame, I love you.

Suzanne [*aside*]. Make-believe.

Prosper [*apart*]. Ah! Of course! Make-believe! [*Aloud.*] And I call monsieur to witness this mutual affection.

Suzanne [*aside*]. Enough! Enough!

Prosper. And I will marry you, madame, on my word of honor—I will marry you when you will.

Vanhove. At last!

Suzanne [*aside*]. Always in make-believe.

Prosper [*aside*]. Ah! Of course! Make-believe in good earnest. In good earnest! [*Aloud.*] Come to my arms, Suzanne, come to my arms.

Suzanne [*drawing back*]. Oh! But——

Vanhove [*pushing her into* PROSPER's *arms*]. Never mind us, Suzanne. It's all in the family.

Prosper [*embracing her*]. Ah! My dear Suzanne!

Suzanne. Ah! Prosper! [*Aside.*] Ah! Traitor!

Prosper. Get out of this if you can!

Enter THIRION, BUSONIER, COLOMBA, MARTHE, *the three hunters,* BAPTISTE, *and* HENRI.

Vanhove. Gentlemen, I have the honor of announcing the marriage of my cousin, Suzanne, with Monsieur Prosper Block.

All. Ah!

Suzanne. What! Already? [*All surround them and congratulate them.*]

Thirion [*in the foreground, holding the scrap of blue paper in his hand. He is slightly intoxicated*]. A letter to Colomba! A letter that I seized without being seen, at the moment when the waitress was slipping it under her plate. Ah! The emotion!—the champagne! I am suffocated. Let me read. [*Reads.*] "I leave tonight, but far or near, my love—" He calls Colomba his love. Ah, wretch!—If I knew! And no signature! [*Folds the paper.*]

Vanhove [*coming down with a cup of coffee*]. Don't you take coffee, Thirion? [THIRION *tries to put on a good face.*] What a face! [*To* PROSPER.] Just look!

Thirion. An idea! The master of the house! He must know the handwriting of everybody here. [*To* VANHOVE, *giving him the folded paper.*] Who wrote that?

Vanhove. That? [*Reads.*] "I have returned"——

Thirion. "I have returned!" He says that he is leaving.

Vanhove. "They want me to study for my bachelor's degree"——

Thirion. His bachelor's degree? No, no—it reads "My love"——

Vanhove. "My bachelor's degree"—It's written in lead pencil.

Thirion. No, no! [*Takes the folded paper and hands it back opened.*] There! There!

Prosper [*recognizing the letter*]. The letter! [*Snatches it from* VANHOVE.]

Vanhove [*laughing*]. Come, let's see it.

Prosper. No, you shall not see it.

Vanhove [*still laughing at* THIRION]. Hey?

Thirion. What does this mean?

Prosper. It means that I admit nobody here into my confidence.

Thirion. It's he! He wrote it.

Vanhove. This letter—

Prosper. Well, yes—I wrote it! What of it?

Thirion. You! My friend! Under my roof! To declare his passion for Colomba——

Vanhove [*jumping*]. Eh?

Prosper [*shrugging his shoulders*]. What nonsense!

Vanhove. But, sir, this is monstrous! This morning you ask for the hand of Marthe; this evening you promise to marry Suzanne; and you still find time to love——

Thirion. Colomba!

Colomba [*coming forward*]. Yes, dear?

Prosper. What nonsense! Who's thinking of loving Colomba?

Thirion. You, wretch!

Prosper. Do keep still!

Thirion. You call her "my love!"

Prosper. It's a lie!

Vanhove. Your proof, sir.

Prosper [*embarrassed*]. My proof! [*Showing the letter to* SUZANNE.]

Suzanne. The letter!

Clarisse. The letter!

Prosper. My proof?—is that I call upon Mademoiselle Suzanne, my future wife, gentlemen, to take cognizance at once. [*Offers the letter to* SUZANNE.]

Vanhove [*snatching the letter*]. So be it! Suzanne!

Suzanne [*laughing*]. Quite unnecessary, my friend. I know what it is.

Vanhove. You know?

Suzanne. A mere bit of nonsense. Burn it.

Vanhove. Take care, Suzanne. Your happiness is at stake.

Suzanne [*picking up a lighted candle from the table*].
Burn! Burn!

Vanhove. You wish it? [*To* PROSPER.] You are a happy
man to marry a woman—[*Lights the paper and throws it
on the ground.*]

Prosper [*watching the paper burn*]. Ah, you rogue! You've
given us enough trouble.

Thirion. All the same it was written "my love!"

Colomba. What's that?

Suzanne. Good news. We're going to marry Marthe and
Paul!

Paul [*rushing from his hiding place*]. What joy!

Colomba. He was there all the time!

Paul [*kissing* MARTHE'S *hand*]. Ah, how happy I am.

Prosper [*to* SUZANNE]. And I!

Suzanne. You! You're going to start for Honolulu!

Prosper. With my wife, yes.

Suzanne. Never!

Clarisse. Ah! My dear Suzanne!

Prosper. Ah! My dear Suzanne!

Suzanne. I see it's decreed I am to sacrifice myself for
everybody—and all on account of a letter——

Prosper. Ah, dear little scrap of paper—don't scold it!

Suzanne. A pretty chase it has led us.

APPENDIX

I. Selected Bibliography

The Well-Made Play

Archer, William, and C. H. Herford. Introductions to *The Works of Henrik Ibsen*. Viking Edition. Vols. 1 and 6. New York, Chas. Scribner's Sons, 1911.

Archer, William. *Playmaking, A Manual of Craftsmanship*. New York, Dodd, Mead & Co., 1934.

Bentley, Eric. "The Ill-Made Play," in *The Dramatic Event*. Boston, Beacon Press, 1956 (paperback edition).

———. "Homage to Scribe," in *What Is Theatre?* Boston, Beacon Press, 1956.

Crane, Milton. "Pygmalion: Bernard Shaw's Dramatic Theory and Practice," *PMLA* 66:879-885 (Dec., 1951).

Ellehauge, Martin. "The Initial Stages in the Development of the English Problem Play," *Englische Studien* 66:373-401. (Leipzig, 1931-32).

Engstrom, Elmer. "Shaw and the Well-Made Play." Unpublished Master's Thesis. Columbia University, 1948.

Fergusson, Francis. "The Theatricality of Shaw and Pirandello," in *The Idea of a Theater*. Princeton, Princeton University Press, 1949 (Doubleday Anchor Books, 1955).

Montague, C. E. "The Well-Made Play," in *Dramatic Values*. New York, Doubleday, Page & Co., 1925.

Nicoll, Allardyce. *A History of Early Nineteenth-Century Drama, 1800-1850*. Vol. 1. Cambridge, Eng., Cambridge University Press, 1930.

Savin, Maynard. *Thomas Wm. Robertson: His Plays and Stagecraft*. Brown University Studies, XIII. Providence, R. I., Brown University Press, 1950.

Scribe, Eugène. "Discours prononcé pour sa réception à l'Académie Française, 28 Jan., 1836," in *Oeuvres Complètes* . . . . Vol. 1. Paris, E. Dentu, 1874.

Shaw, George Bernard. "My Way with a Play," in *British Thought*. Edited by Ivor Brown. New York, The Gresham Press, 1947.

————. Preface to *Three Plays by Brieux*. New York, Brentano's, 1911.

Stanton, Stephen S. *English Drama and the French Well-Made Play, 1815-1915*. Doctoral Dissertation. Columbia University, 1955.

Stuart, Donald C. *The Development of Dramatic Art*. Chap. 17. New York, D. Appleton & Co., 1928.

Tolles, Winton. *Tom Taylor and the Victorian Drama*. New York, Columbia University Press, 1940.

van Druten, John. *Playwright at Work*. New York, Harper & Bros., 1953.

Eugène Scribe

Arvin, Neil C. *Eugène Scribe and the French Theatre, 1815-1860*. Cambridge, Mass., Harvard University Press, 1924.
Historical background of the well-made play and analyses of Scribe's plays. Contains extensive bibliography.

Allard, Louis. *La Comédie de Moeurs en France au XIXe. Siècle*. Vol. 1, Cambridge, Mass., Harvard University Press, 1923; Vol. 2, Paris, 1933.

————. *Esquisses Parisiennes en les Temps Heureux, 1830-1848*. Montréal, Canada, Les Editions Variétés, 1943.

Benoist, Antoine. "Le Théâtre de Scribe: les Comédies Historiques," in *Revue des Cours et Conférences* 3:417-422 (14 Fev., 1895); 3:449-464 (21 Fev., 1895).

Bentley, Eric. "Homage to Scribe" (review of "The Queen's Gambit"), in *What Is Theatre?* Boston, Beacon Press, 1956.

Brunetière, Ferdinand. "Scribe et Musset" (1892), in *Les Epoques du Théâtre Français*. Paris, 1896.
Discusses Scribe's resourcefulness and the injustice done him.

Doumic, René. *De Scribe à Ibsen*. Paris, Delaplane, 1896.

Engstrom, Elmer. "Shaw and the Well-Made Play." Unpublished Master's Thesis. Columbia University, 1948.
Contains excellent analysis of Scribe's "Une Chaîne."

Epagny, Jean d'. *Molière et Scribe*. Paris, A. Durand, 1865.

Legouvé, Ernest. *Soixante Ans de Souvenirs.* Vol. 2, chap. 4. Paris, Hetzel et Cie., 1887. Translated as *Sixty Years of Recollections*, by A. D. Vandam. Vol. 2, chap. 4. London, Eden, Remington & Co., 1893.

Lintillac, Eugène. *Histoire Genérale du Théâtre en France* (*La Comédie de la Revolution au Second Empire.*) Vols. 4 and 5. (Vol. 5: "La Comédie de Moeurs de Scribe à Augier.") Paris, Flammarion, 1910.
Defends Scribe's style and dramatic form as suitable to the *comédie-vaudeville*; praises his use of this form (with all its limitations) in the comedy of manners.

Sarcey, Francisque. *Quarante Ans de Théâtre*. Vol. 4: essays on Scribe (1868-1883). Paris, F. Didot et Cie., 1901.

Stanton, Stephen S. *English Drama and the French Well-Made Play, 1815-1915*. Doctoral Dissertation. Columbia University, 1955.
Analyzes Scribe's "Bertrand et Raton," explains his technique and purpose, and discusses his impact upon English drama of the nineteenth century. Contains analytical summaries of 25 plays by Scribe.

Stuart, Donald C. *The Development of Dramatic Art.* Chap. 17. New York, D. Appleton & Co., 1928.

Alexandre Dumas, fils

Arvin, Neil C. *Alexandre Dumas, fils*. Chap. 2. Paris, Presses Universitaires de France, 1939.

Doumic, René. *Portraits d'Ecrivains*. Paris, Delaplane, 1892.

Dumas, Alexandre, *fils*. Preface (1868) to "Un Père Prodigue" (1859), in *European Theories of the Drama*, edited by Barrett H. Clark. New York, 1947.

Filon, Augustin. "L'âge de Dumas et d'Augier," in *De Dumas à Rostand*. Paris, 1898.

Hamilton, Clayton. "The Career of *Camille*," in *Seen on the Stage* (1920). Reprinted in *The Theory of the Theatre*. New York, Henry Holt & Co., 1939.

Lancaster, C. M. "Dumas the Younger and French Dramatic Forms Existing in 1850," *Poet Lore* 51:345-352 (Winter, 1945).

Matthews, Brander. *French Dramatists of the Nineteenth Century*. 5th edition. Chap. 6. New York, Charles Scribner's Sons, 1914.

Moses, Montrose J. "Stage History of Famous Plays: 'La Dame aux Camélias,' " *The Theatre* 6:64-68 (March, 1906).

Page, Philip. "The Camellias and the Hump" (review of the Reynolds-Playfair "The Lady of the Camellias"), *The Saturday Review* (London), 290-291 (March 8, 1930).

Perkins, Merle L. "Matilda Heron's 'Camille,' " *Comparative Literature* 7:338-343 (Fall, 1955).

Saunders, Edith. "Patron Saint of Courtesans," *The Twentieth Century* 157:140-147 (Aug., 1955).

Seillière, Ernest. "Emile Augier contre Dumas *fils*," *La Minerve Française* 6:676-693 (Paris, 1920).

Sewell, J. E. "Dumas with Apologies" (review of the Reynolds-Playfair "The Lady of the Camellias"), *The New Statesman* (London), (April 12, 1930).

Smith, Hugh A. *Main Currents of Modern French Drama.* Chap. 7. New York, Henry Holt & Co., 1925.

Taylor, Frank A. *The Theatre of Alexandre Dumas fils.* Chaps. 4 and 6. Oxford, Eng., The Clarendon Press, 1937.

Zucker, A. E. and P. de F. Henderson. " 'Camille' as the Translation of 'La Dame aux Camélias,' " *Modern Language Notes* 49:472-476 (Nov., 1934).

Emile Augier

Clark, Barrett H. "Emile Augier," *The Drama* 5:440-457 (Aug., 1915).

Filon, Augustin. *De Dumas à Rostand.* Paris, 1898.

Fitch, Girdler B. "Emile Augier and the Intrusion Plot," *PMLA* 63:274-280 (March, 1948).

Gaillard, Henri, de Champris. *Emile Augier et la Comédie Sociale.* Chap. 2. Paris, Grasset, 1910.

Guthrie, W. N. "Emile Augier," *The Drama* 1:3-26 (Nov., 1911).

Matthews, Brander. *French Dramatists of the Nineteenth Century.* 5th edition. Chap. 5. New York, Charles Scribner's Sons, 1914.

Seillière, Ernest. *Emile Augier contre Dumas fils. La Minerve Française* 6:676-693 (Paris, 1920).

Smith, Hugh A. *Main Currents of Modern French Drama.*
Chap. 8. New York, Henry Holt & Co., 1925.

Victorien Sardou

Blanc, Charles. "Discours en Réponse au Discours Prononcé par M. Victorien Sardou, pour sa Réception à
l'Académie Française, le 23 Mai, 1878." Paris, Didier
et Cie., 1878.

Clark, Barrett H. Introduction to Sardou's *Patrie!* (translated by Barrett H. Clark). Garden City, N. Y., Doubleday, Page & Co., 1915.

Doumic, René. *Portraits d'Ecrivains.* Paris, Delaplane,
1892.

Hart, Jerome A. *Sardou and the Sardou Plays.* Philadelphia,
J. B. Lippincott Co., 1913.

Hornblow, Arthur. "Contemporary French Playwrights,"
Cosmopolitan Magazine 15:108 (May, 1893).

Lenotre, G. "Victorien Sardou," *Revue des Deux Mondes*
4:779-805 (1931).

Matthews, Brander. *French Drama of the Nineteenth Century.* 5th edition. Chap. 7. New York, Charles Scribner's Sons, 1914.

Montague, C. E. "The Well-Made Play," in *Dramatic
Values.* New York, Doubleday, Page & Co., 1925, pp.
32-33. (Analysis of Sardou's "La Sorcière" reprinted
in John van Druten, *Playwright at Work.* New York,
Harper & Bros., 1953, pp. 32-33.)

Mouly, Georges. *La Vie Prodigieuse de Victorien Sardou
d'après des Documents Inédits.* Paris, 1931.

Praviel, Armand. "Victorien Sardou," *Le Correspondant*
324:515-528 (Aug. 25, 1931).

Rebell, Hughes. *Victorien Sardou, le Théâtre et l'Epoque.*
Paris, 1903.

Sardou, Victorien, *Discours Prononcé à l'Académie Française.* Paris, Didier et Cie., 1878.

Shaw, George Bernard. *Dramatic Opinions and Essays.*
London, Constable & Co., 1909. 2 vols. (passim).

Smith, Hugh A. *Main Currents of Modern French Drama.*
Chap. 9. New York, Henry Holt & Co., 1925.

II. English Versions Available
in the United States[1]

Reference Works: F. K. W. Drury, *Drury's Guide to Best Plays*, 1953; I. T. E. Firkins, *Index to Plays: 1800-1926*, 1927; *Index to Plays* (Supplement), 1935; *International Index to Periodicals*. Vols. 1-14. (1907-1956); J. H. Ottemiller, *Index to Plays in Collections*, 1951; F. S. Boas, *The Player's Library: The Catalogue of the Library of the British Drama League*, 1954.

Libraries Consulted: The New York Public Library; the Libraries of Columbia University, Barnard College, Harvard University, The University of Michigan, and The Library of Congress.

For Records of Stage Performance: H. W. Schoenberger, *American Adaptations of French Plays on the New York and Philadelphia Stages from 1790-1833.* University of Pennsylvania, 1924; R. H. Ware, *American Adaptations . . . from 1834 to the Civil War*, University of Pennsylvania, 1930; George C. D. Odell, *Annals of the New York Stage.* Vols. 3-15. New York, Columbia University Press, 1928-1949. Marvin Felheim, *The Theater of Augustin Daly: An Account of the Late Nineteenth-Century American Stage.* Chap. 5. Cambridge, Mass., Harvard University Press, 1956; Alexander Hamilton Mason, 4th. *French Theatre in New York: A List of Plays, 1899-1939.* New York, Columbia University Press, 1940.

Key to Acting Editions and Libraries:
Initials representing acting editions are followed by volume number, unless number of individual play is given. More information about the plays of Scribe listed below will be found in Arvin, Appendix A.

---

[1] The editor does not claim to have listed *all* the English versions existing in America of *all* the plays by the authors included in this volume. This list is intended only as a "reader's guide" to a good many versions which could otherwise be located only with difficulty and great expense of time. Until science invents a new kind of Geiger counter which will reveal old scripts in the stacks of libraries, human toil (and fallibility!) must remain the only means of hunting down this elusive material.

AND	*The Acting National Drama* (London).
BPP	*Baker's Professional Plays* (W. H. Baker Co., Boston).
CBT	*Cumberland's British Theatre.*
FAE	*French's Acting Edition* (Samuel French, Inc., N. Y.) (Samuel French, Ltd., London.)
FAEP	*French's Acting Edition of Plays.*
FMD	*French's Minor Drama.*
FSD	*French's Standard Drama.*
HUL	Harvard University Library, Cambridge, Mass.
LAEP	*Lacy's Acting Edition of Plays* (T. H. Lacy Co., London).
LOC	The Library of Congress, Washington, D. C.
MMAD	*Miller's Modern Acting Drama.*
NYPL	The New York Public Library.
NYPLTC	Theatre Collection, New York Public Library.
ONYT	*Olwine's New York Theatre.*
RAEAP	*Roorbach's American Edition of Acting Plays* (N. Y.).
SAD	*Sergel's Acting Drama* (The Dramatic Publishing Co., Chicago).
SBT	*Spencer's Boston Theatre.*
WAD	*Wemyss' Acting Drama.*
WWESP	*Wm. Warren Edition of Standard Plays* (W. H. Baker Co., Boston).

Eugène Scribe

ONE-ACTS

Le Solliciteur (1817). Tr. as *The Solicitor* (1932) by Sylvia Wolfsie.[2]

L'Ours et le Pacha (1820). Tr. as *The Pasha & the Bear* (1932), Wolfsie.[3]

Michel et Christine (1821). Ad. as *Love in Humble Life* (1822), J. H. Payne. LAEP, 21; CBT, 11.

[2] Barnard College Library, N. Y.
[3] Loc. cit.

Le Gastronome sans Argent (1821). Ad. as *A Race for a Dinner* (1828), J. T. G. Rodwell. CBT, 19.

Le Vieux Garçon et la Petite Fille (1822). Ad. as *Old & Young* (n.d.), by ? CBT, 30.

Le Menteur Véridique (1823). Tr. as *He Lies Like Truth* (1828), by F. Kimpton. LAEP, 75.

Le Coiffeur et le Perruquier (1824). Tr. as *The Hairdresser & the Barber* (1932), Wolfsie.

Les Premières Amours (1825). Tr. as *First Love* (1873), L. J. Hollenius. LOC, NYPL only.

La Chatte Métamorphosée en Femme (1827). Ad. as *The Woman That Was a Cat* (1859), W. E. Suter. LAEP, 72.

La Protectrice (1830). Ad. as *The Daughter* (185-?), Thos. H. Bayly. LAEP, 1; FMD, no. 115.

La Frontière de Savoie (1834). Ad. as *A Peculiar Position* (1837), J. R. Planché. AND, 1.

TWO OR MORE ACTS

Une Visite à Bedlam (1818). Tr. as *A Roland for an Oliver* (1819), Thos. Morton, Sr. SBT, 1.

Le Plus Beaux Jour de la Vie (1825). Ad. as *The Happiest Day of My Life* (1829), J. B. Buckstone. CBT, 23.

La Lune de Miel (1826). Ad. as *A Russian Honeymoon* (1890), Constance C. (Mrs. Burton) Harrison. SAD.

Bertrand et Raton (1833). Tr. as *A School for Politicians* (1840), by ? LOC, HUL only.

Le Moulin de Javelle (1833). Tr. as *The Regent* (1835), by ? MMAD, 31.

L'Ambitieux (1834). Tr. as *Ambition* (1835), by ? Lewis. LOC, HUL only.

Le Verre d'Eau (1840). Ad. as *The Glass of Water* (1863), W. E. Suter. LAEP, 79. Tr. as *The Glass of Water* (1936), DeWitt Bodeen.

Adrienne Lecouvreur (1849). Ad. as *The Reigning Favorite* (1850), John Oxenford. LAEP, 1. Ad. as *Adrienne Lecouvreur* (1881), Sarah Bernhardt (generally available). Tr. Viviane de Charrière (1942).[4]

Bataille de Dames (1851). Tr. as *The Ladies' Battle* (1851), Reade (?). FMD, no. 226; LAEP, no. 47;

[4] Barnard College Library, N. Y.

FAEP, 108; SBT, 15. Tr. T. W. Robertson. *LAEP,*
4; also in *Principal Dram. Wks.* Vol. 1. London,
1889. Ad. as *The Queen's Gambit* (1955), Maurice
Valency. N. Y., Sam'l French, Inc., 1956.
Les Doigts de Fée (1858). Ad. as *The World of Fashion*
(18—?), John Oxenford. *LAEP,* 55.

Alexandre Dumas, fils

La Dame aux Camélias (1852). Ad. as *Camille, or the Fate
of a Coquette* (1853), John H. Wilkins. Prompt-book
in verse and prose. NYPLTC only. Ad. Matilda Heron
(1856). *FSD,* no. 129; *SAD,* no. 316. Ad. as *Camille,
or the Fate of a Coquette—a Magic Play* (1856), by
"a gentleman of Philadelphia" [Wilkins?]. *ONYT,*
no. 10. Tr. as *The Lady of the Camellias* (1880), F. A.
Schwab. N. Y., Rullman ("The Bernhardt Edition").
Tr. as *Camille, the Lady of the Camellias* (1907),
Mildred Aldrich. BPP. Tr. as *The Lady of the Camellias* (1930), Edith Reynolds & Nigel Playfair. London,
Ernest Benn, Ltd., 1930. Tr. as *Camille, the Lady of
the Camellias* (1931), Henriette Metcalfe. N. Y.,
Sam'l French, Inc., 1931.
Le Demi-Monde (1855). Tr. Harold Harper (pseud.)
(1933). In *World Drama,* ed. B. H. Clark. N. Y.,
Dover Pub. Inc., 1933 (paperback edition, 1956).
Le Question d'Argent (1857). Tr. as *The Money Question*
(1915), by students of Tufts College. *Poet Lore* 26:
129-227 (Mar., 1915).
Le Fils Naturel (1858). Tr. T. L. Oxley. London, Kerby
and Endean, 1879. NYPL.
L'Ami des Femmes (1864). Ad. as *The Woman's Friend*
(1928), L. J. Slevin. Reproduced fr. typewritten copy.
NYPL only.
La Princesse Georges (1871). Tr. by ? N. Y., Rullman,
1881. NYPL.
Monsieur Alphonse (1873). Ad. Augustin Daly. N. Y.,
1886. NYPL.
La Femme de Claude (1873). Tr. as *The Wife of Claude,*
Chas. Alfred Byrne. N. Y., Rullman, 1905 (as repr.
by Mme. Sarah Bernhardt and Co.). NYPL.
L'Etrangère (1876). Ad. as *The Foreigner,* by ? N. Y.

Rullman, 1881 ("Sarah Bernhardt season in U. S."). NYPL.

Denise (1885). Ad. Augustin Daly (1885). N. Y., Rullman, 1888. NYPL.

Les Danicheff (188-?). Ad. as *The Danicheffs, or Married by Force* (188-?), Arthur Shirley. *LAEP*, 129.

Emile Augier

ONE-ACTS

L'Habit Vert. Tr. as *The Green Coat*, B. H. Clark. London, S. French, 1915. Also in *The World's Best Plays Series*, N. Y., S. French.

Le Post-Scriptum. Tr. as *The Post-Script*, B. H. Clark. In *Four Plays by Augier.* N. Y., Alfred A. Knopf, 1915.

TWO OR MORE ACTS

L'Aventurière (1848). Ad. as *The Adventuress*, by ? N. Y., Rullman, 1888 (Coquelin-Hading ed.). NYPL.

Gabrielle (1849). Ad. as *Good for Evil, or A Wife's Trial* (also as *Home Truths* (1860). *LAEP*, 43.

Le Mariage d'Olympe (1855). Ad. as *The Marriage Game* (1901), Clyde Fitch. LOC; owned by American Play Co., N. Y. Tr. as *Olympe's Marriage*, B. H. Clark. In *Four Plays by Augier*, tr. B. H. Clark. N. Y., Alfred A. Knopf, Inc., 1915. Also in *The Drama* 5 (1915).

Le Gendre de Monsieur Poirier (1855). Tr. as *Monsieur Poirier's Son-in-Law.* B. H. Clark. In *Four Plays by Augier*, tr. B. H. Clark. N. Y., Alfred A. Knopf, Inc., 1915. Also in *World Drama*, ed. B. H. Clark. N. Y., Dover Pub. Inc., 1933 (paperback ed., 1955).

Les Lionnes Pauvres (1858). Ad. as *A False Step*. Arthur Matthison. London, S. French, 1878. *FAEP*, 113.

Les Effrontés (1861). Tr. as *Faces of Brass*, Frederic Lyster. N. Y., Rullman, c. 1888 (Coquelin-Hading ed.). NYPL.

Le Fils de Giboyer (1862). Tr. as *Giboyer's Son*, Bénedict Papot. *The Drama* 1:27-137 (Nov., 1911).

Paul Forestier (1868). Ad. as *Paul Forrester.* N. Y., The New York Printing Co., 1871.

Les Fourchambault (1878). Tr. as *The House of Four-*

chambault, B. H. Clark. In *Four Plays by Augier*, tr. B. H. Clark. N. Y., Alfred A. Knopf, Inc., 1915.

Victorien Sardou

Les Pattes de Mouche (1860). Ad. (1) as *A Scrap of Paper* (1861), J. P. Simpson. FSD, no. 399; FAE, no. 756; WWESP. Ad. (2) as *A Scrap of Paper, or The Adventures of a Love Letter* (1889), J. P. Simpson (with English chars. & setting). RAEAP, no. 2. Tr. Léonie Gilmour. In *Dram. Masterpieces*. Vol. 2, N. Y., Colonial Press, 1900.

Nos Intimes (1861). Ad. as *Friends or Foes?* H. Wigan. LAEP, 54. Ad. as *Our Friends*, G. March. FAEP, 115.

La Perle Noire (1862). Tr. as *The Black Pearl*, B. H. Clark. N. Y., S. French, Inc., 1915. Also in *The World's Best Plays, by Celebrated European Authors*, ed. B. H. Clark.

Nos bons Villageois (1866). Ad. as *Hazardous Ground*, Augustin Daly. N. Y., S. French, 1868. WAD, no. 4.

La Maison Neuve (1866). Ad. as *Mayfair*, A. W. Pinero. London, 1885.

Séraphine (1868). Ad. Dion Boucicault. London, 1869 (?) NYPL.

Patrie! (1869). Tr. B. H. Clark. Garden City, N. Y., Doubleday, Page & Co., 1915. Also in *Plays for the College Theater*, ed. G. H. Leverton. N. Y., 1932.

L'Oncle Sam (1873). Ad. as *Americans Abroad* (1892), Abby S. Richardson. Prompt-book; typewritten. NYPL only.

Dora (1877). Ad. as *Diplomacy* (1878), Saville & Bolton Rowe. Prompt-book; typewritten. NYPL only.

Les Bourgeois de Pont-Arcy (1878). Ad. as *Duty*, J. Albery. FAEP, 127. Also in *Dram. Wks. of J. Albery*, ed. Wyndham Albery. Vol. 2. London, Davies, 1939.

Daniel Rochat (1880). Tr. J. V. Pritchard. FSD, no. 379.

Divorçons (1880). Ad. as *Cyprienne*, M. Mayo. N. Y., S. French, Inc., 1941. Tr. as *Let's Get a Divorce*, by ? Chicago, c. 1909. SAD, no. 602.

Théodora (1884). Argument of play. N. Y., Rullman, 1890.

La Tosca (1887). Ad. as *The Tragedy of La Tosca,* Walter Howgrave. London, Drane's Ltd., 1925. Opera libretto tr. W. Beatty-Kingston. London, G. Ricordi & Co., Ltd., 1900.

Madame Sans-Gêne (1893). Ad. as *Madam Devil-May-Care* (1901), C. H. Meltzer. N. Y., S. French, Inc., 1939 (revised).

La Sorcière (1903). Tr. as *The Sorceress,* Chas. H. Weissert. With Introduction by the translator. Boston, R. G. Badger, 1917. Argument of play. N. Y., Rullman, 1905.